STATE-BY-STATE GUIDE TO WOMEN'S LEGAL RIGHTS

SHANA ALEXANDER'S

STATE-BY-STATE GUIDE TO

WOMEN'S LEGAL RIGHTS

Barbara Brudno
Professor of Law, UCLA
Legal Consultant

Published by Wollstonecraft Incorporated

PUBLISHER'S NOTE:
In this book we have made every effort to include the most recent legislative changes affecting women in the United States. With each printing, information is updated in an area of the law that is changing almost daily. Attorneys General of all fifty states have been asked to review the book and inform us of any possible errors or changes that may have taken place in their states since the material was compiled.

STAFF FOR THIS BOOK

Annette Welles, Editor-in-Chief
Irwin Glusker and Associates, Design
Georgia Griggs, Editor
Fred M. Kleeberg Associates, Production
Helaine Tollin French, Illustration
Computer Typesetting Services, Composition

LEGAL STAFF

Barbara Brudno, Professor of Law, UCLA, Legal Consultant
Gilda R. Cohen, Attorney at Law
Debbie Reinberg, Legal Researcher
Mary Ledding, Legal Researcher

SPECIAL THANKS TO:

Eleanor Bice, County of Los Angeles, Department of Adoptions
Ursula M. Gallagher, Children's Bureau—HEW
Stephen Lachs, Public Defenders Office, Los Angeles County
David Leavitt, Attorney at Law
Stanley Weinstein, Attorney at Law

FIRST EDITION—Second Printing

Copyright © Shana Alexander 1975

Printed in the United States of America

Wollstonecraft Incorporated
6399 Wilshire Boulevard
Los Angeles California 90048

Wollstonecraft books are distributed by Price/Stern/Sloan Publishers Inc.

Library of Congress Cataloging in Publication Data

Alexander, Shana.
    Shana Alexander's State-by-State guide to women's legal rights.

    1. Women—Legal status, laws, etc.—United States—
States. I. Title.
KF478.Z95A4   346:.73'013   74-10169
ISBN 0-88381-008-5
ISBN 0-88381-009-3 pbk.

For Fanny

Contents

Introduction

I was named after my great-grandmother, or, rather, two of them. Each one was named Shana; each was a peasant woman and knew her place: obey her husband, bear children, keep house, keep quiet.

My two grandmothers also shared the same name: Fanny. Both Fannys were baby girls when they left the old country, but in the new land each Fanny still knew her place. Each dutifully became the near child-bride of an older man, kept house, bore children, etcetera. If you had asked either Fanny what she believed her legal rights were, she wouldn't have known what you were talking about. A woman didn't have rights, she had duties; she was expected—and she *expected herself*—to be dutiful daughter, dutiful wife and mother.

A critical difference between the Shanas and the Fannys was that the Fannys could read and write. They read the same things, the Bible and the newspaper, and wrote the same things, letters and lists. Their letters were full of gossip, foreboding, sorrow, and loss. The lists on the other hand were sunbursts of organized optimism: favorite delicacies, winning numbers, happy birthdays, hat and glove sizes of children and grandchildren.

I remember one Fanny small and one stout, one with blue-gray eyes and one with amazing violet, and both smelling wonderfully of baby powder—or could that perhaps have been *me?* Anyway, in my childish memory my grandmothers are very clear. The Fanny in Chicago is at her kitchen table, chopping herring and singing to her canary; the Hollywood Fanny has just announced an expedition to Grauman's Chinese Theater. "Look up!" she directs us, ages four and seven, tapping the newspaper neatly folded back to the movie page. "Look up!" She is so proud that already we can read and write, and even tell time from the wonderful upside-down crystal ball watch suspended on the shelf of her bosom by a black silken cord.

The son and daughter of the two Fannys—that is, my own mother and father—became professional writers, one a composer, the other a critic. My sister is a special kind of technical writer and *her* eleven-year-old daughter, Soft-Hearted Hannah, named in wry salute to one of my father's songs, writes and publishes her own monthly magazine, *Kid's Lib*. My daughter Kathy is a poet and mathematician. What a tribe of scribblers!

I include here this brief family history for reasons other than mere family pride. The double coincidences of those names—the two Shanas followed by the two Fannys—is a reminder that, only a generation or two back, women were scarcely differentiated one from the next, let alone regarded as people able to think and act for themselves, on their own, independent of men. Surely this is one reason why so few books explaining and listing the legal rights of women have been published.

Even today, most women have only the scantiest notion of what their legal rights are. If I had myself realized the tangled thicket of ignorance, prejudice, stupidity, and gross neglect which I was about to hack my way into, I might never have attempted to put this book together. But even though by then I myself had had to wrestle with every aspect of the law covered in this book with the exception of widowhood and crime. I was still not, in the words of the final chapter, a "full citizen." I still did not fully understand my own condition in law. One astounding fact I learned in the course of writing this book, or rather of causing it to be compiled, is that when two people marry they become in the eyes of the law one person, and that one person is the husband!

Though today the woman's movement has set women's law to mutating with the speed of fruit flies—even now, and in every state, when a woman marries she legally to some degree ceases to exist. Only the loss of her husband through death or divorce can bring about the full restoration of her legal self.

God bless the two Fannys! From them I must have inherited the lifelong urge to write down and look up. Each day I still like to look up my horoscope, the weather, my ideal weight, quotations, stock tables, yellow pages, Thoughts for Today, movie pages, what to cook, what to see, what to do, and what Dear Abby says *not* to do. As for all my lists . . . chagrin forbids mention. Even a list of lists would fill pages.

This book is addressed to that side of all women which forever struggles to make order out of chaos, to plan, to divine and get braced for the future by the opposed but complementary acts of looking up and writing down. The activity in itself seems to make one feel a bit more secure, to make life a little tidier, less inchoate, and more comprehensible. Looking up is a way of finding out without having to ask, or of understanding *what* to ask. It permits the oblique approach to problems that today's woman, no longer sure of her place—often exalted but just as often dizzied by her recent, rapid "liberation"—can find reassuring. It encourages the still timid but newly independent mind.

As woman's place began to change three-fourths of a century or so ago, looking up became big business in this country. Newspapers added a special "women's page": columns of recipes, fashions, household tips, and domestic advice garnished the traditional announcements of birth, marriage, death. These women's pages were the neighborhood shrines to Looking Up. The great temples of the new religion became the powerful ladies' magazines.

For a brief, uncomfortable period in 1969 and 1970 I served the most exalted of these great temples, *McCall's* magazine, as temporary high priestess. In part, my own affection and long-running familiarity with traditional women's-page fare led me to accept the editorship of the magazine. Nor were vanity and greed entirely absent from my calculations. But a new and powerful sense of sisterhood was working in me too. I wanted to *help women,* to help them cope with the mounting stress of their daily lives. After having spent a score of years as a woman working full time in the man's world of newsmagazines, and living full time in the woman's world of wife-and-motherhood, I saw in *McCall's* a possibility of at last bringing the two separate sides of my life into harmonious, fruitful collaboration. Instead they collided, and by 1971 there was a sickening crash.

I didn't realize until after I'd signed on for this stormy voyage that I was the seventh editor of *McCall's* in the past ten years, nor that I was to be the first woman editor of the world's largest women's magazine in fifty years. But certainly I knew that what all women's magazines were giving women to read was largely illusion, fantasy, and too often cruel deception. Too many glossy photos of wall-to-wall artichokes, cosmeticked casseroles, popcorn hairdos; too many recipes they couldn't afford the time to make (it took our own staff experts several days to produce that sublime suckling pig, or the tuna-noodle casserole crowned with baroque whorls of instant reconstituted potato); too many fashions they couldn't afford to buy; too many dress patterns they lacked the time and skill to sew.

I wanted to feed them reality, and clothe them with armor against the exploitation of women's needs and dreams which I knew abounded in the closed, essentially fake world of ladies' magazines. The women's books, as they are called, are slick-paper ghettos whose sole reason for existence is to sell products to women; that is, to deliver the cheapest-possible all-female audience to mass marketers of breakfast foods, sloppy joes, electric fry pans, vaginal deodorants, training bras, johnny mops, diet drinks, and other essentials of American life.

I wanted to remake our magazine to serve the real needs of real women, rather than the marketing needs of the advertisers who kept us in business. But there were no precedents for accomplishing such a miraculous conversion. There was no place one could go to follow Fanny's advice and look up. Nor did I see any tradition to look up *to*. Rather, increasingly, in those early days of "liberation," as womanpower began to stir and the mass of women themselves began to change, I saw a tendency on the part of management of *all* the ladies' magazines—ours was no worse than others, indeed better than most—to look down on all women.

In the same way that political radicals and visionaries in the nineteenth century had looked forward to the gradual withering away of the state, I came to long for the withering away of the ladies' magazine as a last, vestigial remnant of a hypocritical, discriminatory, chauvinist, hamstrung, pre-pill age. Not surprisingly, what withered away first was me. One morning without warning I awoke to find Ms. Editor Number Eight sitting in my ladylike gray velvet editor's chair.

The relationship between any editor and management is a lot like that between husband and wife. It can take a lot of strain for the sake of circulation and profit, and it can also drive people to drink, even suicide or murder. At *McCall's* it drove us both up the wall, and we split; or rather, to express the situation in the new language I have learned in the course of assembling this book, we arranged a no-fault divorce based on grounds of irreconcilable differences.

My last good editorial idea before our sudden split had been to try to devise a way to make women more aware of their legal rights in their own areas of special concern—marriage, divorce, child custody, division of property, abortion, equal pay, and so on. What the magazine eventually produced was a folio of highly decorative but also highly unreadable charts. Once again fancy graphics had been substituted for content. Like the artichokes the charts were beautiful, even astonishing, but not much help to the ordinary reader—to the average woman wondering about an ordinary problem of life, but too poor, too ignorant, or too timid to consult a lawyer as readily as a man might.

When management and I got around to the division of our community property, I asked for—and was generously given—custody of one but-slightly-used idea. I wanted greatly to expand and refurbish the material, and put it into a form which would do people some good.

I wanted simply to compile an orderly, logical explanation and listing of women's legal rights, written not in legalese but in ordinary English, so that any inquiring, doubtful, troubled, or just curious woman in any state in the union could, if she cared to, follow my grandmother's advice and look herself up.

That's when I discovered that no one before had ever attempted such a fool task. A lawyer would have had more sense. But after a few false starts I learned that one book on the subject did exist, *Women and the Law,* by Professor Leo Kanowitz. This was not a guidebook or a listing but a scholarly general survey of the field, only a few years in print and yet in the sudden rush of history already hopelessly out of date. I went to see Professor Kanowitz, and eventually he and his law students at the University of New Mexico agreed to tackle the massive amount of law-library work that was our necessary starting place.

And so the fun began: three years of research in law libraries and statute books, three years of cataloguing and compiling, of revising and rewriting, three years of translating impenetrable legalese into reasonably simple English. The problem was tangled, thorny, and vast; your queries and letters will tell us how well we have succeeded.

My desire to catalogue, classify, and simplify was complicated by the fact that the law is not dead parchment but a living body of opinion that changes daily as courts hand down new rulings, and legislatures write new statutes and repeal old ones. Further, it is doubtful whether any area of the law has been revised so extensively, and so rapidly, as women's rights law in the past three or four years, let us say since 1970–71 when the Equal Rights Amendment was passed by Congress and sent to the states for ratification.

Statute law and case law were changing as we went to press in January 1975; they are changing now. Although this book attempts to present a general overview of various current state laws and Supreme Court rulings that relate to women, it makes no claim to being all-inclusive. As the title says, it is a *guide,* not an encyclopedia. Nor is it a legal reference work. The eleven introductory chapters which precede each set of state-by-state listings of laws offer some insight into why the law has evolved as it has. These essays also identify general differences between the laws from state to state, spot new trends and recent changes, and point out those areas in the law which most urgently need reform.

All information is as recent and as accurate as possible, but it must be remembered that courts and legislatures daily amend old laws and enact new ones. The law changes and flows like water, and in a period when the stream of women's rights law has become a sudden rushing torrent it would be almost impossible, even with hundreds of researchers and a computer to boot, to supply up-to-the-minute information about every law affecting women in every state. To be relatively current is the best one can hope for.

The final essay, "Am I a Full Citizen?," does review the major recent Supreme Court decisions that relate to women's rights, and offers a general synthesis of society's current attitudes about women—both discriminatory and protective—which continue to influence the enactment, enforcement, and interpretation of the law. This chapter also discusses why the Equal Rights Amendment is needed, and what the difficulties have been in getting the ERA ratified by the necessary three-quarters of the state legislatures; as of this writing it is still some four states shy of that mark.

A few words of background and history. American law at the state level has its origins in the English system of common law, which was adopted as the basis for our law in colonial times. Common law was built up in England over the centuries in a seemingly haphazard way, case by case. As a situation arose, it was judged in the courts on the basis of what was considered reasonable in terms of prevailing custom and usage; in the words of Sir Edward Coke, "Reason is the life of the law, nay the common law itself is nothing but reason." Occasionally, acts of Parliament were used to define a crime or set a penalty. These rulings then became the precedent on which to base later decisions in similar cases. The decisions were recorded so that they could be used for reference, but the laws themselves were *not* recorded; the principle—the actual law—was considered to be implicit in the decision and had to be inferred from it.

During the nineteenth century in the United States, it was decided to "codify" the common law—that is, legislative bodies in each state examined each area of the common law, extracted the basic principle on which the common-law decisions were based, modified it as necessary, and then included it in a systematically arranged collection of statutes that had been sanctioned by the legislative and executive branches of the government in each state. These collections are known as codes, and are divided into two main categories, penal and civil. Thus was the common law transformed into statute law, and that is why many statutes closely resemble the common law on which they are based. For example, the definition of rape used in most current state statutes—"carnal knowledge of a woman forcibly and against her will"—is the same wording that was used in common law.

Statutory law, however, does not cover every conceivable aspect of a given situation, because each state legislature over the years has made its own individual judgment as to which parts of the common law it will include in its codes, and what changes would be made. This is why laws may differ from state to state. Before state statutes were enacted, the common law applied to everyone throughout the country. Therefore the absence of a statute covering a particular situation does not mean there is no law relating to that situation. When no statute exists, the relevant common law still applies and is still enforceable.

"Case law" keeps the old common-law tradition alive and very active in the present day. The statutes are interpreted every time a judicial decision is made in any area of the law. These decisions are then appended to a state's statutes; that is, when you look at a particular statute, immediately following it will be the cases that relate to it. The case-law decisions do not change the basic law; they show how the law has been applied in a specific case.

A lawyer preparing a case, therefore, must be familiar not only with the relevant statutes but also with all the case law (precedents) that relate to them. Since many of these decisions may wholly or partially contradict others in the same area, further interpretation is constantly going on. It is here that the attorney's skill comes into play: the lawyer tries to make the most persuasive case for the acceptance of the interpretation he or she feels is most applicable in the present instance. In a trial, opposing lawyers often cite conflicting precedents to support their own interpretation of the law in the case at hand. It is then up to the judge or jury, or both, to weigh these arguments, along with the evidence, before making a decision. This decision in turn becomes a part of the case law for that statute.

Of course, state laws are no longer limited to the areas covered by common law. State legislators are continually enacting brand-new legislation to meet the needs of the residents of their states, and of necessity have moved far beyond the limits set by common law two or three centuries ago. But the conceptual basis of state laws is rooted in the common-law tradition.

Federal legislation, on the other hand, is not based on common law. It is an entirely new body of statutory law created over the years by our national legislature (the Senate and House of Representatives). Federal laws must have the approval of the President, who as head of the executive branch of government must sign each bill before it can become law.

Any law, state or federal, may be challenged on constitutional grounds and its validity tested under the terms of a state's constitution or the U.S. Constitution. The review of a law's constitutionality is begun—and sometimes ends—in high state courts or low federal courts, but if it is appealed to and accepted for review by the U.S. Supreme Court a final verdict will be given there. Even at this level, though, a majority decision may not be "definitive"—that is, the justices who concur with the majority opinion may nevertheless not agree with all the reasons given by the writer of that opinion. They will then write their own opinions, based on different reasoning but still reaching the same conclusion. Such rulings will thus be liable to differing interpretations in lower courts when similar cases are deliberated, as is true, for example, with the Court's decision in *Stanley v. Illinois,* discussed in Chapters 2 and 3.

Suits brought on constitutional grounds differ from those brought in both criminal and civil cases in that they are not attempting to find whether someone is guilty or innocent, or liable for damages. They are designed solely to give the judicial branch of government (the courts) a chance to rule on the constitutionality of a law created by the legislative branch. Sometimes the decisions on constitutional issues are so sweeping that not only is the state statute challenged in the suit rendered unconstitutional, but so are all similar laws in other states. This is exactly what happened with the 1973 U.S. Supreme Court decisions on abortion. It may take a while for state legislators to respond and to revise their statutes in accordance with the Supreme Court decision, but in the meantime the unconstitutional state laws cannot be enforced even though they are still on the books.

Outside my window as I write a flock of pheasants—five females, two cocks—ambles across the field. The females are so dowdy, drab, dun-colored, and diligent in their pecking, so hopelessly plodding compared to the handsome high-stepping ring-neck males, that for an atavistic moment I wonder anew whether and how the human female will ever transcend the lower, more dependent, less rights-ful station to which her reproductive nature has until the last-minute invention of The Pill confined her. Still, one must try, and this book is a first, sometimes faltering step.

It has been the usual labor of love and frustration wherein many people struggle in uneven unison to perform a task that had never been done before, and to do it under the pressures of deadlines, unfamiliarity with the material, differences of interpretation, and so on, and all of it made more difficult because the law changes daily as refracted through the eyes of jurymen and women, and pounded up under the gavels of judges.

In a project of this kind thanks are due and overdue in myriad directions. I must especially thank David J. Mahoney, President of Norton Simon, Inc., and Edward E. Fitzgerald, then President of the McCall Publishing Company, for generously nurturing me in difficult times; Jerome Hardy and Howard Stein of the Dreyfus Fund for being angels in both senses of the word; Professor Leo Kanowitz, now with the Law School of the University of California at Berkeley, and his students, for hundreds of hours of legal spade work; the Wollstonecraft staff for vigilant and painstaking supervision and revision of this work; and most particularly Barbara Brudno, Professor of Law at UCLA Law School, for the courage, patience, clear-headedness, and tenacity to ride herd on all the rest of us. Most of all, I thank the two Fannys for passing on to a grateful granddaughter the habit and passion to look up. That heritage has produced a book I hope will serve not only the Fanny in me, but the Fanny in us all.

—*Shana Alexander*
Wainscott, New York

1
When I Get Married

Under common law—the ancient unwritten law of England on which American law is based—a husband and wife were regarded as one person, and that one person was the husband. As a result of this concept of the "unity of the spouses," a woman who married surrendered much of her legal identity. The control and management of her real property, as well as the profits from any leases she held, went to her husband. He also became the absolute owner of all personal property she brought into the marriage, and only he could recover her legal claims against others.

A wife was not allowed to contract on her own with a third party. This is the origin of some modern-day restrictions still in force that do not permit a wife to get credit without her husband's consent or to buy or sell property on her own behalf. She could neither sue a third party for personal injuries or losses nor be sued by others unless her husband was included in the lawsuit. Moreover, a married woman could not enter into contracts with or sue her husband.

Men also were subject to certain economic restrictions when they married. For example, a wife's "dower right" entitled her to inherit a one-third interest in all her husband's real estate for life. This right made it difficult for a husband to sell or give away any of his property without his wife's consent, even though he alone had control over the couple's property and the sole obligation to support his wife and their children.

British ownership laws and restraints on contracts were considered intolerably repressive to American women. So in 1830 in Mississippi, and soon in other states, a series of new laws was passed. These laws, known as Married Women's Property Acts, gave wives the right to contract and to sue and be sued on their own, apart from their husbands. Wives could now manage and control any property they acquired prior to the marriage. They could work outside the home, keeping any money they earned, without permission of their husbands.

Although today some version of the Married Women's Property Acts exists in all fifty states and the District of Columbia, many unfair practices still have not been eliminated from American law. The differences in legal status of a woman before and after marriage often continue to discriminate against her. But in the welter of other things a woman about to be married seldom stops to think about the impending changes in her legal rights and responsibilities. The choosing of a dress, the pattern of a plate take precedence over thinking about and investigating the legal implications of marriage. A wedding ring may still legally tether a woman.

When a woman marries, the most immediate change in her legal status is her name. With the exception of Louisiana, all states assume a bride's legal surname will become that of her husband, although there are very few laws to that effect. Only eight states—Alabama, Alaska, Indiana, Kentucky, Hawaii, Nevada, Oregon, and Vermont—have legal restrictions on this issue.

Most states recognize the common-law right to change one's name without having to go through the necessity of legal proceedings as long as the change is not for fraudulent or illegal purposes. Those states that provide legal procedures to change one's

name do so in addition to the common-law right. In most states, therefore, it is legal for a woman to continue to use her maiden name.

In the few states that restrict the common-law right, some of the formal procedures leave it to the court's discretion whether to grant the name change to a married woman. Some states won't grant the change unless it is consistent with the public interest or in the best interests of the people involved. Thus a married woman might have a problem if a conservative judge finds it not in the "best interest" of the husband or wife for her to keep her maiden name.

Marriage also affects a person's legal domicile—that is, the place where one lives and to which, when absent, he or she intends to return. While this place is usually one's immediate residence, it is not unusual for Domicile to be in one state and Residence in another.

In general, all men and all unmarried adult women automatically establish domicile by residing in the place where they intend to make their home. But a married woman has no such right. Under the common law and the laws of most states, her domicile is her husband's, provided his choice is reasonable. He may not, for instance, insist that the only place for his wife to live is in his parents' home. But if a wife remains in the family's Virginia home while her husband takes a job and residence in Montana, for example, the wife's domicile by law is Montana.

The location of a legal domicile is important for many reasons. It determines which court has jurisdiction over divorce suits, probate matters, guardianships, and taxation. Domicile also determines one's right to vote and hold public office, receive welfare, or be eligible for privileged tuition at state educational institutions; it also affects one's obligation for jury duty.

A few states do permit a married woman to have an independent domicile for all purposes; a few more states allow her to have

one if she is living apart from her husband for good cause and by mutual consent. But nearly half the states deny her the right to maintain a separate domicile. (See "rights of wife" in state-by-state guide.)

The passage of Married Women's Property Acts and comparable laws has expanded the right of married women to enter into contracts. This right, nonetheless, is not granted in all fifty states. In Michigan, for example, a wife cannot enter into a contract making her own property liable for debts jointly assumed with her husband. In Kentucky a wife may contract at will but, with some exceptions, cannot contractually guarantee another's financial obligations unless her husband also agrees to be liable. A wife in Alabama or Georgia may not contract to guarantee her husband's debts.

Alabama and Kentucky prohibit a wife from contracting to sell or lease her separate real property without her husband's written approval. There is inequality in such a law—a husband does not need his wife's permission to sell or lease *his* real property. However, in community-property states, where the wife is considered a joint owner in one-half the property acquired during marriage, neither marriage partner can sell community property without the other's consent.

Perhaps the most revolutionary right granted under the Married Women's Property Acts is the right of a woman to keep her own property after marriage and the right to get and keep new property during her marriage. The English common law gave absolute dominion to the husband. This was mercifully modified by the Married Women's Property Acts, which allowed a wife to keep and control her own property. But these acts still have not achieved the equality that women are demanding in contemporary society.

Marriage is after all and above all a partnership. Yet only the eight states with community-property laws—Arizona, California, Idaho, Louisiana, Nevada, New Mexico, Texas, and Washington—regard marriage as a type of partnership. These laws, however, affect only mutual rights in property acquired after marriage; they do not make the wife an equal partner for all legal purposes.

The community-property system sees each spouse as contributing—either within the home or outside it—to the financial well-being of the marriage, and emphasizes the equal right of both husband and wife in property acquired during the marriage. But in practice this principle is often more honored in the breach than in the observance. Perhaps the most significant feature of the community-property system is that the earnings of both husband and wife are considered the community property of both during the marriage. Each has, theoretically at least, a one-half interest in those earnings. Even so, until recently laws in all eight community-property states gave the husband the right to manage and control this community property, including a wife's earnings unless she kept them in a separate bank account. If a wife put her own earnings in the bank account she shared with her husband, he could use that money to join a men's health club or to pay his own gambling debts. Here is another example of the old common-law notion that husband and wife are one, the

"one" being the husband. Since 1972, however, legislative changes in Arizona, California, and Texas provide for equal management and control of all community property.

While many laws have been improved by the Married Women's Property Acts and other statutes, the laws governing the duties of support between husband and wife still reflect values of the past and result in discrimination against husbands as well as wives. Twenty-six states have no provisions for a wife to support her husband under any circumstances. Ten states provide that a wife must support her husband out of her separate property when he is unable, because of illness or accident, to support himself. Six states compel the wife to support her husband when he is in need. Eight states and the District of Columbia have enacted "Poor Persons" legislation to solve this problem. These statutes provide that certain relatives—including a wife or husband—must support other relatives in need. Often these laws are part of public assistance or welfare laws and provide penalties for nonsupport.

The precise legal duty of a husband to support his wife is rarely defined so long as the marriage is stable and the spouses are living together. This is because the courts refuse to intervene except in cases of marital breakdown. Thus even if a husband refuses to give his wife a cent for her own personal needs—clothing, for example—she cannot, as long as she continues living with her husband, get a court order to compel him to provide her with reasonable support money. Her only recourse is to institute a suit for a legal separation or divorce. The rationale behind the courts' refusal to intervene is their inability to supervise day-to-day problems between husband and wife. However, when a legal separation, an annulment, or a divorce is contemplated, and when the partners themselves cannot reach a financial agreement, the court will fix the exact amount of support a husband must pay his wife, or, more often, his former wife. (See Chapter 5.)

Husbands and wives used to be absolutely prohibited from suing each other, whatever the circumstances, including intentional infliction of serious physical injury. When a husband and wife were considered one person in the eyes of the law, to have permitted suits by a person against himself would have been an anomaly. The right of husbands and wives to sue each other has been modified in the last century, although again vestiges of old rules are still found in many states.

More than a third of the states allow spouses to sue each other if one of them physically injures the other. The courts no longer voice the platitude that to permit husbands and wives to sue one another would "disturb domestic harmony." This quaint law permitted a husband to beat his wife and cause her permanent injury, disfigurement, and untold pain and suffering. But it did not allow her to sue him because such a suit could destroy the "peace of the home." Even today, though, in half the states spouses cannot sue each other even for willful injury, let alone injury that was caused by negligence—that is, failure to use reasonable care.

If a husband or wife injures the other negligently, as opposed to willfully, the injured person will have even less success in winning a suit in those states where suit can be brought. Most negligent injuries result from automobile accidents or other activities covered by insurance. Our suspicious society fears that if suits are permitted between spouses for accidental injuries, too many fraudulent claims will be filed. It is often argued that husbands and wives would cooperate to take advantage of insurance companies. This same reasoning has also been applied in cases of children suing their parents (see Chapter 2). But in the growing number of states that now allow injury suits between spouses there seems to be no special abuse of insurance companies.

All states now permit both wives and husbands who have been injured by a third party to sue for damages. However, a husband, but not a wife, traditionally has been allowed to sue a third person for "loss of consortium." Loss of consortium is the loss of "conjugal" rights to enjoy a spouse's physical, sexual, and psychological well-being. If a wife or husband is injured so that one may not enjoy her or his conjugal rights, twenty-eight states and the District of Columbia permit either spouse to bring suit for loss of consortium; sixteen permit only the husband to sue a third party for his loss. This inequality in legal rights arising out of personal injuries to one of the spouses has been eliminated in seven states (Connecticut, Louisiana, Massachusetts, North Carolina, Rhode Island, Utah, and Virginia), which have abolished the right of either spouse to bring a lawsuit on the grounds of loss of consortium.

When marriage goes into court and mounts the witness stand, another legal twist occurs. Under the laws of evidence, anyone called as a witness in a trial has a right, as well as a duty, to answer all relevant questions unless protected by a special privilege, such as the constitutional privilege against self-incrimination. Married couples, much like parties in a confidential relationship between attorney-client and priest-confessor, receive special treatment.

A husband-and-wife relationship presupposes a privilege of uninhibited communication, without which they would presumably confide in each other only at their peril. However, the statutes vary widely on husband and wife testimonial privilege. Some hold that the privilege is personal to the *witness* only, and that if the witness wants to testify for or against the spouse, the spouse has no right to object. Other statutes hold that the witness may only testify for or

against the spouse with the spouse's consent. Generally, a husband or wife need not testify against his or her spouse unless he/she wants to do so. But in a criminal trial if the witness desires to testify and the other spouse has given consent, then the witness must do so as if he/she were not married (see laws, Chapter 9).

Many of the laws governing relationships between husbands and wives have been criticized because of their sexual bias. With the trend toward equal treatment without regard to sex, discrepancies between the legal status of wives and husbands are slowly being changed. The "one-person" view of marriage, while still present, is dimming. But because the ways of the law are wondrous slow, differences in women's and men's legal status both before and after marriage are likely to be with us for a long time.

1
When I Get Married
The Law
State by State

ALABAMA

Support: Husband has primary duty to support wife. Wife is not obligated to support husband if he is unable.

Spousal litigation: 1. Wife may sue husband for personal injuries. **2.** Husband may recover for loss of wife's consortium. Wife may not recover for loss of husband's consortium.

Rights of wife: 1. Generally, wife may enter into contracts and engage in business on the same basis as her husband, but she may not contract to guarantee her husband's debts and she may not sell property unless her husband joins her in the deed—a restriction not placed on the husband. **2.** Wife may use maiden name without restrictions. **3.** Wife may retain separate domicile for voting if couple is living in a temporary abode and husband has voting residence elsewhere.

Common-law marriage: Allowed.

ALASKA

Support: Husband and wife are jointly responsible for support of the family. Wife must support husband if he is in need.

Spousal litigation: 1. Husband and wife may sue each other for personal injuries. **2.** Husband may recover for loss of wife's consortium. Wife may not recover for loss of husband's consortium.

Rights of wife: 1. Wife may enter into contracts, sell property, and engage in business on exactly the same basis as her husband. **2.** Wife whose name is changed by marriage must re-register to vote. **3.** Wife may retain separate domicile for voting.

Common-law marriage: Not valid.

ARIZONA

Support: Husband has primary duty to support

wife. Wife is not obligated to support husband if he is unable.

Spousal litigation: 1. Husband and wife may not sue each other for personal injuries. **2.** Husband may recover for loss of wife's consortium. Wife may recover for loss of husband's consortium.

Rights of wife: 1. Wife may enter into contracts, sell property, and engage in business on exactly the same basis as her husband. **2.** Wife whose name is changed by marriage must re-register to vote. **3.** Wife may not retain separate domicile for voting.

Common-law marriage: Not valid.

ARKANSAS

Support: Husband has primary duty to support wife. Wife is not obligated to support husband if he is unable.

Spousal litigation: 1. Husband and wife may sue each other for personal injuries. **2.** Husband may recover for loss of wife's consortium. Wife may recover for loss of husband's consortium.

Rights of wife: 1. Wife may enter into contracts, sell property, and engage in business on exactly the same basis as her husband. **2.** Wife may use her maiden name without restrictions. **3.** Wife may retain separate domicile for voting.

Common-law marriage: Not valid.

CALIFORNIA

Support: Husband has primary duty to support wife. If husband is unable to support himself, wife must support him out of her separate property if he has no separate property or there is no community property.

Spousal litigation: 1. Husband and wife may sue each other for personal injuries. **2.** Husband may recover for loss of wife's consortium. Wife may recover for loss of husband's consortium.

Rights of wife: 1. Wife may enter into contracts, sell property, and engage in business on exactly the same basis as her husband. **2.** Wife may not use maiden name without restrictions. **3.** Wife

may retain separate domicile for voting.

Common-law marriage: Not valid.

COLORADO

Support: Husband has primary duty to support wife. Wife is not obligated to support husband if he is unable.

Spousal litigation: 1. Wife may sue husband for personal injuries. **2.** Husband may recover for loss of wife's consortium. Wife may recover for loss of husband's consortium.

Rights of wife: 1. Wife may enter into contracts, sell property, and engage in business on exactly the same basis as her husband. **2.** Wife may not use maiden name without restrictions. **3.** Wife may not retain separate domicile for voting.

Common-law marriage: Status of law uncertain.

CONNECTICUT

Support: Husband has primary duty to support wife. Wife must support husband only to prevent him from going on welfare.

Spousal litigation: 1. Husband and wife may sue each other for personal injuries. **2.** Right to bring consortium suits has been abolished.

Rights of wife: 1. Wife may enter into contracts, sell property, and engage in business on exactly the same basis as her husband. **2.** Wife must list maiden name and married name on voter registration forms. **3.** Wife must meet residency requirements on her own and cannot obtain them through husband.

Common-law marriage: Not valid.

DELAWARE

Support: Husband has primary duty to support wife. Wife must support husband if he is unable, but his parents' obligation comes before hers.

Spousal litigation: 1. Husband and wife may not sue each other for personal injuries. **2.** Husband may recover for loss of wife's consortium. Wife may recover for loss of husband's consortium.

Rights of wife: 1. Wife may enter into contracts,

sell property, and engage in business on exactly the same basis as her husband. **2.** Wife who changes her name by marriage must re-register to vote. **3.** A married woman has the same domicile as her husband if he is domiciled in the state. If he is not, her domicile at the time of marriage continues to be her domicile.
Common-law marriage: Not valid.

DISTRICT OF COLUMBIA

Support: The husband or wife of a public assistance applicant or recipient may be required to support his or her spouse depending on his or her financial responsibility.
Spousal litigation: 1. Husband and wife may not sue each other for personal injuries. **2.** Husband may recover for loss of wife's consortium. Wife may recover for loss of husband's consortium.
Rights of wife: 1. Wife may enter into contracts, sell property, and engage in business on exactly

the same basis as her husband. **2.** Wife may use maiden name without restrictions. **3.** No statute on domicile.
Common-law marriage: Allowed.

FLORIDA

Support: Husband has primary duty to support wife. Wife is not obligated to support husband if he is unable.

Spousal litigation: 1. Husband and wife may not sue each other for personal injuries. **2.** Husband may recover for loss of wife's consortium. Wife may recover for loss of husband's consortium.
Rights of wife: 1. Wife may enter into contracts, sell property, and engage in business on exactly the same basis as her husband. **2.** Wife may use maiden name without restrictions. **3.** Wife may not retain separate domicile for voting.
Common-law marriage: Allowed.

GEORGIA

Support: Husband has primary duty to support wife. Wife is not obligated to support husband if he is unable.
Spousal litigation: 1. Husband and wife may not sue each other for personal injuries. **2.** Husband may recover for loss of wife's consortium. Wife may recover for loss of husband's consortium.
Rights of wife: 1. Generally, wife may enter into contracts, sell property, and engage in business on the same basis as her husband, but she may not contract to guarantee her husband's debts. **2.** Wife may use maiden name without restrictions. **3.** Wife may not retain separate domicile for voting.
Common-law marriage: Allowed.

HAWAII

Support: Husband has primary duty to support wife. Wife is not obligated to support husband if he is unable.
Spousal litigation: 1. Husband and wife may not sue each other for personal injuries. **2.** Husband may recover for loss of wife's consortium. Wife may recover for loss of husband's consortium.
Rights of wife: 1. Wife may enter into contracts, sell property, and engage in business on exactly the same basis as her husband. **2.** Wife may not use maiden name without restrictions. **3.** Wife may retain separate domicile for voting only if husband is not a resident of the state.
Common-law marriage: Not valid.

IDAHO

Support: Husband has primary duty to support wife. If husband is unable to support himself, wife must support him out of her separate property if he has no separate property or there is no community property.

Spousal litigation: 1. Husband and wife may sue each other for personal injuries. **2.** Husband may recover for loss of wife's consortium. Wife may not recover for loss of husband's consortium.

Rights of wife: 1. Wife may enter into contracts, sell property, and engage in business on exactly the same basis as her husband. **2.** Wife may use maiden name without restrictions. **3.** Wife may not retain separate domicile for voting.

Common-law marriage: Allowed.

ILLINOIS

Support: Husband has primary duty to support wife. Wife must support husband when he is in need.

Spousal litigation: 1. Husband and wife may not sue each other for personal injuries. **2.** Husband may recover for loss of wife's consortium. Wife may recover for loss of husband's consortium.

Rights of wife: 1. Wife may enter into contracts, sell property, and engage in business on exactly the same basis as her husband. **2.** Wife may not use maiden name without restrictions. **3.** Wife

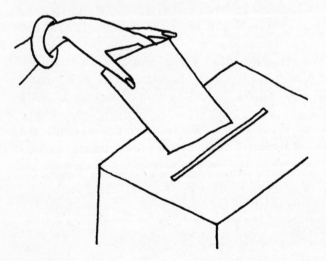

may retain separate domicile for voting.

Common-law marriage: Not valid.

INDIANA

Support: Husband has primary duty to support wife. Wife is not obligated to support husband if he is unable.

Spousal litigation: 1. Husband and wife may not sue each other for personal injuries. **2.** Husband may recover for loss of wife's consortium. Wife may recover for loss of husband's consortium.

Rights of wife: 1. Wife may enter into contracts, sell property, and engage in business on exactly the same basis as her husband. **2.** Wife who is a professional woman may vote or be a candidate under the name used in the profession. **3.** Wife may retain separate domicile for voting.

Common-law marriage: Not valid.

IOWA

Support: Husband has primary duty to support wife. Wife is not obligated to support husband if he is unable.

Spousal litigation: 1. Husband and wife may not sue each other for personal injuries caused by negligence. **2.** Husband may recover for loss of wife's consortium. Wife may recover for loss of husband's consortium.

Rights of wife: 1. Wife may enter into contracts, sell property, and engage in business on exactly the same basis as her husband. **2.** Wife may not use maiden name without restrictions. **3.** Wife may retain separate domicile for voting.

Common-law marriage: Allowed.

KANSAS

Support: Both husband and wife must support the other spouse if he or she is in "necessitous circumstances."

Spousal litigation: 1. Husband and wife may not sue each other for personal injuries. **2.** Husband may recover for loss of wife's consortium. Wife may not recover for loss of husband's consortium.

Rights of wife: 1. Wife may enter into contracts, sell property, and engage in business on exactly the same basis as her husband. **2.** Wife may not have her name changed. **3.** Wife may not retain separate domicile for voting.
Common-law marriage: Allowed.

KENTUCKY

Support: Husband has primary duty to support wife. Wife is not obligated to support husband if he is unable.
Spousal litigation: 1. Husband and wife may sue each other for personal injuries. **2.** Husband may recover for loss of wife's consortium. Wife may recover for loss of husband's consortium.
Rights of wife: 1. Generally, wife may enter into contracts and engage in business on the same basis as her husband, but she may not contract to guarantee her husband's debts and she may not sell property unless her husband joins her in the deed—a restriction not placed on the husband. **2.** Wife may not have her name changed. **3.** Wife may retain separate domicile for voting.
Common-law marriage: Not valid.

LOUISIANA

Support: Husband has primary duty to support wife. Wife is not obligated to support husband if he is unable.
Spousal litigation: 1. Wife may not sue husband for personal injuries. **2.** Right to bring consortium suits has been abolished.
Rights of wife: 1. Wife may enter into contracts, sell property, and engage in business on exactly the same basis as her husband. **2.** Wife may use maiden name without restrictions. **3.** Wife may not retain separate domicile for voting.
Common-law marriage: Not valid.

MAINE

Support: Husband has primary duty to support wife. Wife is not obligated to support husband if he is unable.

Spousal litigation: 1. Husband and wife may not sue each other for personal injuries. **2.** Husband may recover for loss of wife's consortium. Wife may recover for loss of husband's consortium.
Rights of wife: 1. Wife may enter into contracts, sell property, and engage in business on the same basis as her husband, except that she may not sell property given to her by her husband unless he joins her in the deed (unless the property was given to her as payment for a debt he owed her). **2.** Wife's voter registration will automatically be corrected to her married name. **3.** Wife may retain separate domicile for voting.
Common-law marriage: Not valid.

MARYLAND

Support: Husband has primary duty to support wife. Wife is not obligated to support husband if he is unable.
Spousal litigation: 1. Wife may not sue husband for personal injuries. **2.** Husband may recover for loss of wife's consortium. Wife may not recover for loss of husband's consortium.
Rights of wife: 1. Wife may enter into contracts, sell property, and engage in business on exactly the same basis as her husband. **2.** Wife may use maiden name without restrictions. **3.** Wife may not retain separate domicile for voting.
Common-law marriage: Not valid.

MASSACHUSETTS

Support: Husband has primary duty to support wife. Wife is not obligated to support husband if he is unable.
Spousal litigation: 1. Husband and wife may not sue each other for personal injuries. **2.** Right to bring consortium suits has been abolished.
Rights of wife: 1. Wife may enter into contracts, sell property, and engage in business on exactly the same basis as her husband. **2.** Wife who changes her name by marriage must re-register to vote. **3.** Wife may retain separate domicile for voting.
Common-law marriage: Not valid.

MICHIGAN

Support: Husband has primary duty to support wife. Wife must support husband if he is likely to become a public charge.

Spousal litigation: 1. Husband and wife may not sue each other for personal injuries. 2. Husband may recover for loss of wife's consortium. Wife may recover for loss of husband's consortium.

Rights of wife: 1. Generally, wife may enter into contracts, sell property, and engage in business on the same basis as her husband, but she may not agree to make her property liable for debts jointly assumed with her husband. 2. Wife is not required to re-register for voting after marriage, but when husband petitions for a name change, the court automatically includes wife in the petition. 3. Wife may retain separate domicile for voting.

Common-law marriage: Not valid.

MINNESOTA

Support: Husband has primary duty to support wife. Wife is not obligated to support husband if he is unable.

Spousal litigation: 1. Husband and wife may sue each other for personal injuries. 2. Husband may recover for loss of wife's consortium. Wife may recover for loss of husband's consortium.

Rights of wife: 1. Wife may enter into contracts, sell property, and engage in business on exactly the same basis as her husband. 2. Wife may not use maiden name without restrictions. 3. Wife must fulfill residency requirements on her own, not by virtue of marrying a resident.

Common-law marriage: Not valid.

MISSISSIPPI

Support: Husband has primary duty to support wife. Wife is not obligated to support husband if he is unable.

Spousal litigation: 1. Husband and wife may not sue each other for personal injuries. 2. Husband may recover for loss of wife's consortium. Wife may recover for loss of husband's consortium.

Rights of wife: 1. Wife may enter into contracts, sell property, and engage in business on exactly the same basis as her husband. 2. Wife may use maiden name without restrictions. 3. Wife may not retain separate domicile for voting.

Common-law marriage: Not valid.

MISSOURI

Support: Husband has primary duty to support wife. Wife is not obligated to support husband if he is unable.

Spousal litigation: 1. Husband and wife may not sue each other for personal injuries. 2. Husband may recover for loss of wife's consortium. Wife may recover for loss of husband's consortium.

Rights of wife: 1. Wife may enter into contracts, sell property, and engage in business on exactly the same basis as her husband. 2. Wife may not use maiden name without restrictions. 3. Wife may not retain separate domicile for voting.

Common-law marriage: Not valid.

MONTANA

Support: Husband has primary duty to support wife. If husband is unable to support himself, wife must support him out of her separate property if he has no separate property.

Spousal litigation: 1. Husband and wife may not sue each other for personal injuries. 2. Husband may recover for loss of wife's consortium. Wife may recover for loss of husband's consortium.

Rights of wife: 1. Wife may enter into contracts, sell property, and engage in business on exactly the same basis as her husband. 2. Wife may use separate name without restrictions. 3. Wife may not retain separate domicile for voting.

Common-law marriage: Allowed.

NEBRASKA

Support: Husband has primary duty to support wife. Wife is not obligated to support husband if he is unable.

Spousal litigation: 1. Husband and wife may not sue each other for personal injuries. **2.** Husband may recover for loss of wife's consortium. Wife may recover for loss of husband's consortium.
Rights of wife: 1. Wife may enter into contracts, sell property, and engage in business on exactly the same basis as her husband. **2.** Wife must re-register to vote if her name is changed by marriage. **3.** Wife may not retain separate domicile for voting.
Common-law marriage: Not valid.

NEVADA

Support: Husband has primary duty to support wife. If husband is unable to support himself, wife must support him out of her separate property if he has no separate property or there is no community property.
Spousal litigation: 1. Husband and wife may sue each other for personal injuries. **2.** Husband may recover for loss of wife's consortium. Wife may not recover for loss of husband's consortium.
Rights of wife: 1. Wife may enter into contracts, sell property, and engage in business on exactly the same basis as her husband. **2.** Wife may not use maiden name without restrictions. **3.** Wife may not retain separate domicile for voting.
Common-law marriage: Not valid.

NEW HAMPSHIRE

Support: Husband has primary duty to support wife. Wife is liable to the state for funds expended on a husband who cannot support himself.
Spousal litigation: 1. Husband and wife may sue each other for personal injuries. **2.** Husband may recover for loss of wife's consortium. Wife may recover for loss of husband's consortium.
Rights of wife: 1. Wife may enter into contracts, sell property, and engage in business on exactly the same basis as her husband. **2.** Wife may use maiden name without restrictions. **3.** Wife may not retain separate domicile for voting.

Common-law marriage: Not valid.

NEW JERSEY

Support: Husband has primary duty to support wife. Wife must support husband if he is likely to become a public charge.
Spousal litigation: 1. Husband and wife may sue each other for personal injuries. **2.** Husband may recover for loss of wife's consortium. Wife may recover for loss of husband's consortium.
Rights of wife: 1. Wife may enter into contracts, sell property, and engage in business on exactly the same basis as her husband. **2.** Wife who changes name due to marriage must re-register to vote. A female notary who marries must sign her surname, hyphen, husband's surname. **3.** Wife may retain separate domicile for voting.
Common-law marriage: Not valid.

NEW MEXICO

Support: Husband has primary duty to support wife. If husband is unable to support himself, wife must support him out of her separate property if he has no separate property or there is no community property.
Spousal litigation: 1. Husband and wife may not

sue each other for personal injuries. **2.** Husband may recover for loss of wife's consortium. Wife may not recover for negligently caused loss of husband's consortium.

Rights of wife: 1. Wife may enter into contracts, sell property, and engage in business on exactly the same basis as her husband. **2.** Wife need not indicate marital status when registering to vote, but must sign her given name, middle name or initial, married surname. **3.** Wife may not retain separate domicile for voting.

Common-law marriage: Not valid.

NEW YORK

Support: Husband has primary duty to support wife. Wife must support husband if he is likely to become a public charge.

Spousal litigation: 1. Husband and wife may sue each other for personal injuries. **2.** Husband may recover for loss of wife's consortium. Wife may recover for loss of husband's consortium.

Rights of wife: 1. Wife may enter into contracts, sell property, and engage in business on exactly the same basis as her husband. **2.** Wife may choose to vote under maiden name, but there is an 1881 decision on the books which holds that upon marriage a wife's maiden name is lost and husband's surname is her legal name. **3.** Wife may retain separate domicile for voting.

Common-law marriage: Not valid.

NORTH CAROLINA

Support: Husband has primary duty to support wife. Wife is not obligated to support husband if he is unable.

Spousal litigation: 1. Husband and wife may sue each other for personal injuries. **2.** Right to bring consortium suits has been abolished.

Rights of wife: 1. Wife may enter into contracts, sell property, and engage in business on exactly the same basis as her husband. **2.** Wife may not use maiden name without restrictions. **3.** Wife may not retain separate domicile for voting.

Common-law marriage: Not valid.

NORTH DAKOTA

Support: Husband has primary duty to support wife. If husband is unable to support himself, wife must support him out of her separate property if he has no separate property.

Spousal litigation: 1. Wife may sue husband for personal injuries. **2.** Husband may recover for loss of wife's consortium. Wife may not recover for loss of husband's consortium.

Rights of wife: 1. Wife may enter into contracts, sell property, and engage in business on exactly the same basis as her husband. **2.** Wife may use maiden name without restrictions. **3.** Wife may retain separate domicile for voting.

Common-law marriage: Not valid.

OHIO

Support: Husband has primary duty to support wife. Wife must support husband if he is in need.

Spousal litigation: 1. Husband and wife may not sue each other for personal injuries. **2.** Husband

may recover for loss of wife's consortium. Wife may recover for loss of husband's consortium.

Rights of wife: 1. Wife may enter into contracts, sell property, and engage in business on exactly the same basis as her husband. **2.** Wife's voter registration is automatically canceled upon marriage, and she must re-register under married name unless she has agreed to maintain her maiden name, has advised the proper authorities of her decision, and has used her maiden name consistently so that it could be said that she never changed her name. **3.** Wife may retain separate domicile for voting.

Common-law marriage: Allowed.

OKLAHOMA

Support: Husband has primary duty to support wife. If husband is unable to support himself, wife must support him out of her separate property if he has no separate property.

Spousal litigation: 1. Husband and wife may sue each other for personal injuries. **2.** Husband may recover for loss of wife's consortium. Wife may not recover for loss of husband's consortium.

Rights of wife: 1. Wife may enter into contracts, sell property, and engage in business on exactly the same basis as her husband. **2.** Wife may not use maiden name without restrictions. **3.** Wife may not retain separate domicile for voting.

Common-law marriage: Allowed.

OREGON

Support: Husband has primary duty to support wife. Wife is not obligated to support husband if he is unable.

Spousal litigation: 1. Husband and wife may sue each other for personal injuries caused by willful conduct, but not if they are caused by negligence. **2.** Husband may recover for loss of wife's consortium. Wife may recover for loss of husband's consortium.

Rights of wife: 1. Wife may enter into contracts, sell property, and engage in business on exactly the same basis as her husband. **2.** Wife must re-register to vote if her name is changed by marriage. **3.** Wife may not retain separate domicile for voting.

Common-law marriage: Not valid.

PENNSYLVANIA

Support: Husband has primary duty to support

wife. Wife must support husband if he is likely to become a public charge.

Spousal litigation: 1. Husband and wife may not sue each other for personal injuries. **2.** Husband may recover for loss of wife's consortium. Wife may not recover for loss of husband's consortium.

Rights of wife: 1. Wife may enter into contracts, sell property, and engage in business on exactly the same basis as her husband. **2.** Wife may use maiden name without restrictions. **3.** Wife may not retain separate domicile for voting.

Common-law marriage: Allowed.

RHODE ISLAND

Support: Husband has primary duty to support wife. Wife is not obligated to support husband if he is unable.

Spousal litigation: 1. Husband and wife may not sue each other for personal injuries caused by negligence. **2.** Right to bring consortium suits has been abolished.

Rights of wife: 1. Wife may enter into contracts, sell property, and engage in business on exactly the same basis as her husband. **2.** Wife may not use maiden name without restrictions. **3.** Wife may not retain separate domicile for voting.

Common-law marriage: Allowed.

SOUTH CAROLINA

Support: Husband has primary duty to support wife. Wife is not obligated to support husband if he is unable.

Spousal litigation: 1. Husband and wife may sue each other for personal injuries. **2.** Husband may recover for loss of wife's consortium. Wife may not recover for loss of husband's consortium.

Rights of wife: 1. Wife may enter into contracts, sell property, and engage in business on exactly the same basis as her husband. **2.** Wife may use maiden name without restrictions. **3.** Wife may not retain separate domicile for voting.

Common-law marriage: Allowed.

SOUTH DAKOTA

Support: Husband has primary duty to support wife. If husband is unable to support himself, wife must support him out of her separate property if he has no separate property.

Spousal litigation: 1. Husband and wife may sue each other for personal injuries. **2.** Husband may recover for loss of wife's consortium. Wife may recover for loss of husband's consortium.

Rights of wife: 1. Wife may enter into contracts, sell property, and engage in business on exactly the same basis as her husband. **2.** Wife may not use maiden name without restrictions. **3.** Wife may not retain separate domicile for voting.

Common-law marriage: Not valid.

TENNESSEE

Support: Husband has primary duty to support wife. Wife is not obligated to support husband if he is unable.

Spousal litigation: 1. Husband and wife may not sue each other for personal injuries. **2.** Husband may recover for loss of wife's consortium. Wife may recover for loss of husband's consortium.

Rights of wife: 1. Wife may enter into contracts, sell property, and engage in business on exactly the same basis as her husband. **2.** Wife must re-register to vote if her name is changed by marriage. **3.** Wife may retain separate domicile for voting.

Common-law marriage: Not valid.

TEXAS

Support: Husband has primary duty to support wife. Wife must support husband if he is in need.

Spousal litigation: 1. Wife may not sue husband for personal injuries. **2.** Husband may recover for loss of wife's consortium. Wife may not recover for loss of husband's consortium.

Rights of wife: 1. Wife may enter into contracts, sell property, and engage in business on exactly the same basis as her husband. **2.** Wife may use maiden name without restrictions. **3.** Wife may

not retain separate domicile for voting.

Common-law marriage: Allowed.

UTAH

Support: Husband has primary duty to support wife. Wife must support husband if he is in need.

Spousal litigation: 1. Wife may not sue husband for personal injuries caused by negligence. **2.** Right to bring consortium suits has been abolished.

Rights of wife: 1. Wife may enter into contracts,

sell property, and engage in business on exactly the same basis as her husband. **2.** Wife may use maiden name without restrictions. **3.** Wife may not retain separate domicile for voting.

Common-law marriage: Not valid.

VERMONT

Support: Husband has primary duty to support wife. If husband is unable to support himself, wife must support him out of her separate property if he has no separate property.

Spousal litigation: 1. Husband and wife may not sue each other for personal injuries. **2.** Husband may recover for loss of wife's consortium. Wife may not recover for loss of husband's consortium.

Rights of wife: 1. Wife may enter into contracts, sell property, and engage in business on exactly the same basis as her husband. **2.** Married person

needs consent of his or her spouse to change name, but if a married man changes his name it becomes his wife's name. **3.** Wife may not retain separate domicile for voting.
Common-law marriage: Not valid.

VIRGINIA

Support: Husband has primary duty to support wife. If husband is unable to support himself, wife must support him out of her separate property if he has no separate property.
Spousal litigation: 1. Husband and wife may sue each other for personal injuries arising from automobile accidents. **2.** Right to bring consortium suits has been abolished.
Rights of wife: 1. Wife may enter into contracts, sell property, and engage in business on exactly the same basis as her husband. **2.** Wife must notify voter registrar when her name is changed by marriage. **3.** Wife may not retain separate domicile for voting.
Common-law marriage: Not valid.

WASHINGTON

Support: Husband has primary duty to support wife. Wife is not obligated to support husband if he is unable.
Spousal litigation: 1. Husband and wife may sue each other for personal injuries. **2.** Husband may recover for loss of wife's consortium. Wife may not recover for loss of husband's consortium.
Rights of wife: 1. Wife may enter into contracts, sell property, and engage in business on exactly the same basis as her husband. **2.** Wife may use maiden name without restrictions. **3.** Wife may not retain separate domicile for voting.
Common-law marriage: Not valid.

WEST VIRGINIA

Support: Husband has primary duty to support wife. Wife is not obligated to support husband if he is unable.
Spousal litigation: 1. Husband and wife may sue each other for personal injuries. **2.** Husband may

recover for loss of wife's consortium. Wife may recover for loss of husband's consortium.
Rights of wife: 1. Wife may enter into contracts, sell property, and engage in business on exactly the same basis as her husband. **2.** Wife may not use maiden name without restrictions. **3.** Wife may not retain separate domicile for voting.
Common-law marriage: Not valid.

WISCONSIN

Support: Husband has primary duty to support wife. Wife must support husband if he is likely to become a public charge.
Spousal litigation: 1. Wife may sue husband for personal injuries. Husband may sue wife for personal injuries caused by her wrongful act, neglect, or default. **2.** Husband may recover for loss of wife's consortium. Wife may recover for loss of husband's consortium
Rights of wife: 1. Wife may enter into contracts, sell property, and engage in business on exactly the same basis as her husband. **2.** Wife may use maiden name without restrictions. **3.** Wife may retain separate domicile for voting.
Common-law marriage: Not valid.

WYOMING

Support: Husband has primary duty to support wife. Wife is not obligated to support husband if he is unable.
Spousal litigation: 1. Wife may not sue husband for personal injuries caused by negligence, but there is uncertainty as to whether such suits are disallowed only because of the absence of insurance or whether they are disallowed in all circumstances. **2.** Husband may recover for loss of wife's consortium. Wife may not recover for loss of husband's consortium.
Rights of wife: 1. Wife may enter into contracts, sell property, and engage in business on exactly the same basis as her husband. **2.** Wife who is a notary public must inform the secretary of state of her choice not to adopt her husband's name. **3.** Wife may retain separate domicile for voting.
Common-law marriage: Not valid.

2
When I Have Children

The right to have children is inalienable. But since few human acts escape either the protection or the confinement of laws, creating a child brings its parents face to face with previously unconsidered legal responsibilities. In its own right, the child exists in law. Once a man and a woman have given life to a child, they take on both rights and responsibilities toward that child.

While the law does not dictate who may or may not have children (except where it permits sterilization of some habitual criminals), it can and does punish mothers and fathers whose performance in child care falls below standards imposed by society. Fortunately, society's standards are accepted by most parents, who observe them without being aware that they are legally bound to do so.

It is questionable whether any laws can make irresponsible parents responsible. But laws do provide some means of protecting the rights of children, even to the extent of removing them from their natural (biological) parents when those parents are not living up to their basic obligations to support, nurture, and educate the child. Some states place the support duty entirely on the father, calling on the mother only if he is unable to shoulder it alone. Others totally relieve the mother of this duty, whether she be rich or poor. But thirty-one states and the District of Columbia bind both parents equally. Several states still retain vestiges of Elizabethan poor laws, which obliged all family members to support those adults or children unable to support themselves.

Just as courts are reluctant to intervene in marital disputes over adequate support and treatment (see Chapter 1), so are they reluctant to intervene in disputes concerning parental obligations, unless parents are not providing their children with necessities. But the definition of "necessity" depends in large degree on the parents' means, and affluent parents are by custom required to provide their children with far more than bare essentials. Thus, for example, in New York a twenty-year-old college student sued her father when he cut off her support after she moved from a dormitory to a private apartment. She won the first round, but on appeal the decision was reversed. The court maintained that though the daughter had a right to choose her own style of living, her father had no obligation to support it if he disapproved of it. Poverty necessarily has other standards—how can poor parents be forced to give a child more than they can afford?

The law, therefore, distinguishes between those parents who *will not* and those who *cannot* support their minor children. It is a crime in almost every state to desert young children who are dependent, unless the parent can demonstrate that he or she is truly unable to provide for their support or there is reasonable excuse for desertion. However, if a parent is unable to provide a decent minimal degree of support, he or she (or both) may be declared unfit by the court, and temporarily or permanently lose custody of the child.

The support duty applies only to minor children, but if the child is a college student many states extend this obligation. If a child is physically or mentally disabled, support obligations may continue indefinitely. Penalties for breaking child-support laws are relatively light; the courts recognize the fact that throwing parents into jail will rarely help the child.

Every state has legal provisions to remove minor children from the custody of unfit or unsuitable parents. If the parents have been found legally insane or convicted of particular crimes or found to have contributed to a child's delinquency, the children may be placed in institutions or foster homes on court order. Except in extreme cases, a child is not removed from his or her parents' custody before the court acts. In these situations the juvenile court system begins an action known as "loss-of-parental-rights" proceedings, which tend mainly and often unfairly to affect racial minorities and the poor.

Children born of unwed parents are said to be "illegitimate," though a more honest view might see only the parents "illegitimate" and the child "innocent." Legitimacy is determined in four ways. In the first, if the mother is married—either at the time her child was conceived or at its birth—eleven states (California, Colorado, Idaho, Kentucky, Louisiana, Montana, Nevada, North Dakota, Oregon, South Dakota, Wisconsin) presume her legal husband is the child's father. In some of these states, this determination may be modified if the spouses were not cohabiting (sharing the same bed) when the child was conceived, or if blood-test evidence disproves the husband's paternity. Another way to establish legitimacy is for the father to follow the state's required procedures to "legitimate" (publicly acknowledge) the child as his even if he and the child's mother were not married at the time of conception or birth. A child also becomes legitimate if its parents subsequently marry.

Finally, an illegitimate child can be declared legitimate if a nonbiological father adopts his wife's child. Louisiana's laws on illegitimacy differ from those of every other state in both concept and language (see page 51). Louisiana is the only state to legally sanction the use of the term "bastard" for certain kinds of illegitimate children.

Since no system of laws can limit childbearing to married couples, children of unwed parents must be provided for. According to the common law, the natural mother has the legal right to custody, care, and control of her illegitimate children. She always has a duty to support such children; no state has yet done away with this duty. However, as a result of statute and recent

U.S. Supreme Court decisions holding that discriminations based on illegitimacy violate the equal protection clause of the Fourteenth Amendment, the natural father of an illegitimate child has the same support obligation as if the child were legitimate. The problem is one of proof and enforcement. If the alleged natural father refuses to provide support, the mother must institute paternity proceedings on her child's behalf to establish both the fact of paternity and the amount of support obligation. In the latter situation,

the court proceedings are comparable to those followed when natural parents divorce and the parent who does not have custody of the child must provide financial support.

While the father of an illegitimate child has support obligations comparable to those due a legitimate child, until the Supreme Court's 1972 decision in the case of *Stanley v. Illinois* he did not have any custody or related rights, as do both the father and mother of a legitimate child. The Court strengthened an unwed father's rights by ruling that he must be allowed to have the opportunity to a hearing to decide whether he should assume custody of his illegitimate child if the mother dies, rather than having the state take custody. The decision does not remove primary support and custody from an unwed mother or give the father full rights, but it recognizes his standing if he does in fact wish to be recognized. (The *Stanley* ruling also affects adoption consents; see Chapter 3.)

Coupled with obligations and duties to their young, parents also enjoy privileges and rights over their children. Nearly every state gives both natural parents of legitimate children mutual rights of custody and control over the earnings and services of their minor children—a right which these days is not often asserted but is nonetheless available. Statutes vary widely. Louisiana gives the parents no right to a child's earnings, and two states, Hawaii and Wyoming, have no statute on this aspect of the law. But in Florida the law is very precise. A mother and father may appropriate no more than one thousand of their child-earned dollars.

When a child harms or destroys property

or injures another person, it is usually pointless to try to recover damages from the child, so forty-three states hold parents "vicariously liable"—that is, financially responsible—as if they personally had committed the wrong. The extent of this legal responsibility is limited by state law. The amount of money parents can be sued for in each of the child's destructive acts ranges from $100 in Minnesota to $2000 in Alaska, California, Nevada, and Ohio. Seven states—Arizona, Louisiana, Massachusetts, Mississippi, New Hampshire, Tennessee, Utah—and the District of Columbia have no laws imposing financial responsibility, but all states hold parents responsible if they neglect their parental duty to supervise the child.

When a child is no longer a minor, usually at eighteen or twenty-one, and is physically and mentally capable, the parents are relieved of legal obligations as well as rights they acquired at the child's birth. Many parents continue to help and support their grown children, but they do so through love or habit, not by constraint of law. In some states parents are freed of obligations toward a minor who marries before becoming an adult. But about half the states hold that marriage neither frees a child from its parents' authority nor confers adulthood.

Many courts, however, have freed children from parental authority in special cases and declared them "emancipated minors." Minors may be emancipated, for example, if they are not adequately cared for by their parents, if they acquire greater financial resources than their parents and manage to support themselves, or if they leave home and have an independent residence.

Parental authority is not the only authority governing minors. "Guardianship," which may or may not rest with a child's parents, also is concerned with custody rights and support duties as well as management of a minor's property, money, and legal claims.

There are various systems of guardianship within the family. Under English common law, the natural father was also the guardian of his child. In America, most states have decided to recognize both father and mother as joint guardians, providing the parents are living together. If the father dies or abandons the family, the mother becomes guardian. A few states will give the father the greater power, but most often both parents equally govern their child. If relatives or persons other than the natural parents assume guardianship of a child, special legal proceedings (similar to those of adoption) are necessary.

The law distinguishes between two types of guardianship; the guardian of the child's physical being may not always be the same person as the guardian of the child's separate estate. For example, guardians of a child's physical being may be his or her natural parents, while guardians of the same child's separate estate may be a financial institution. When minor children have inherited or earned substantial personal wealth, their property may be given to a bank, trustee, or other person to administer, rather than to the natural parents.

A much more acute problem concerning guardianship comes up when parents are divorced or separated. In the remarriage of a divorced parent who has partial or complete child custody and receives child-support payments, no state imposes a support obligation on the stepparent. The natural parent who has been providing child support must continue to do so. If, however, the stepparent wants to adopt the child, consent of the "replaced" parent is required. If consent is given, the natural parent permanently gives up all parental rights and duties.

In a legal separation or divorce, if parents do not agree, the court must decide which parent can provide the best home for the child. It is customary, other things being equal, to give young children to the mother and permit older children to live with their father, because he is supposedly in a better position to supervise their higher education. In fact, however, about 90 per cent of all children of divorced or separated parents live with their mothers. Sometimes custody is joint, with the child spending approximately 50 per cent of the time living with each parent. However, even if custody is given to one parent only, the other parent usually is awarded visitation rights. (Also see Chapter 5.)

From time to time state legislators try to discourage childbearing among certain groups of people. Thus a bill was recently introduced in the New York legislature requiring unmarried welfare mothers of three or more children to submit to sterilization in order to continue to receive welfare benefits. In another case, a judge in California attempted to impose sterilization as a condition of probation for a young mother who was a drug addict. Neither of these attempts to impose morality by judicial or legislative edict survived challenges to their constitutionality.

When the state does try to legislate morality it is likely to be at the expense of the poor. An example of one way this is done is through the most widespread type of welfare assistance—the Aid to Families with Dependent Children (AFDC) program, established as part of the federal Social Security Act in 1935. AFDC is designed to give financial aid to "needy" children and their families. A child is needy, according to the program's criteria, if one of his or her parents—usually the father—is continually absent from home, is completely incapacitated, or is dead, and if the family's income falls below minimum levels set by each state.

An early example of states' using the AFDC program to regulate the morality of welfare recipients was to deny AFDC assistance to an otherwise eligible child solely because his or her mother gave birth to an illegitimate child or had an ongoing "illicit" sexual relationship, or because the child's home environment was judged by welfare officials to be "unsuitable." Recent U.S. Supreme Court decisions have held such state disqualifications illegal under the governing federal AFDC laws.

The Court, however, has upheld other state practices that subject AFDC recipients to pressures that those who do not receive welfare do not have to endure. For example, a welfare caseworker is permitted to search an AFDC family's home every six months for evidence that the family is not living up (or down) to the program's requirements even though the authorities may have no reason whatsoever to believe the family is abusing the program. This practice was held by the Supreme Court to be an exception to the Fourth Amendment's requirement that a search warrant is necessary before one's home may be searched.

Another problem faced by AFDC families in the states that do not have the optional AFDC-UF program (described below) is that assistance will be denied to an otherwise eligible family if an unemployed father is living in the home, even if the family's need is caused by the father's inability to find work. Inadequate as the assistance is, it is better than nothing, and often it is better than the salary an unskilled, uneducated man would receive if he could find work. Thus, many critics charge, the AFDC program encourages families to break up because an unemployed father—unless he is totally incapacitated—must desert his family for it to be eligible for AFDC. Clearly this is contrary to accepted morality as well as to the AFDC guidelines' stated goal of "strengthening family ties."

The "Catch-22" quality of this requirement has prompted twenty-four states to enact an optional companion AFDC program. Under AFDC-UF (unemployed father), an eligible child's father is permitted to live with his family if he is not working as long as he participates in mandatory work and training programs specified in the federal regulations. The least the other states could do is adopt AFDC-UF, even though it only partially alleviates some of the inequities and humiliations the poor are subjected to because of the nature of our welfare programs.

While the law discourages childbearing in certain circumstances, it traditionally encourages married couples to have children.

If a person marries with the intention of not having children and fraudulently fails to tell his or her spouse until after the ceremony, this may be grounds for annulment or divorce. But what if a man marries with the intention of having children and finds he is sterile and unable to father a child? Sterility can be overcome by two types of artificial insemination: AIH (artificial insemination, husband), in which the husband's sperm is used to impregnate the wife, and AID (artificial insemination, donor), in which a donor other than the husband supplies the sperm. With AIH there is little need for special regulation, but AID presents several legal problems.

In AID the husband must sign an agreement for the use of the donor's sperm. He then becomes legally responsible for the child, as though it were his own physical offspring. Sometimes a husband has later tried to avoid financial responsibility for his AID children, but the courts have held him to be the legal father. However, if artificial insemination is used without the husband's consent or without his knowledge, then he may use this as a ground for divorce, and will not be held responsible for supporting the child.

In the past, doctors were so discreet about performing artificial insemination that they often made no record of it at all. New York was one of the first states to require legal records of the procedure in order to control possible carriers of congenital disease and to allow legal supervision of AID. Today seven states (California, Florida, Georgia, New York, North Carolina, Oklahoma, Virginia) have laws on artificial insemination.

2
When I Have Children
The Law
State by State

ALABAMA

Parental support: Both parents have joint obligation. Parents who willfully neglect their dependent children are guilty of a crime.

Guardianship: Father is guardian. If he dies or is living apart from family, mother is guardian.

Right to minor's earnings: Father is entitled. If he dies or is living apart from family, mother has right.

Parental liability: Parents are responsible for willful damage to property by their children.

Obligation to support poor relatives: The parents, grandparents, children, and grandchildren of persons unable to support themselves are required to support them to the best of their ability.

Obligation of stepparents: Stepfather is required to support a stepchild if he has publicly acknowledged the child and treated it as his own, even though he does not have custody of the child.

Legitimation: Marriage of the parents or father's written acknowledgment of paternity, in court proceedings, legitimates a child.

Artificial insemination: No statute.

Aid to Families with Dependent Children (AFDC) law: Does *not* have provision to provide benefits to families if an able-bodied unemployed father is living with the family.

ALASKA

Parental support: Both parents have joint obligation. Parents who willfully neglect their dependent children are guilty of a crime.

Guardianship: No statute.

Right to minor's earnings: Father is entitled. If he dies or is living apart from family, mother has right.

Parental liability: Parents are responsible for willful damage to property by their children under 18.

Obligation to support poor relatives: The parents of persons unable to support themselves are required to support them; children have the same obligation to their parents.

Obligation of stepparents: No statute.

Legitimation: Marriage of the parents, father's written acknowledgment of paternity, or the court's judgment of paternity legitimates a child.

45

Artificial insemination: No statute.

Aid to Families with Dependent Children (AFDC) law: Does *not* have provision to provide benefits to families if an able-bodied unemployed father is living with the family.

ARIZONA

Parental support: Both parents have joint obligation. Parents who willfully neglect their dependent children are guilty of a crime.

Guardianship: Both parents are joint guardians.

Right to minor's earnings: Father is entitled. If he dies or is living apart from family, mother has right.

Parental liability: Parents are responsible, with the children, for willful damage to property and injury to persons by their minor children.

Obligation to support poor relatives: No statute.

Obligation of stepparents: Stepfather is not required to support his stepchildren, although he may be made legally responsible if his actions indicate he has assumed support.

Legitimation: Any child is considered the legitimate and natural child of its parents even if born out of wedlock.

Artificial insemination: No statute.

Aid to Families with Dependent Children (AFDC) law: Does *not* have provision to provide benefits to families if an able-bodied unemployed father is living with the family.

ARKANSAS

Parental support: Both parents have joint obligation. Parents who willfully neglect their children under 16, or physically or mentally handicapped children of any age, are guilty of a crime.

Guardianship: Both parents are joint guardians.

Right to minor's earnings: Father is entitled. If he dies or is living apart from family, mother has right.

Parental liability: Parents are responsible for willful damage to property by their minor children.

Obligation to support poor relatives: The parents of persons unable to support themselves, or who are incompetent or insane, are required to support them to the best of their ability; children have the same obligation to their parents.

Obligation of stepparents: No statute.

Legitimation: Marriage of the parents and father's recognition of the child as his own legitimates a child.

Artificial insemination: No statute.

Aid to Families with Dependent Children (AFDC) law: Does *not* have provision to provide benefits to families if an able-bodied unemployed father is living with the family.

CALIFORNIA

Parental support: Father has primary obligation but mother must assist if he is unable. Parents who willfully neglect their dependent children are guilty of a crime.

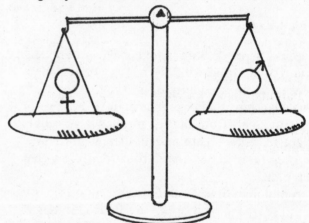

Guardianship: Both parents are joint guardians.

Right to minor's earnings: Both parents are equally entitled.

Parental liability: Parents are liable for willful damage to property and injury to persons by their minor children.

Obligation to support poor relatives: The parents of persons unable to support themselves are required to support them to the best of their ability; children have the same obligation to their parents.

Obligation of stepparents: Stepfather is required to support his stepchildren. However, if he takes stepchildren into his family and acts as a father to them, they have no obligation to reimburse him for his support.

Legitimation: Marriage of the parents legitimates a child. Any child born during wedlock is presumed to be legitimate.

Artificial insemination: A child born by artificial insemination to which the husband consented in writing is legitimate if the child was born during wedlock or within three hundred days of the dissolution of the marriage.

Aid to Families with Dependent Children (AFDC) law: Does have provision to provide benefits to families if an unemployed father is living with the family (AFDC-UF).

COLORADO

Parental support: Father has primary obligation. A father who neglects his dependent children is guilty of a crime.

Guardianship: Both parents are joint guardians.

Right to minor's earnings: Both parents are equally entitled.

Parental liability: Parents are responsible for willful damage to property by their minor children.

Obligation to support poor relatives: Adult children are required to support parents who are unable to support themselves.

Obligation of stepparents: No statute.

Legitimation: Marriage of the parents and father's recognition of the child as his own legitimates a child. Any child born during wedlock is presumed to be legitimate.

Artificial insemination: No statute.

Aid to Families with Dependent Children (AFDC) law: Does have provision to provide benefits to families if an unemployed father is living with the family (AFDC-UF).

CONNECTICUT

Parental support: Father has primary obligation. Parents who willfully neglect their dependent children are guilty of a crime.

Guardianship: Both parents are joint guardians.

Right to minor's earnings: Both parents are equally entitled unless the child has been supported by welfare for three years preceding his or her 18th birthday.

Parental liability: Parents are responsible for willful damage to property and injury to persons by their minor children.

Obligation to support poor relatives: The husband, wife, parents, and children of persons unable to support themselves are required to support them to the best of their ability.

Obligation of stepparents: No statute.

Legitimation: Marriage of the parents legitimates a child.

Artificial insemination: No statute.

Aid to Families with Dependent Children (AFDC) law: Does *not* have provision to provide benefits to families if an able-bodied unemployed father is living with the family.

DELAWARE

Parental support: Father has primary obligation. Parents who willfully neglect their dependent children are guilty of a crime.

Guardianship: Both parents are joint guardians.

Right to minor's earnings: Both parents are equally entitled.

Parental liability: Parents are responsible for willful damage to property by their minor children.

Obligation to support poor relatives: The husband, wife, parents, and children of persons unable to support themselves are required to support them.

Obligation of stepparents: No statute.

Legitimation: Marriage of the parents or father's written acknowledgment of paternity legitimates a child.

Artificial insemination: No statute.

Aid to Families with Dependent Children (AFDC) law: Does have provision to provide benefits to families if an unemployed father is living with the family (AFDC-UF).

DISTRICT OF COLUMBIA

Parental support: Both parents have joint obligation. Parents who willfully neglect their children under 16 are guilty of a crime.
Guardianship: Both parents are joint guardians.
Right to minor's earnings: Father is entitled if he is supporting the family.
Parental liability: Parents are not liable for the misconduct of their children.
Obligation to support poor relatives: The husband, wife, parents, and adult children of persons receiving public assistance or who need public assistance are required to support them.
Obligation of stepparents: No statute.
Legitimation: Marriage of the parents and father's acknowledgment of paternity or the court's judgment of paternity legitimates a child.
Artificial insemination: No statute.
Aid to Families with Dependent Children (AFDC) law: Does have provision to provide benefits to families if an unemployed father is living with the family (AFDC-UF).

FLORIDA

Parental support: Father has primary obligation. Parents who willfully neglect their dependent children are guilty of a crime.
Guardianship: Both parents are joint guardians.
Right to minor's earnings: Both parents are equally entitled to up to $1000 of a dependent child's earnings.
Parental liability: Parents are responsible for willful damage to property by their minor children.
Obligation to support poor relatives: No statute.
Obligation of stepparents: No statute.
Legitimation: Marriage of the parents legitimates a child.
Artificial insemination: A child born by artificial insemination to which both husband and wife consented in writing is legitimate, if the child was born during wedlock.
Aid to Families with Dependent Children (AFDC) law: Does *not* have provision to provide benefits to families if an able-bodied unemployed father is living with the family.

GEORGIA

Parental support: Father has primary obligation.
Guardianship: Father is guardian. If he dies or is living apart from family, mother is guardian.
Right to minor's earnings: Father is entitled unless he agrees to give the right to a third party, consents to the child's adoption, abandons the child or fails to provide for it, allows the child to keep its earnings (this is revokable at any time), permits the child to marry, or is guilty of cruel treatment of the child.
Parental liability: Parents are responsible for willful damage to property and injury to persons by their minor children.
Obligation to support poor relatives: The parents of persons unable to support themselves are required to support them to the best of their ability; children have the same obligation to their parents.
Obligation of stepparents: No statute.
Legitimation: Marriage of the parents or father's written acknowledgment of paternity, in court proceedings, legitimates a child.
Artificial insemination: A child born by artificial insemination to which both husband and wife consented in writing is legitimate, if the child was born during wedlock or after divorce but within the normal period of gestation.
Aid to Families with Dependent Children (AFDC) law: Does *not* have provision to provide benefits to families if an able-bodied unemployed father is living with the family.

HAWAII

Parental support: Both parents have joint obligation.
Guardianship: Both parents are joint guardians.
Right to minor's earnings: No statute.
Parental liability: Parents are responsible for willful damage to property and injury to persons by their minor children.

Obligation to support poor relatives: No statute.
Obligation of stepparents: Stepparent is required to support a stepchild if the child has been deserted by its parents, is in need, or is living with the stepparent.
Legitimation: Marriage of the parents legitimates a child.
Artificial insemination: No statute.
Aid to Families with Dependent Children (AFDC) law: Does have provision to provide benefits to families if an unemployed father is living with the family (AFDC-UF).

IDAHO

Parental support: Both parents have joint obligation.
Guardianship: Both parents are joint guardians.
Right to minor's earnings: Both parents are equally entitled. If father is living apart from family and mother is supporting the children, she has the sole right.
Parental liability: Parents are responsible for willful damage to property by their minor children.
Obligation to support poor relatives: The parents of persons unable to support themselves are required to support them to the best of their ability; children have the same obligation to their parents.
Obligation of stepparents: No statute.

Legitimation: Marriage of the parents legitimates a child. Any child born during wedlock is presumed to be legitimate. Also, the father of an illegitimate child, by publicly acknowledging his paternity and receiving it into his family—with the consent of his wife, if he is married—thereby adopts a child and legitimates it.
Artificial insemination: No statute.
Aid to Families with Dependent Children (AFDC) law: Does *not* have provision to provide benefits to families if an able-bodied unemployed father is living with the family.

ILLINOIS

Parental support: Both parents have joint obligation. A father is liable for the support of his dependent children even if he is divorced or separated from his wife. Parents who willfully neglect their dependent children are guilty of a crime.
Guardianship: Both parents are joint guardians.
Right to minor's earnings: Both parents are equally entitled.
Parental liability: Parents are responsible for willful damage to property and injury to persons by their minor children.
Obligation to support poor relatives: No statute.
Obligation of stepparents: No statute.
Legitimation: Marriage of the parents and father's acknowledgment of paternity legitimates a child.
Artificial insemination: No statute.
Aid to Families with Dependent Children (AFDC) law: Does have provision to provide benefits to families if an unemployed father is living with the family (AFDC-UF).

INDIANA

Parental support: Both parents have joint obligation. Parents who willfully neglect their dependent children are guilty of a crime.
Guardianship: Both parents are joint guardians.
Right to minor's earnings: Both parents are equally entitled.

Parental liability: Parents are responsible for willful damage to property by their minor children.

Obligation to support poor relatives: Adult children are required to support parents who are unable to support themselves.

Obligation of stepparents: Stepfather is required to support his wife's children if they are living with him and if otherwise they would have to receive public assistance. This obligation does not relieve the natural father of his support obligation.

Legitimation: Marriage of the parents legitimates a child.

Artificial insemination: No statute.

Aid to Families with Dependent Children (AFDC) law: Does *not* have provision to provide benefits to families if an able-bodied unemployed father is living with the family.

IOWA

Parental support: Both parents have joint obligation. Parents who willfully neglect their children under 16 are guilty of a crime.

Guardianship: Both parents are joint guardians.

Right to a minor's earnings: Both parents are equally entitled.

Parental liability: Parents are responsible for the unlawful acts of their minor children.

Obligation to support poor relatives: The parents

of persons unable to support themselves are required to support them; children have the same obligation to their parents.

Obligation of stepparents: No statute.

Legitimation: Marriage of the parents legitimates a child.

Artificial insemination: No statute.

Aid to Families with Dependent Children (AFDC) law: Does have provision to provide benefits to families if an unemployed father is living with the family (AFDC-UF).

KANSAS

Parental support: Both parents have joint obligation. Parents who willfully neglect their children under 16 are guilty of a crime.

Guardianship: Both parents are joint guardians.

Right to minor's earnings: Both parents are equally entitled.

Parental liability: Parents are responsible for willful damage to property by their minor children if children are living with them.

Obligation to support poor relatives: The husband, wife, parents, and children of persons admitted to the state hospital for the insane are required to support them.

Obligation of stepparents: Stepfather is not required to support stepchildren. However, if he voluntarily assumes their care and support, they have no obligation to reimburse him.

Legitimation: Marriage of the parents legitimates a child.

Artificial insemination: No statute.

Aid to Families with Dependent Children (AFDC) law: Does have provision to provide benefits to families if an unemployed father is living with the family (AFDC-UF).

KENTUCKY

Parental support: Father has primary obligation. Parents who willfully neglect their children under 14 or abandon children under 6 are guilty of a crime.

Guardianship: Both parents are joint guardians.

Right to minor's earnings: Both parents are equally entitled.

Parental liability: Parents are responsible for willful damage to property by their minor children.

Obligation to support poor relatives: Children over 18 whose parents are unable to support themselves are required to support them to the best of their ability.

Obligation of stepparents: No statute.

Legitimation: Marriage of the parents and father's recognition of the child as his own legitimates a child. Any child born during wedlock or within ten months thereafter is presumed to be legitimate.

Artificial insemination: No statute.

Aid to Families with Dependent Children (AFDC) law: Does *not* have provision to provide benefits to families if an able-bodied unemployed father is living with the family.

LOUISIANA

Parental support: Both parents have joint obligation.

Guardianship: Both parents are joint guardians. In case of differences between the parents, however, the authority of the father prevails.

Right to a minor's earnings: Neither parent is entitled to any money a dependent child may earn by his or her own labor and industry.

Parental liability: Parents are not responsible for the misconduct of their minor children.

Obligation to support poor relatives: No statute.

Obligation of stepparents: No statute.

Legitimation: A natural father or mother can legitimate their natural child by declaration before a notary or the court, but this acknowledgment can be made only if the parents could have been married legally at the time of conception, or it can be made later if they do legally marry. Illegitimate children who have been acknowledged by their father are called natural children; those who have not been so acknowledged are called bastards. Natural children do not have the same rights as legitimate children in terms of inheritance, etc. Any child born during wedlock is presumed to be legitimate.

Artificial insemination: No statute.

Aid to Families with Dependent Children (AFDC) law: Does *not* have provision to provide benefits to families if an able-bodied unemployed father is living with the family.

MAINE

Parental support: Both parents have joint obligation. Parents who willfully neglect their dependent children are guilty of a crime.

Guardianship: Both parents are joint guardians.

Right to minor's earnings: Both parents are equally entitled.

Parental liability: Parents are responsible for willful damage to property and injury to persons by their children aged 7 to 17.

Obligation to support poor relatives: Adult children whose parents are unable to support themselves are required to support them to the best of their ability.

Obligation of stepparents: No statute.

Legitimation: Marriage of the parents or father's acknowledgment of paternity before a justice of the peace or notary public legitimates a child.

Artificial insemination: No statute.

Aid to Families with Dependent Children (AFDC) law: Does *not* have provision to provide benefits to families if an able-bodied unemployed father is living with the family.

MARYLAND

Parental support: Both parents have joint obligation.

Guardianship: Both parents are joint guardians.

Right to minor's earnings: Both parents are equally entitled.

Parental liability: Parents are responsible for willful damage to property or injury to persons by their minor children.

Obligation to support poor relatives: Children whose parents are unable to support themselves are required to support them to the best of their ability.

Obligation of stepparents: No statute.

Legitimation: Father's written acknowledgment of paternity, his public recognition of the child as his own, the court's judgment of paternity, or marriage of the parents and father's acknowledgment of paternity legitimates a child.

Artificial insemination: No statute.

Aid to Families with Dependent Children (AFDC) law: Does have provision to provide benefits to families if an unemployed father is living with the family (AFDC-UF).

MASSACHUSETTS

Parental support: Both parents have joint obligation. A mother who deserts or refuses to support her children under 16 or willfully fails to provide for her children of any age is guilty of a crime.

Guardianship: Both parents are joint guardians.

Right to minor's earnings: Father is entitled. If he dies or is living apart from his family, mother is entitled.

Parental liability: Parents are not responsible for the misconduct of their minor children.

Obligation to poor relatives: The parents of persons unable to support themselves are required to support them; children have the same obligation to their parents.

Obligation of stepparents: No statute.

Legitimation: Marriage of the parents and father's recognition of the child as his own or the court's judgment of paternity legitimates a child.

Artificial insemination: No statute.

Aid to Families with Dependent Children (AFDC) law: Does have provision to provide benefits to families if an unemployed father is living with the family (AFDC-UF).

MICHIGAN

Parental support: Both parents have joint obligation. A father who deserts his children under 17 is guilty of a crime.

Guardianship: Both parents are joint guardians.

Right to minor's earnings: Both parents are equally entitled, but if one is exclusively supporting the child that parent is entitled before the other parent. However, the child may keep its earnings if the parents do not notify the child's employer to give the earnings to them.

Parental liability: Parents are responsible for willful damage to property and injury to persons by their minor children.

Obligation to support poor relatives: Adult children whose parents are unable to support themselves are required to support them to the best of their ability.

Obligation of stepparents: No statute.

Legitimation: Marriage of the parents or written acknowledgment of paternity by both parents legitimates a child.

Artificial insemination: No statute.

Aid to Families with Dependent Children (AFDC) law: Does have provision to provide benefits to families if an unemployed father is living with the family (AFDC-UF).

MINNESOTA

Parental support: Father has primary obligation, but mother must assist if he is unable and if children are unable to support themselves.

Guardianship: Both parents are joint guardians.

Right to minor's earnings: Both parents are equally entitled. However, the child may keep its earnings if the parents do not notify the child's employer to give the earnings to them.

Parental liability: Parents are responsible for willful damage to property and injury to persons by their minor children.

Obligation to support poor relatives: No statute.

Obligation of stepparents: No statute.

Legitimation: Marriage of the parents legitimates a child.

Artificial insemination: No statute.

Aid to Families with Dependent Children (AFDC) law: Does have provision to provide benefits to families if an unemployed father is living with the family (AFDC-UF).

MISSISSIPPI

Parental support: Both parents have joint obligation. Parents who willfully neglect their children under 16 are guilty of a crime.

Guardianship: Both parents are joint guardians.

Right to minor's earnings: Both parents are equally entitled.

Liability of parents: Parents are not responsible for the misconduct of their minor children.

Obligation to support poor relatives: The parents, grandparents, brothers, sisters, children, and grandchildren of persons unable to support themselves and who are likely to need public assistance are required to support them.

Obligation of stepparents: No statute.

Legitimation: Marriage of the parents and father's acknowledgment of paternity legitimates a child.

Artificial insemination: No statute.

Aid to Families with Dependent Children (AFDC) law: Does *not* have provision to provide benefits to families if an able-bodied unemployed father is living with the family.

MISSOURI

Parental support: Both parents have joint obligation. Parents who willfully neglect their children under 16 are guilty of a crime.

Guardianship: Both parents are joint guardians.

Right to a minor's earnings: Both parents are equally entitled. If the wife is living apart from her husband and is supporting the children, she has sole right.

Parental liability: Parents are responsible for willful damage to property by their minor children.

Obligation to support poor relatives: No statute.

Obligation of stepparents: No statute.

Legitimation: Marriage of the parents and father's recognition of the child as his legitimates a child.

Artificial insemination: No statute.

Aid to Families with Dependent Children (AFDC) law: Does *not* have provision to provide benefits to families if an able-bodied unemployed father is living with the family.

MONTANA

Parental support: Both parents have joint obligation. Parents who willfully neglect their children under 16 are guilty of a crime.

Guardianship: Both parents are joint guardians.

Right to minor's earnings: Both parents are equally entitled. However, the child may keep its earnings if the parents do not notify the child's employer to give the earnings to them.

Parental liability: Parents are responsible for willful damage to property by their minor children.

Obligation to support poor relatives: The parents of persons unable to support themselves are required to support them to the best of their ability; children have the same obligation to their parents.

Obligation of stepparents: Stepfather is required to support his stepchildren. However, if he takes stepchildren into his family and acts as a father to them, they have no obligation to reimburse him for his support.

Legitimation: Marriage of the parents legitimates a child. Any child born during wedlock is presumed to be legitimate.

Artificial insemination: No statute.

Aid to Families with Dependent Children (AFDC)

law: Does *not* have provision to provide benefits to families if an able-bodied unemployed father is living with the family.

NEBRASKA

Parental support: Father has primary obligation. Parents who willfully neglect their children under 16 are guilty of a crime.

Guardianship: Both parents are joint guardians.

Right to minor's earnings: Both parents are equally entitled.

Parental liability: Parents are responsible for willful damage to property and injury to persons by their minor children.

Obligation to support poor relatives: No statute.

Obligation of stepparents: Stepparent is required to support a stepchild to the same extent as a natural or adoptive parent.

Legitimation: Marriage of the parents legitimates a child.

Artificial insemination: No statute.

Aid to Families with Dependent Children (AFDC) law: Does have provision to provide benefits to families if an unemployed father is living with the family (AFDC-UF).

NEVADA

Parental support: Both parents have joint obligation. Parents who willfully neglect their children under 18 are guilty of a crime.

Guardianship: Both parents are joint guardians.

Right to minor's earnings: Both parents are equally entitled. If the wife is living apart from her husband and is supporting the children, she has sole right.

Parental liability: Parents are responsible for willful damage to property and injury to persons by their minor children.

Obligation to support poor relatives: The parents, grandparents, brothers, sisters, children, and grandchildren of persons unable to support themselves and who are likely to need public assistance are required to support them. However, the married daughter of such persons is

not required to contribute to their support unless she has income constituting her separate property.

Obligation of stepparents: No statute.

Legitimation: Marriage of the parents legitimates a child. Any child born during wedlock, if the husband is not impotent, is presumed to be legitimate.

Artificial insemination: No statute.

Aid to Families with Dependent Children (AFDC) law: Does *not* have provision to provide benefits to families if an able-bodied unemployed father is living with the family.

NEW HAMPSHIRE

Parental support: Both parents have joint obligation. Parents who willfully neglect their children under 16, or under 21 if children are physically or mentally handicapped, are guilty of a crime.

Parental custody: Both parents have joint custody.

Right to minor's earnings: Both parents are equally entitled.

Parental liability: Parents are not liable for the misconduct of their minor children.

Obligation to support poor relatives: The husband, wife, parents, and children of persons unable to support themselves are required to support them to the best of their ability.

Obligation of stepparents: Stepparent is required to support a stepchild who would otherwise have to receive public assistance.

Legitimation: Marriage of the parents and acknowledgment of the child as their own legitimates a child.

Artificial insemination: No statute.

Aid to Families with Dependent Children (AFDC) law: Does *not* have provision to provide benefits to families if an able-bodied unemployed father is living with the family.

NEW JERSEY

Parental support: Both parents have joint obligation.

Guardianship: Both parents are joint guardians. If the father has failed to support a child under 14 for five years, however, and the mother has done so, she is sole guardian.

Right to minor's earnings: Both parents are equally entitled.

Parental liability: Parents are responsible for willful damage to property by their minor children.

Obligation to support poor relatives: The parents, grandparents, children, and grandchildren of persons unable to support themselves are required to support them to the best of their ability.

Obligation of stepparents: No statute.

Legitimation: Marriage of the parents and recognition—and treatment—of the child as their own legitimates a child.

Artificial insemination: No statute.

Aid to Families with Dependent Children (AFDC) law: Does *not* have provision to provide benefits to families if an able-bodied unemployed father is living with the family.

NEW MEXICO

Parental support: Both parents have joint obligation.

Guardianship: Both parents are joint guardians.

Right to minor's earnings: Both parents are equally entitled.

Parental liability: Parents are responsible for willful damage to property and injury to persons by their minor children.

Obligation to support poor relatives: No statute.

Obligation of stepparents: No statute.

Legitimation: Marriage of the parents or their written acknowledgment recognizing the child as an heir legitimates the child.

Artificial insemination: No statute.

Aid to Families with Dependent Children (AFDC) law: Does *not* have provision to provide benefits to families if an able-bodied unemployed father is living with the family.

NEW YORK

Parental support: Father has primary obligation but mother must assist if he is unable.

Guardianship: Both parents are joint guardians.

Right to minor's earnings: Both parents are equally entitled.

Parental liability: Parents are responsible for willful damage to property by their children aged 10 to 18.

Obligation to support poor relatives: The parents, grandparents, husband, wife, and children of persons in need of public assistance are required to support them to the best of their ability.

Obligation of stepparents: Stepparent is required to support a stepchild who would otherwise have to receive public assistance.

Legitimation: Marriage of the parents legitimates a child.

Artificial insemination: A child born by artificial insemination to which both husband and wife consented in writing is legitimate, if the child was born during wedlock.

Aid to Families with Dependent Children (AFDC) law: Does have provision to provide benefits to families if an unemployed father is living with the family (AFDC-UF).

NORTH CAROLINA

Parental support: Both parents have joint obligation. Parents who willfully neglect their dependent children are guilty of a crime.

Guardianship: Father is guardian. If he dies or is living apart from family, mother is guardian.

Right to minor's earnings: Father is entitled. If he dies or is living apart from family, mother is entitled.

Parental liability: Parents are liable for willful damage to property by their minor children.

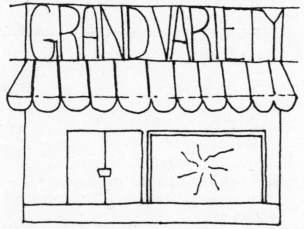

Obligation to support poor relatives: Children whose parents are unable to support themselves are required to support them if they are able to after providing for their immediate family.

Obligation of stepparents: No statute.

Legitimation: Marriage of the parents or father's written acknowledgment of paternity, in court proceedings, legitimates a child.

Artificial insemination: A child born by artificial insemination to which both husband and wife consented in writing is legitimate.

Aid to Families with Dependent Children (AFDC) law: Does *not* have provision to provide benefits to families if an able-bodied unemployed father is living with the family.

NORTH DAKOTA

Parental support: Both parents have joint obligation. Parents who willfully neglect their dependent children are guilty of a crime.

Guardianship: Both parents are joint guardians.

Right to minor's earnings: Both parents are equally entitled.

Parental liability: Parents are responsible for willful damage to property by their minor children.

Obligation to support poor relatives: The parents, grandparents, children, and grandchildren of persons unable to support themselves are required to support them to the best of their ability.

Obligation of stepparents: No statute.

Legitimation: Marriage of the parents legitimates a child. Any child born during wedlock is presumed to be legitimate.

Artificial insemination: No statute.

Aid to Families with Dependent Children (AFDC) law: Does *not* have provision to provide benefits to families if an able-bodied unemployed father is living with the family.

OHIO

Parental support: Father has primary obligation but mother must assist if he is unable.

Guardianship: Both parents are joint guardians.

Right to minor's earnings: Both parents are equally entitled.

Parental liability: Parents are responsible for willful damage to property and assault by their minor children.

Obligation to support poor relatives: No statute.

Obligation of stepparents: No statute.

Legitimation: Marriage of the parents and father's acknowledgment of paternity legitimates a child.

Artificial insemination: No statute.

Aid to Families with Dependent Children (AFDC) law: Does have provision to provide benefits to families if an unemployed father is living with the family (AFDC-UF).

OKLAHOMA

Parental support: Father has primary obligation but mother must assist if he is unable.

Guardianship: Father is guardian. If he dies or is living apart from family, mother is guardian.

Right to minor's earnings: Father is entitled. If

he dies or is living apart from family, mother has right.

Parental liability: Parents are responsible for willful damage to property by their minor children.

Obligation to support poor relatives: The parents of persons unable to support themselves are required to support them to the best of their ability; children have the same obligation to their parents. The promise of an adult child to support a parent is binding.

Obligation of stepparents: Stepfather is required to support his stepchildren. However, if he takes stepchildren into his family and acts as a father to them, they have no obligation to reimburse him for his support.

Legitimation: Marriage of the parents legitimates a child. Also, the father of an illegitimate child, by publicly acknowledging his paternity and receiving it into his family—with the consent of his wife, if he is married—thereby adopts a child and legitimates it.

Artificial insemination: A child born by artificial insemination to which both husband and wife consented in writing is legitimate.

Aid to Families with Dependent Children (AFDC) law: Does have provision to provide benefits to families if an unemployed father is living with the family (AFDC-UF).

OREGON

Parental support: Both parents have joint obligation. Parents who willfully neglect their children under 18 are guilty of a crime.

Guardianship: Both parents are joint guardians.

Right to minor's earnings: Both parents are equally entitled.

Parental liability: Parents are responsible for willful damage to property and injury to persons by their minor children.

Obligation to support poor relatives: The parents of persons unable to support themselves are required to support them; children have the same obligation to their parents.

Obligation of stepparents: Stepparent is required to support stepchildren if they have been deserted by their parents or their parents are dead, if they are in need, or if they are living with the stepparent.

Legitimation: Marriage of the parents legitimates a child. Any child born during wedlock is presumed to be legitimate.

Artificial insemination: No statute.

Aid to Families with Dependent Children (AFDC) law: Does have provision to provide benefits to families if an unemployed father is living with the family (AFDC-UF).

PENNSYLVANIA

Parental support: Father has primary responsibility.

Guardianship: Both parents are joint guardians.

Right to minor's earnings: Both parents are equally entitled.

Parental liability: Parents are responsible for willful damage to property and injury to persons by their minor children.

Obligation to support poor relatives: The husband, wife, parents, and children of persons unable to support themselves are required to support them to the best of their ability.

Obligation of stepparents: No statute.

Legitimation: Marriage of the parents legitimates a child.

Artificial insemination: No statute.

Aid to Families with Dependent Children (AFDC) law: Does have provision to provide benefits to families if an employed father is living with the family (AFDC-UF).

RHODE ISLAND

Parental support: Father has primary obligation but mother must assist if he is unable. Parents who willfully neglect their dependent children are guilty of a crime.

Guardianship: Both parents are joint guardians.

Right to minor's earnings: Both parents are equally entitled.

Parental liability: Parents are responsible for willful damage to property or injury to persons by their minor children.

Obligation to support poor relatives: Adult children whose parents are unable to support themselves are required to support them to the best of their ability.

Obligation of stepparents: No statute.

Legitimation: Marriage of the parents legitimates a child.

Artificial insemination: No statute.

Aid to Families with Dependent Children (AFDC) law: Does have provision to provide benefits to families if an unemployed father is living with the family (AFDC-UF).

SOUTH CAROLINA

Parental support: Father has primary obligation but mother must assist if he is unable. A father who willfully neglects his dependent children is guilty of a crime.

Guardianship: Both parents are joint guardians.

Right to minor's earnings: Both parents are equally entitled.

Parental liability: Parents are responsible for willful damage to property by their minor children.

Obligation to support poor relatives: No statute.

Obligation of stepparents: No statute.

Legitimation: Marriage of the parents or father's written acknowledgment of paternity, in court proceedings, legitimates a child.

Artificial insemination: No statute.

Aid to Families with Dependent Children (AFDC) law: Does *not* have provision to provide benefits to families if an able-bodied unemployed father is living with the family.

SOUTH DAKOTA

Parental support: Father has primary obligation but mother must assist if he is unable. Parents who willfully neglect their children under 16 are guilty of a crime.

Guardianship: Both parents are joint guardians.

Right to minor's earnings: Both parents are equally entitled.

Parental liability: Parents are responsible for willful damage to property by their minor children.

Obligation to support poor relatives: The parents of persons unable to support themselves are required to support them to the best of their ability; children have the same obligation to their parents.

Obligation of stepparents: Stepfather is required to support his wife's children if they are living with him. This obligation does not relieve the natural or adoptive parents of their support obligation.

Legitimation: Marriage of the parents legitimates a child. Also, the father of an illegitimate child, by publicly acknowledging his paternity and receiving it into his family—with the consent of his wife, if he is married—thereby adopts and legitimates it. Any child born during wedlock is presumed to be legitimate.

Artificial insemination: No statute.

Aid to Families with Dependent Children (AFDC) law: Does *not* have provision to provide benefits to families if an able-bodied unemployed father is living with the family.

TENNESSEE

Parental support: Both parents have joint obligation. Parents who willfully neglect their children under 18 are guilty of a crime.

Guardianship: Both parents are joint guardians.

Right to minor's earnings: Both parents are equally entitled.

Parental liability: Parents are not liable for the misconduct of their minor children.

Obligation to support poor relatives: No statute.

Obligation of stepparents: No statute.

Legitimation: Marriage of the parents legitimates a child. Either parent may make written application to the court to legitimate a child.

Artificial insemination: No statute.

Aid to Families with Dependent Children (AFDC)

law: Does *not* have provision to provide benefits to families if an able-bodied unemployed father is living with the family.

TEXAS

Parental support: Both parents have joint obligation. Parents who willfully neglect their dependent children are guilty of a crime.
Guardianship: Father is guardian. If he dies or is living apart from family, mother is guardian.
Right to minor's earnings: Both parents are equally entitled.
Parental liability: Parents are responsible for willful damage to property by their minor children.

Obligation to support poor relatives: The husband, wife, and parents of persons admitted to the state hospital for the insane are required to support them.
Obligation of stepparents: No statute.
Legitimation: Marriage of the parents legitimates a child.
Artificial insemination: No statute.
Aid to Families with Dependent Children (AFDC) law: Does *not* have provision to provide benefits to families if an able-bodied unemployed father is living with the family.

UTAH

Parental support: Both parents have joint obligation. Parents who willfully neglect their dependent children are guilty of a crime.
Guardianship: Both parents are joint guardians.
Right to minor's earnings: Both parents are equally entitled.
Parental liability: Parents are not liable for the misconduct of their minor children.
Obligation to support poor relatives: The parents, grandparents, brothers, sisters, children, and grandchildren of persons unable to support themselves are required to support them.
Obligation of stepparents: No statute.
Legitimation: Marriage of the parents legitimates a child. Also, the father of an illegitimate child, by publicly acknowledging his paternity and receiving it into his family—with the consent of his wife, if he is married—thereby adopts a child and legitimates it.
Artificial insemination: No statute.
Aid to Families with Dependent Children (AFDC) law: Does have provision to provide benefits to families if an unemployed father is living with the family (AFDC-UF).

VERMONT

Parental support: Father has primary obligation. Parents who willfully neglect their dependent children are guilty of a crime.
Guardianship: Both parents are joint guardians.
Right to minor's earnings: Father is entitled. If he dies or is living apart from family, mother has right.
Parental liability: Parents are liable for willful damage to property and injury to persons by their minor children.
Obligation to support poor relatives: Adult children whose parents are unable to support themselves are required to support them to the best of their ability.
Obligation of stepparents: Stepparent is required

to support a stepchild to the same extent as a natural or adoptive parent for as long as he or she is the spouse of the child's natural or adoptive parent.

Legitimation: Marriage of the parents and father's recognition of the child as his own legitimates a child.

Artificial insemination: No statute.

Aid to Families with Dependent Children (AFDC) law: Does have provision to provide benefits to families if an unemployed father is living with the family (AFDC-UF).

VIRGINIA

Parental support: Both parents have joint obligation. Parents who willfully neglect their dependent children are guilty of a crime.

Guardianship: Both parents are joint guardians.

Right to minor's earnings: Both parents are equally entitled.

Parental liability: Parents are responsible for willful damage to property by their minor children.

Obligation to support poor relatives: Children over 17 whose parents are unable to support themselves are required to support them if they are able to after providing for their immediate family.

Obligation of stepparents: No statute.

Legitimation: Marriage of the parents and father's recognition of the child as his own legitimates a child.

Artificial insemination: A child born by artificial insemination to which both husband and wife consented in writing is legitimate, if the child was born during wedlock.

Aid to Families with Dependent Children (AFDC) law: Does *not* have provision to provide benefits to families if an able-bodied unemployed father is living with the family.

WASHINGTON

Parental support: Father has primary obligation. Parents who willfully neglect their dependent children are guilty of a crime.

Guardianship: Both parents are joint guardians.

Right to minor's earnings: Both parents are equally entitled.

Parental liability: Parents are responsible for willful damage to property by their minor children.

Obligation to support poor relatives: No statute.

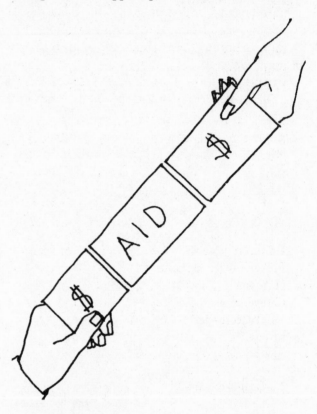

Obligation of stepparents: Stepparent is required to support a stepchild to the same extent as a natural parent for as long as he or she is the spouse of the child's natural parent.

Legitimation: Marriage of the parents legitimates a child. If a father gives written acknowledgment of his paternity, the child is considered legitimate for purposes of intestate succession.

Artificial insemination: No statute.

Aid to Families with Dependent Children (AFDC) law: Does have provision to provide benefits to families if an unemployed father is living with the family (AFDC-UF).

WEST VIRGINIA

Parental support: Father has primary obligation. Parents who willfully neglect their dependent children are guilty of a crime.

Guardianship: Both parents are joint guardians.

Right to minor's earnings: Both parents are equally entitled.

Parental liability: Parents are responsible for willful damage to property by their minor children.

Obligation to support poor relatives: No statute.

Obligation of stepparents: No statute.

Legitimation: Marriage of the parents legitimates a child.

Artificial insemination: No statute.

Aid to Families with Dependent Children (AFDC) law: Does have provision to provide benefits to families it an unemployed father is living with the family (AFDC-UF).

WISCONSIN

Parental support: Father has primary obligation. Parents who willfully neglect their dependent children are guilty of a crime.

Guardianship: Both parents are joint guardians.

Right to minor's earnings: Father is entitled. If he dies or is living apart from family, mother has right. If parents refuse to support a child, they have no right to its earnings.

Parental liability: Parents are responsible for willful damage to property and injury to persons by their minor children.

Obligation to support poor relatives: No statute.

Obligation of stepparents: No statute.

Legitimation: Any child born during wedlock is presumed to be legitimate.

Artificial insemination: No statute.

Aid to Families with Dependent Children (AFDC) law: Does have provision to provide benefits to families if an unemployed father is living with the family (AFDC-UF).

WYOMING

Parental support: Both parents have joint obligation. Parents who willfully neglect their dependent children are guilty of a crime.

Guardianship: Both parents are joint guardians.

Right to minor's earnings: No statute.

Parental liability: Parents are responsible for willful damage to property by their children aged 10 to 17.

Obligation to support poor relatives: No statute.

Obligation of stepparents: No statute.

Legitimation: Marriage of the parents legitimates a child.

Artificial insemination: No statute.

Aid to Families with Dependent Children (AFDC) law: Does *not* have provision to provide benefits to families if an able-bodied unemployed father is living with the family.

3
When I Adopt a Child

A very important way that parents and children are brought together is through the process of adoption. A child who has been adopted is in every sense a full member of his or her new family. Once an adoption is final, all legal ties to the child's natural parents are severed, and the new parents are issued a birth certificate listing them as the child's parents, with no qualifications. An adopted child has all the obligations and privileges of a natural child, including inheritance rights. The legal responsibilities of parents and children discussed in Chapter 2 apply to all families, whether or not the children are adopted.

But although the law eliminates all legal differences between adopted children and natural children, there are psychological aspects to adoption which cannot be legislated. It is of course important that the adopted child and his or her parents accept their relationship as natural and immutable, and most of them do. But sometimes natural parents and children see families of adoptive parents and children as somehow different from themselves. This tendency can be cruel and destructive.

An obvious remedy, it might seem, would be never to tell a child that he or she is adopted. The trouble is that it doesn't work. Experience has shown that the likelihood is great that through neighbors, relatives, or some other channel the child will discover the truth, with results that can be psychologically devastating. Not only are one's parents suddenly "not" one's parents, but the child has been lied to about it. (Many adoptive parents would not choose this course in any case because they reject any intimate human relationships based on deception, not truth.)

More open family attitudes, shifting values, and increasingly humane and realistic adoption practices can be expected gradually to obliterate these emotional and idiosyncratic distinctions between the natural and the adopted child.

Adoption practices are actually governed less by state adoption laws than by what judges and, more particularly, adoption agencies conceive to be in the best interest of the child. Many people do not realize that, by and large, the laws themselves are not restrictive in the criteria they set for adoptive parents.

For example, no law expressly prohibits single adults from adopting children. The adoption statutes of thirty-four states say "any adult" or "any person" is eligible, or make no reference at all to marital status or, in fact, to any personal criteria. Statutes in the other seventeen states specifically include unmarried persons as acceptable prospective adoptive parents. Delaware, Maine, New York, Rhode Island, and Wisconsin require an effort to match the religious faith of the child with that of the adoptive parents, but all qualify this requirement in some way—if it is "practicable" or if it does not cause "undue hardship" for those trying to place the child. Massachusetts' law says religious matching is necessary only if requested by the child's natural parents, and even then only if practicable.

Only two states—Louisiana and Texas— explicitly state that adoptive parents and child must be members of the same race. Two others mention racial matching indirectly: Missouri says the "hereditary background" of all parties must be investigated,

Kentucky that the adoption may be annulled if within five years "the adoptee reveals traces of ethnological ancestry different from those of the adoptive parents."

Indiana is the only state to outline in its statutes the conditions that must be satisfied before an adoption is permitted: "(1) the best interest of the child; (2) suitability of adopting parents; (3) proper consents; (4) proper investigative reports." Although the other states are not this specific in their laws, it is safe to assume their standards are similar, and most states have laws governing adoption procedures and outlawing so-called "black-market" adoptions.

Since the laws do not define such terms as "best interest," "suitable," and "proper," however, a great deal is left to the discretion of the agencies which set the standards, and to the judges who grant adoption decrees. Until recently, these criteria were very narrowly interpreted. The adoptive parents had to be a childless married couple, neither of whom had ever been divorced or touched with any scandal, and they had to be able to prove they were biologically incapable of having children of their own. They also had to be of the same religious faith as the child's natural parents, and of the same race as the child. They could not be "too old"—usually not more than thirty-five. Further, their financial status was carefully scrutinized. The prospective mother could not be working outside the home, and the agency had to be satisfied that the father would be able to support the child, with all the middle-class amenities, until he or she came of age. Painstaking efforts were also made to match physical characteristics of parents and child—

blue-eyed child with blue-eyed parents, olive-skinned parents with olive-skinned baby, and so forth.

The relaxation of these criteria during the last decade represents only one of a number of cyclical changes in adoption practices. There were no provisions at all for adoption in the English common law on which our laws are based. Through the eighteenth and nineteenth centuries in England the practice was to apprentice homeless destitute children to families who needed help in the household, on the farm, or in the husband's occupation. Far from being adopted—as we know it, anyway—these children were treated as indentured servants. Those who were not taken into homes on this basis got by as best they could on the streets, living by their wits and begging or stealing. We have met many of these children in the works of Charles Dickens and John Gay.

The apprentice system was carried over to America, but by the middle of the nineteenth century the problem of homeless children had become severe, and sympathy began to grow for those who had been abused as apprentices. Also, by this time the United States was home to a growing number of immigrants from Europe. They brought with them a tradition of adoption based on Roman law, in which a child taken into a home was made a full member of its adoptive family. In 1851 Massachusetts became the first state to enact an adoption law; by 1929 all states had done so. (England, on the other hand, had no adoption laws of any kind until 1926.)

Basically, the statutes set up the legal procedure for severing the ties of the natural parents and making the child a full member of his or her adoptive family. The steps include: (1) obtaining the natural parents' consent to have the child made available for adoption; (2) receiving an application from the persons who want to adopt a child; (3) conducting an investigation by a public or private adoption agency into the suitability of the applicants as adoptive parents; (4) a judicial hearing at which the interlocutory decree is granted, which indicates that the judge is satisfied that the consents are valid and that the investigation of the prospective parents has shown them to be satisfactory; (5) placing the child with the adoptive family; and (6) granting the final decree after the interlocutory period and issuing a new birth certificate for the child in the name of the adoptive parents, at which point all rights of the natural parents regarding the child are irrevocably terminated. All records relating to the adoption are then sealed, and may not be examined by anyone except on the basis of a court order.

Even with these statutory safeguards, people were still somewhat leery of taking a child whose background they knew nothing about.

After World War II, however, there was a dramatic shift in favor of adoption, so much so that the supply of people who wanted to adopt exceeded the supply of adoptable children. This situation was responsible for the inauguration of the stringent criteria for adoptive parents mentioned earlier. Prospective adoptive parents were screened very carefully; it took months or years before they were approved, during which time they might be subjected to sudden visits from adoption agency caseworkers prying into any aspect of their lives. Even after they were certified as qualified, a couple often had to wait a year or more before an "appropriate" baby was found.

It was in order to circumvent these often silly or humiliating investigations and eliminate the waiting period that private (nonagency) adoptions began to flourish. There are two kinds of nonagency adoptions. In the first kind, the so-called black-market adoptions, all legalities are bypassed. Amounts ranging up to $25,000 may be paid for a baby, usually to an unwed mother through a lawyer, doctor, nurse, or friend who takes a percentage of the payment as a "commission" for his or her services. Some married couples also sell unwanted children. Birth certificates are forged in the name of the adopting parents, and the whole transaction is kept out of legal channels. Black-market adoptions are illegal in every state, because they do not protect the child's rights.

The other kind of nonagency adoption—sometimes called "gray market" adoptions, but more often referred to as independent adoptions—are legal in every state except Connecticut, Delaware, and Illinois, where all adoptions must be handled through licensed agencies. In independent adoptions the arrangements are made directly between the natural and adoptive parents, but the legalities are not bypassed. All necessary consents are obtained; all parties go to court to have the proper changes made in birth certificates and adoption decrees issued; and all abide by the state's statutory waiting period before the adoption becomes final. Further, in most states the adoptive parents are investigated by an authorized government agency to make sure they will provide a suitable home for the child, as is done in agency adoptions. Customarily the adoptive parents pay for the mother's medical expenses during pregnancy and childbirth.

Some adoption agencies charge the adoptive parents for their services, but—especially in agencies operated by city, county, or state authorities—the fees can be adjusted to an adopting family's ability to pay. Often there is no charge if a family seems right for a particular child but cannot afford a fee.

Gradually during the 1950's the emphasis in adoption practices shifted to finding a good home for a child rather than a "perfect" infant for "perfect" parents. Adoption agencies also began making more active efforts to find permanent homes for children once thought to be unadoptable—those who are older, or physically handicapped or emotionally disturbed, or members of racial minorities, or siblings who cannot be separated from each other. At about the same time, the number of prospective adoptive parents decreased. Publicity about the difficulties of dealing with adoption agencies drove them either to resort to the black market or independent adoptions, or to give up the idea altogether.

By the mid-1960's the difficulty in finding adoptive parents was becoming acute. Simultaneously the supply of healthy white infants—the most-wanted category of adoptive child—diminished drastically because of the increased use of birth control and the fact that more unwed mothers were keeping their babies instead of giving them up. At the same time, agencies and the public began to assume a more enlightened attitude toward finding homes for "hard to place" children. As a result, agencies now actively try to recruit adoptive parents for older, handicapped, and minority children, and make real efforts to remove legal restrictions so that children in institutions and temporary foster homes can be freed for permanent adoption.

Through television programs and newspaper features, agencies let the public know about children who need homes, and the standards for adoptive parents are explained. In a growing number of states, short-term government- or agency-sponsored subsidies are given to parents who will permanently adopt children who need extensive medical care or treatment for emotional problems. Similar arrangements are made for foster parents who could not otherwise afford to care for a child at home on a permanent basis.

Today an agency investigates prospective parents to make sure they really want to adopt, and that they are not so emotionally unstable as to be harmful to the child. Further, most agencies try to find families that will be able to give each child the kind of love and understanding all children need—not necessarily a separate bedroom or a college education, but a warm environment in which the child can grow and feel secure.

Agencies in most states no longer automatically rule out interracial adoptions, and most do not insist on matching the religion of parent and child unless the child is old enough to have an established religious preference. The fact that there may be other children in the family is no longer a drawback, nor is a mother who works outside the home a deterrent. It is still rare for an unmarried man or woman to adopt a child, but sometimes a single person is actually preferred as a parent for an older child.

One reason so many children languish in institutions, or bounce from foster home to foster home, is that many parents who have abandoned or neglected their children nevertheless refuse to free them for adoption. Lack of parental consent is especially frustrating when it blocks an adoption by foster parents who have been caring for a child on a temporary basis. Thus a large part of a good agency's work is trying to locate a child's natural parents and convince them to give their consent if they cannot—or will not—take responsibility for the child themselves. If this is not possible, the agency will nearly always take steps to have parental rights involuntarily terminated in court so that the child can be made available for adoption. Even then, though, there is no guarantee that the judge who hears the case will agree that terminating parental rights is in the best interest of the child. All too often a judge seems to have an almost mystical belief in the relationship of biological parents to their offspring even if the natural parents have no realistic plans for taking custody.

The issue of consent is one of the most difficult legal aspects of adoption. Before a child may be adopted, the agency must have obtained the proper consent (also called release, surrender, or relinquishment) from the natural parents. Such consent cannot be withdrawn without a court order, so a natural parent cannot easily reverse the decision if the child has been voluntarily turned over to an adoption agency. If a natural parent does change his or her mind, the case must be taken to court, where a decision will be made based on the judge's interpretation of the relevant statutes, judicial precedents, and the claims of all parties.

Nearly every state requires a waiting period of from six months to a year before an adoption becomes final. After the interlocutory adoption decree has been replaced by a final decree the natural parents have no further claim on the child, who at that time legally becomes a member of the adoptive family on the same basis as if he or she were the biological child of the adoptive parents.

A popular misconception about interlocutory decrees is that they are granted in order to give natural parents a chance to change their minds about letting the child be adopted. On the contrary, the intention is to give *adoptive* parents a chance to change their minds if they realize an adoption is not going to work out. When the adoptive parents do reverse themselves, the child is returned to the care of the agency that handled the adoption. In private adoptions this situation is more complex. If the natural parents do not want to take back the child, he or she will be placed in foster care; then, if the natural parents do not retract their already-given consent, the child is made available for adoption by someone else. Despite all this, until an adoption is completely final a natural parent in most states is not legally prohibited from bringing a suit to get his or her child back. Though it happens only rarely, it is something about which adoptive parents are understandably apprehensive.

Some states have resolved this problem by providing for judicial termination of the rights of the natural parents before a child is made available for adoption. Most adoption authorities feel this is a sound practice because the parent is absolutely barred from changing his or her mind. In any case, no authorized agency, government-sponsored or private, treats consent lightly; all possible efforts are made to get complete, well-thought-out consents from the necessary parties before a child is made available for adoption. For example, reputable agencies no longer accept consents from unwed mothers until after they have left the hospital and have had a chance to reconsider their decision.

The question of consent was made more complex by a 1972 U.S. Supreme Court decision in *Stanley v. Illinois,* which in effect gave the father a say in the custody rights of an illegitimate child. As is often true of Supreme Court decisions, however, it was not definitive (that is, a majority of the justices did not join in one opinion). Thus it is open to different interpretations depending on the judge who is making the rulings at the local level.

So far, only Illinois has a law that says, without qualification, that the father as well as the mother of an illegitimate child must give his consent to adoption. Fourteen states and the District of Columbia say his consent is necessary only if he has acknowledged paternity or it has been otherwise legally established. Twenty-two states require only the mother's consent, and the remaining thirteen have no statutory provisions on this matter.

Because of confusion caused by the *Stanley* ruling, even if a state's law says the consent of the unwed father is not necessary before a child may be made available for adoption, it may nevertheless be required if a judge says so. If the putative father cannot be found, or if he contests the adoption of the child but does not want to take custody himself, or is unfit to do so even if he wants to, freeing the child for adoption can be delayed indefinitely. Undoubtedly the father's role will be clarified judicially sometime in the future, but for the time being it is a very murky area.

Those who are working for reforms in adoption laws and practices would like to see a number of changes. All states should inaugurate the policy—already in effect in nearly half the states—of not making any child available for adoption until the court has terminated all rights of the natural parents who have knowingly and voluntarily given their consent to adoption. There might still be a period between the initial hearing and the final decree, as there is in most of the states that have this provision, but the natural parents could not revoke their consent during that time, even by court order. Extreme care must be taken, of course, to make sure that the natural parents' decision is firm, and not the result of coercion, pressure, or fear.

Along these same lines, all states should

make provision in their laws, as some already have, for court termination of parental rights after a specified time if a child has in effect been abandoned to state care. Such cases have to be carefully evaluated to distinguish between parents who are not genuinely concerned about their child's welfare and those who do care but for financial or other reasons are temporarily incapable of providing for the child themselves. This would free for permanent adoption some of the many children who spend their childhoods being shifted from one foster home or institution to another.

Some critics advocate resolving the problem of an unwed father's consent and custody rights by means of a compromise plan. Any father who wishes to be consulted about what is to become of his illegitimate child would register with a central bureau. When the mother gives her consent to have the child adopted, the adoption agency would check the registry. If the father is registered and his paternity established, he would be given an opportunity to give his consent to the adoption or to present a plan for taking custody of the child himself. An adoption agency would not be obligated to get the consent of a father who did not care enough to register as an interested party, and his parental rights would be severed completely.

Some of the reforms supported by those actively concerned about adoption are included in a bill sponsored by Senator Alan Cranston of California. This legislation, called the Opportunities for Adoption Act, was introduced in the Senate in March 1974, but so far a comparable bill has not been introduced in the House.

The Cranston bill's first provision grants federal subsidies to people who would like to be adoptive parents but cannot afford it. This is similar to arrangements for subsidized adoptions already in operation in about half the states, and might be made contingent on state matching funds. Where such programs are in use, it is considerably easier for agencies to find homes for "hard to place" children.

The second provision would establish a

clearinghouse to keep track, throughout the country, of all children available for adoption and all persons who want to adopt. It would replace a service begun in 1967 by the Child Welfare League, called the Adoption Resource Exchange of North America (ARENA), which acts as a national registry for prospective adoptive parents, and children in need of homes. ARENA is doing a commendable job, but federal sponsorship and support are needed to make the program more effective and broader in scope. Similar services are in operation on a statewide basis in most states.

The third provision of the Cranston bill would allocate federal funds to help adoption agencies pay medical and counseling expenses for expectant mothers planning to have their babies adopted. Those who distrust this plan feel it would put too much pressure on low-income expectant parents, and especially on young unwed mothers, to consent to adoption when they might not really want to. Proponents say it will enable licensed agencies, which offer greater protection to the rights of the child, to compete with independent adoptions, where these expenses are privately paid. Advocates of this measure insist that the federal help would not be dependent on the mother's unqualified decision to give up her child; she need only indicate that she might be willing to do so.

Though reforms and clarifications are still needed, there is no denying that there has been a real change of emphasis in the field of adoption from the restrictive and superficial concepts that prevailed only a few years ago, to honest efforts to find caring families for all the children who need them.

3
When I Adopt a Child
The Law
State by State

ALABAMA

Restrictions on who may adopt: None.

Consents required: Adoptive child if over 14; natural parents unless one (or both) has abandoned the child, cannot be located, or is mentally incompetent; guardian if there is one.

Consents required from unwed parents: Mother; father if paternity has been established.

Termination of natural parents' rights: Judicial termination of rights of natural parents is required before child may be made available for adoption.

Waiting period before adoption is final: Six months.

ALASKA

Restrictions on who may adopt: None.

Consents required: Adoptive child if over 14; natural parents unless one (or both) has abandoned the child, is mentally incompetent, has been imprisoned for at least three years, or has been declared unfit by the court; guardian if there is one.

Consents required from unwed parents: Mother only.

Termination of natural parents' rights: Parental rights are not terminated irrevocably until the adoption becomes final.

Waiting period before adoption is final: Six months.

ARIZONA

Restrictions on who may adopt: None.

Consents required: Adoptive child if over 12; natural parents unless one (or both) is mentally incompetent; guardian if there is one.

Consents required from unwed parents: Mother; father if paternity has been established.

Termination of natural parents' rights: Judicial termination of rights of natural parents is required before child may be made available for adoption.

Waiting period before adoption is final: One year.

ARKANSAS

Restrictions on who may adopt: None.

Consents required: Adoptive child if over 14; natural parents unless one (or both) has abandoned the child or cannot be located; guardian if there is one.

Consents required from unwed parents: Mother; father if paternity has been established.
Termination of natural parents' rights: Parental rights are not terminated irrevocably until the adoption becomes final.
Waiting period before adoption is final: Six months.

CALIFORNIA

Restrictions on who may adopt: Adoptive parent must be at least ten years older than the child.
Consents required: Adoptive child if over 12; natural parents unless one (or both) has abandoned the child or been declared unfit by the court.
Consents required from unwed parents: Mother only.
Termination of natural parents' rights: Parental rights are not terminated irrevocably until the adoption becomes final.
Waiting period before adoption is final: Six months.

COLORADO

Restrictions on who may adopt: None.
Consents required: Adoptive child if over 12; natural parents; guardian if there is one.
Consents required from unwed parents: No statute.
Termination of natural parents' rights: Judicial termination of rights of natural parents is required before child may be made available for adoption.
Waiting period before adoption is final: Six months.

CONNECTICUT

Restrictions on who may adopt: None.
Consents required: Adoptive child if over 14; natural parents; guardian if there is one.
Consents required from unwed parents: No statute.
Termination of natural parents' rights: Parental

rights are not terminated irrevocably until the adoption becomes final.
Waiting period before adoption is final: Final decree may be issued at time of hearing; if interlocutory decree is granted, the waiting period may be no longer than thirteen months.

DELAWARE

Restrictions on who may adopt: At least one of the adoptive parents must be of the same religious faith as the child unless natural parents have waived this requirement; if it will create undue hardship in placing the child, however, this requirement may be waived by the court.
Consents required: Adoptive child if over 14; natural parents unless one (or both) has abandoned the child or been declared unfit by the court; guardian if there is one.
Consents required from unwed parents: Mother only.
Termination of natural parents' rights: Judicial termination of rights is required before child may be made available for adoption.
Waiting period before adoption is final: Final decree may be issued at time of hearing.

DISTRICT OF COLUMBIA

Restrictions on who may adopt: None.
Consents required: Adoptive child if over 14; natural parents, unless one (or both) has been declared unfit by the court; guardian if there is one.
Consents required from unwed parents: Mother; father if paternity has been established.
Termination of natural parents' rights: Parental rights are not terminated irrevocably until the adoption becomes final.
Waiting period before adoption is final: Six months.

FLORIDA

Restrictions on who may adopt: None.
Consents required: Adoptive child if over 12; natural parents; guardian if there is one.

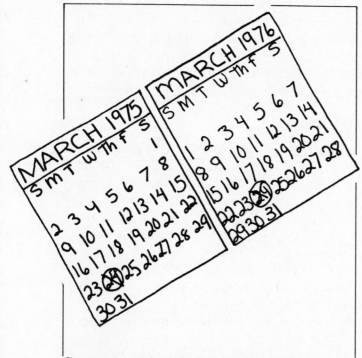

Consents required from unwed parents: Mother only.

Termination of natural parents' rights: Judicial termination of rights of natural parents is required before child may be made available for adoption.

Waiting period before adoption is final: Final decree may be issued at time of hearing.

GEORGIA

Restrictions on who may adopt: Adoptive parent must be at least ten years older than the child.
Consents required: Adoptive child if over 14; natural parents unless one (or both) has abandoned the child or cannot be found; guardian if there is one.
Consents required from unwed parents: Mother only.
Termination of natural parents' rights: Judicial termination of rights of natural parents is required before child may be made available for adoption.
Waiting period before adoption is final: Final decree may be issued at time of hearing.

HAWAII

Restrictions on who may adopt: None.
Consents required: Adoptive child if over 10; natural parents unless one (or both) has abandoned the child, is mentally incompetent, or has not supported or communicated with the child for one year; guardian if there is one.
Consents required from unwed parents: Mother; father if paternity has been established.
Termination of natural parents' rights: Parental rights are not terminated irrevocably until the adoption becomes final.
Waiting period before adoption is final: One year.

IDAHO

Restrictions on who may adopt: Adoptive parent, if under 25, must be at least fifteen years older than the child.
Consents required: Adoptive child if over 12; natural parents; guardian if there is one.
Consents required from unwed parents: Mother only.
Termination of natural parents' rights: Parental rights are not terminated irrevocably until the adoption becomes final.
Waiting period before adoption is final: No statute.

ILLINOIS

Restrictions on who may adopt: None.
Consents required: Adoptive child if over 14; natural parents unless one (or both) is mentally incompetent or has been declared unfit by the court; guardian if there is one.
Consents required from unwed parents: Mother and father.
Termination of natural parents' rights: Judicial termination of rights of natural parents is required before child may be made available for adoption.
Waiting period before adoption is final: Six months.

INDIANA

Restrictions on who may adopt: None, but the religious faith of the adoptive parents and the child must be investigated.

Consents required: Adoptive child if over 14; natural parents unless one (or both) has abandoned the child or has not supported or communicated with the child for a year; guardian if there is one.

Consents required from unwed parents: Mother; father if paternity has been established.

Termination of natural parents' rights: Parental rights are not terminated irrevocably until the adoption becomes final.

Waiting period before adoption is final: No statute.

IOWA

Restrictions on who may adopt: None.

Consents required: Adoptive child if over 14; natural parents unless one (or both) is mentally incompetent, has been imprisoned for a felony, or is the "inmate or keeper of a house of ill fame"; guardian if there is one.

Consents required from unwed parents: No statute.

Termination of natural parents' rights: Parental rights are not terminated irrevocably until the adoption becomes final.

Waiting period before adoption is final: One year.

KANSAS

Restrictions on who may adopt: None.

Consents required: Adoptive child if over 14; natural parents; guardian if there is one.

Consents required from unwed parents: Mother only.

Termination of natural parents' rights: Judicial termination of rights of natural parents is required before child may be made available for adoption.

Waiting period before adoption is final: Final decree may be issued at time of hearing.

KENTUCKY

Restrictions on who may adopt: None; however, the adoption may be annulled if within five years the "adoptee reveals traces of ethnological ancestry different from those of adoptive parents."

Consents required: Adoptive child if over 12; natural parents unless one (or both) has abandoned the child, is mentally incompetent, or has been declared unfit by the court.

Consents required from unwed parents: Mother only.

Termination of natural parents' rights: Parental rights are not terminated irrevocably until the adoption becomes final.

Waiting period before adoption is final: Final decree may be issued at time of hearing.

LOUISIANA

Restrictions on who may adopt: The adoptive child must be of the same race as the adoptive parents.

Consents required: Natural parents unless one (or both) has abandoned the child or been declared unfit by the court. (No statute on consent of adoptive child.)

Consents required from unwed parents: No statute.

Termination of natural parents' rights: Parental rights are not terminated irrevocably until the adoption becomes final.

Waiting period before adoption is final: Six months to one year.

MAINE

Restrictions on who may adopt: The adopting parents must be of the same religious faith as the child "if a suitable family of that faith can be found."

Consents required: Adoptive child if over 14; natural parents unless one (or both) is mentally incompetent or an alcoholic; guardian if there is one.

Consents required from unwed parents: No statute.

Termination of natural parents' rights: Parental rights are not terminated irrevocably until the adoption becomes final.

Waiting period before adoption is final: At discretion of court, but no longer than one year.

MARYLAND

Restrictions on who may adopt: None.

Consents required: Adoptive child if over 10; natural parents unless one (or both) has abandoned the child or is declared unfit by the court; guardian if there is one.

Consents required from unwed parents: Mother; father if paternity has been established.

Termination of natural parents' rights: Judicial termination of rights of natural parents is required before child may be made available for adoption.

Waiting period before adoption is final: Final decree may be issued at time of hearing; if interlocutory decree is granted, the waiting period may be no longer than one year.

MASSACHUSETTS

Restrictions on who may adopt: Religion will be considered if requested by natural parents if it is considered to be in the best interest of the child.

Consents required: Adoptive child if over 12; natural parents except under "certain circumstances" not specified in statute; guardian if there is one.

Consents required from unwed parents: No statute.

Termination of natural parents' rights: Parental rights are not terminated irrevocably until the adoption becomes final.

Waiting period before adoption is final: Six months.

MICHIGAN

Restrictions on who may adopt: None

Consents required: Adoptive child if over 10; natural parents; guardian if there is one.

Consents required from unwed parents: Mother; father if paternity has been established.

Termination of natural parents' rights: Judicial termination of rights of natural parents is required before child may be made available for adoption.

Waiting period before adoption is final: Final decree may be issued at time of hearing, or there may be a one-year waiting period at the request of the adoptive parents.

MINNESOTA

Restrictions on who may adopt: None.

Consents required: Adoptive child if over 14; natural parents unless one (or both) has abandoned the child or is mentally incompetent; guardian if there is one.

Consents required from unwed parents: Mother only.

Termination of natural parents' rights: Judicial termination of rights of natural parents is required before child may be made available for adoption.

Waiting period before adoption is final: Six months.

MISSISSIPPI

Restrictions on who may adopt: None.

Consents required: Adoptive child if over 14; natural parents unless one (or both) has abandoned the child or is mentally incompetent or "morally unfit"; guardian if there is one.

Consents required from unwed parents: Mother; father if paternity has been established.

Termination of natural parents' rights: Parental rights are not terminated irrevocably until the adoption becomes final.

Waiting period before adoption is final: Six months.

MISSOURI

Restrictions on who may adopt: None, but "hereditary background" of all parties must be investigated.

Consents required: Adoptive child if over 13; natural parents unless one (or both) has abandoned the child or is mentally incompetent.

Consents required from unwed parents: Mother only.

Termination of natural parents' rights: Judicial termination of rights of natural parents is required before child may be made available for adoption.

Waiting period before adoption is final: Nine months.

MONTANA

Restrictions on who may adopt: None.

Consents required: Adoptive child if over 10; natural parents unless one (or both) has abandoned or abused the child, is mentally incompetent or an alcoholic, or has not supported the child for one year; guardian if there is one.

Consents required from unwed parents: Mother; father if paternity has been established.

Termination of natural parents' rights: Judicial termination of rights of natural parents is required before child may be made available for adoption.

Waiting period before adoption is final: Six months.

NEBRASKA

Restrictions on who may adopt: None.

Consents required: Adoptive child if over 14; natural parents unless one (or both) has abandoned the child or is mentally incompetent; guardian if there is one.

Consents required from unwed parents: Mother only.

Termination of natural parents' rights: Judicial termination of rights of natural parents is required before child may be made available for adoption.

Waiting period before adoption is final: Six months.

NEVADA

Restrictions on who may adopt: Adoptive parents must be at least ten years older than the child.

Consents required: Adoptive child if over 14; natural parents unless one (or both) is mentally incompetent or has been declared unfit by the court; guardian if there is one.

Consents required from unwed parents: Mother; father if paternity has been established.

Termination of natural parents' rights: Parental rights are not terminated irrevocably until the adoption becomes final.

Waiting period before adoption is final: Six months.

NEW HAMPSHIRE

Restrictions on who may adopt: None.

Consents required: Adoptive child if over 12; natural parents unless one (or both) has abandoned the child or is mentally incompetent; guardian if there is one.

Consents required from unwed parents: Mother only.

Termination of natural parents' rights: Parental rights are not terminated irrevocably until the adoption becomes final.

Waiting period before adoption is final: Six months.

NEW JERSEY

Restrictions on who may adopt: None.
Consents required: No statute.
Consents required from unwed parents: No statute.
Termination of natural parents' rights: Parental rights are not terminated irrevocably until the adoption becomes final.
Waiting period before adoption is final: Six months.

NEW MEXICO

Restrictions on who may adopt: None.
Consents required: Adoptive child if over 10; natural parents unless one (or both) has abandoned the child, is mentally incompetent, or has been declared unfit by the court; guardian if there is one.
Consents required from unwed parents: Mother; father if paternity has been established.
Termination of natural parents' rights: Parental rights are not terminated irrevocably until the adoption becomes final.
Waiting period before adoption is final: Six months.

NEW YORK

Restrictions on who may adopt: Adoptive parents should be of the same religious faith as the child where practicable.
Consents required: Adoptive child if over 14; natural parents unless one (or both) has abandoned or abused the child, is mentally incompetent, imprisoned, or an alcoholic, was divorced on grounds of adultery, or has been declared an unfit parent by the court; guardian if there is one.
Consents required from unwed parents: Mother only.
Termination of natural parents' rights: Judicial termination of rights of natural parents is required before child may be made available for adoption.

Waiting period before adoption is final: Six months.

NORTH CAROLINA

Restrictions on who may adopt: None.
Consents required: Adoptive child if over 12; natural parents unless one (or both) has abandoned the child or has been declared an unfit parent by the court; guardian if there is one.
Consents required from unwed parents: Mother; father if paternity has been established.
Termination of natural parents' rights: Parental rights are not terminated irrevocably until the adoption becomes final.
Waiting period before adoption is final: Six months.

NORTH DAKOTA

Restrictions on who may adopt: None.
Consents required: Adoptive child if over 10; natural parents unless one (or both) has abandoned the child, is mentally incompetent, or has not supported the child for one year; guardian if there is one.
Consents required from unwed parents: Mother; father if paternity has been established.
Termination of natural parents' rights: Judicial termination of rights of natural parents is required before child may be made available for adoption.

Waiting period before adoption is final: Six months.

OHIO

Restrictions on who may adopt: None.
Consents required: Adoptive child if over 12; natural parents unless one (or both) is mentally incompetent or has not supported the child for one year; guardian if there is one.
Consents required from unwed parents: Mother only.
Termination of natural parents' rights: Parental rights are not terminated irrevocably until the adoption becomes final.
Waiting period before adoption is final: Six months.

OKLAHOMA

Restrictions on who may adopt: None
Consents required: Natural parents unless one (or both) has not supported the child for one year, has abused the child, is an alcoholic, or has been declared an unfit parent by the court; guardian if there is one. (No statute on consent of adoptive child.)
Consent of unwed parents: Mother only.
Termination of natural parents' rights: Parental rights are not terminated irrevocably until the adoption becomes final.
Waiting period before adoption is final: Six months.

OREGON

Restrictions on who may adopt: None.
Consents required: Adoptive child if over 14; natural parents unless one (or both) has abandoned the child or has not supported the child for one year; guardian if there is one.
Consent of unwed parents: Mother only.
Termination of natural parents' rights: Parental rights are not terminated irrevocably until the adoption becomes final.

Waiting period before adoption is final: Six months.

PENNSYLVANIA

Restrictions on who may adopt: None.
Consents required: Adoptive child if over 12; natural parents unless one (or both) has abandoned or abused the child or is mentally incompetent; guardian if there is one.
Consents required from unwed parents: Mother only.
Termination of natural parents' rights: Judicial termination of rights of natural parents is required before child may be made available for adoption.
Waiting period before adoption is final: Six months.

RHODE ISLAND

Restrictions on who may adopt: Adoptive parents should be of the same religious faith as the child where practicable.
Consents required: Adoptive child if over 14; natural parents unless one (or both) has abandoned the child, is mentally incompetent, has not supported or maintained contact with the child for one year, has been imprisoned for at least three years, or has been declared unfit by the court; guardian if there is one.
Consents required from unwed parents: No statute.
Termination of natural parents' rights: Parental rights are not terminated irrevocably until the adoption becomes final.
Waiting period before adoption is final: Six months.

SOUTH CAROLINA

Restrictions on who may adopt: None.
Consents required: Natural parents unless one (or both) has been declared unfit by the court. (No statute on consent of adoptive child.)
Consents required from unwed parents: Mother only.

Termination of natural parents' rights: Parental rights are not terminated irrevocably until the adoption becomes final.

Waiting period before adoption is final: Six months.

SOUTH DAKOTA

Restrictions on who may adopt: None.

Consents required: Adoptive child if over 12; natural parents unless one (or both) has abandoned the child, is mentally incompetent or an alcoholic, has been divorced on grounds of adultery, has been imprisoned for at least a year for an offense involving "moral turpitude," or has been declared unfit by the court.

Consents required from unwed parents: No statute.

Termination of natural parents' rights: Parental rights are not terminated irrevocably until the adoption becomes final.

Waiting period before adoption is final: Six months.

TENNESSEE

Restrictions on who may adopt: None.

Consents required: Adoptive child if over 14; natural parents unless one (or both) has abandoned the child.

Consents required from unwed parents: No statute.

Termination of natural parents' rights: Judicial termination of rights of natural parents is required before child may be made available for adoption.

Waiting period before adoption is final: One year.

TEXAS

Restrictions on who may adopt: A white child cannot be adopted by a Negro, or a Negro child by a white person.

Consents required: Adoptive child if over 14; natural parents unless one (or both) has been declared unfit by the court.

Consents required from unwed parents: Mother only.

Termination of natural parents' rights: Parental rights are not terminated irrevocably until the adoption becomes final.

Waiting period before adoption is final: Six months.

UTAH

Restrictions on who may adopt: Adoptive parent must be at least ten years older than the child.

Consents required: Adoptive child if over 12; natural parents unless one (or both) has abandoned the child or been declared unfit by the court.

Consents required from unwed parents: No statute.

Termination of natural parents' rights: Parental rights are not terminated irrevocably until the adoption becomes final.

Waiting period before adoption is final: Six months.

VERMONT

Restrictions on who may adopt: None.

Consents required: Adoptive child if over 14; natural parents; guardian if there is one.

Consents required from unwed parents: No statute.

Termination of natural parents' rights: Judicial termination of rights of natural parents is required before child may be made available for adoption.

Waiting period before adoption is final: Six months.

VIRGINIA

Restrictions on who may adopt: None.

Consents required: Adoptive child if over 14; natural parents.

Consents required from unwed parents: Mother only.

Termination of natural parents' rights: Judicial

termination of rights of natural parents is required before child may be made available for adoption.

Waiting period before adoption is final: Six months.

WASHINGTON

Restrictions on who may adopt: None.

Consents required: Adoptive child if over 14; natural parents unless one (or both) has abandoned the child, is mentally incompetent, or is imprisoned; guardian if there is one.

Consents required from unwed parents: Mother; father if paternity has been established.

Termination of natural parents' rights: Judicial termination of rights of natural parents is required before child may be made available for adoption.

Waiting period before adoption is final: Six months.

WEST VIRGINIA

Restrictions on who may adopt: Adoptive parent must be at least fifteen years older than the child.

Consents required: Adoptive child if over 12; natural parents unless one (or both) has abandoned the child, is mentally incompetent, or has been declared unfit by the court; guardian if there is one.

Consents required from unwed parents: No statute.

Termination of natural parents' rights: Parental rights are not terminated irrrevocably until the adoption becomes final.

Waiting period before adoption is final: Six months.

WISCONSIN

Restrictions on who may adopt: Adoptive parents should be of the same religious faith as the child where practicable.

Consents required: Adoptive child if over 14; natural parents.

Consents required from unwed parents: Mother only.

Termination of natural parents' rights: Judicial termination of rights of natural parents is required before child may be made available for adoption.

Waiting period before adoption is final: Six months.

WYOMING

Restrictions on who may adopt: None.

Consents required: Adoptive child if over 14; natural parents unless one (or both) has abandoned or abused the child, is mentally incompetent, has not supported the child for one year, or has been declared unfit by the court; guardian if there is one.

Consents required from unwed parents: Mother only.

Termination of natural parents' rights: Parental rights are not terminated irrevocably until the adoption becomes final.

Waiting period before adoption is final: Six months.

4

When I Want an Abortion

While the right to have children is fundamental, so is the right *not* to have children. Increasingly today this means the right to terminate an unwanted pregnancy by a medical abortion. No other aspect of the fight for equal rights for women raises such emotional hue and cry, nor creates such anguished ambivalence, as the discussion of abortion.

In January 1973 the U.S. Supreme Court ruled, in *Roe v. Wade,* that the Fourteenth Amendment guarantees the "right of privacy," which encompasses a woman's decision to seek an abortion. Thus any state law that permits abortion *only* to save the life of the mother is unconstitutional.

In *Doe v. Bolton,* a companion case decided at the same time as *Roe v. Wade,* the Supreme Court held unconstitutional those portions of Georgia's abortion laws that required abortion to be performed in specially accredited hospitals, or be approved by a hospital abortion committee, or be concurred in by two physicians other than the woman's doctor. This ruling also prohibited state residence requirements for women who want abortions.

The Court's decisions in these two cases made the laws of nearly every state in this country either entirely or partially unconstitutional. Only New York, in fact, had a law that met the Supreme Court standards in every respect even before the Court's ruling. Nine other states—Alaska, Georgia, Hawaii, Idaho, Indiana, Montana, North Carolina, Tennessee, and Washington—now have laws that place no over-all restrictions on a woman's right to have an abortion, but all are still constitutionally suspect in one or another of their procedural qualifications.

Specifically, the Court held in *Roe v. Wade* that a state could regulate or prohibit abortions only to the following extent:

(a) For the stage prior to approximately the end of the first trimester, the abortion decision must be left to the medical judgment of the pregnant woman's attending physician.

(b) For the stage subsequent to approximately the end of the first trimester, the State, in promoting its interest in the health of the mother, may, if it chooses, regulate the abortion procedure in ways that are reasonably related to maternal health.

(c) For the stage subsequent to viability, the State, in promoting its interest in the potentiality of human life, may, if it chooses, regulate, and even proscribe, abortion except where it is necessary, in appropriate medical judgment, for the preservation of the life or health of the mother.

Roe v. Wade challenged a Texas law which stated that abortion is permitted only to save the life of the mother. "Jane Roe" was a single woman who brought a class-action suit to contest this law. A Texas resident, she wanted an abortion "performed by a competent, licensed physician, under safe, clinical conditions" but could not get one because her life was not in danger, even though she could not afford to go to a state with a more liberal law. A physician, James Hubert Hallford, who had previously been arrested for violating the Texas abortion law, joined Roe in the suit because he felt the Texas abortion law also curtailed the rights of physicians who wanted to be able to perform safe, early abortions without criminal penalties.

The plaintiff in *Doe v. Bolton* was "Mary Doe," who was twenty-two, married, nine weeks pregnant, and had three children. The two older children were in foster homes because she could not support them. She had been advised that an abortion would be less harmful to her than carrying the fetus full term. Further, clearly she could not afford another child. When she applied for an abortion she was turned down by the hospital's abortion committee. She could not afford to go to another state.

Although few states have revised their abortion laws to conform with the two Supreme Court decisions, a number have acknowledged the rulings in other ways. Florida, Illinois, and Nebraska simply repealed their abortion laws and have not replaced them. Michigan and New Jersey left their laws on the books but apparently consider them void as applying to physicians performing abortions within the Supreme Court guidelines; these states would only prosecute laymen who perform abortions. Rhode Island considers its abortion law void, but has taken no further action, and Maryland has held that its abortion laws no longer carry criminal penalties. In the same kind of action, Texas—whose law was the target in *Roe v. Wade*—lifted its law from the criminal statutes and deposited it, unchanged, in the civil statutes. The result is that abortion is no longer a criminal act in Texas although it seems clear that the legislature does not approve of the Court's decision.

Some states, such as Arizona, Connecticut, Missouri, Oklahoma, and South Dakota, have acknowledged their laws' unconstitutionality on various grounds, citing a wide array of state and federal court cases, but have done nothing further. South Dakota in particular seems to be saying—in an exceedingly convoluted manner—that it knows its law cannot be enforced, but it won't give up without a parting shot; it sniffs, in conclusion: "The effective date [of South Dakota's abortion laws] shall be that specific date upon which the *states are given exclusive authority to regulate abortion*"(italics added). Louisiana will not even concede that much. It not only insists that its law is constitutional but declares positively that the "interest of the fetus" takes precedence over that of the mother.

Thus the laws of practically every state, whether they prohibit abortion for any reason except to save the mother's life or are slightly less restrictive, are completely unconstitutional, and therefore unenforceable. This means that if a woman in any of these states can find a doctor willing to perform an abortion and she and the doctor are later subject to criminal prosecution because of it, they have a complete defense based on the unconstitutionality of the laws under which they are being prosecuted. Further, the laws in a number of states allow a woman to get an abortion on the grounds of preserving her "mental health," which can be broadly interpreted. Women in California, Oregon, and the District of Columbia, for example, can obtain early abortions without too much difficulty—and without fear of reprisal—despite seemingly restrictive abortion laws.

What choice does a woman have if she lives in a state with laws that do not permit her to freely choose to have an abortion? She may go to one of the states with more liberal laws, but only if she can afford the time and expense of travel and living away from home. Or she may go to court and specifically challenge her state's abortion law, an obviously impractical solution given the time-consuming nature and expense of any court litigation. Or, if a doctor is willing to share the risk with her, she can go ahead and have the abortion, secure in the belief that neither she nor the doctor can be successfully prosecuted for it because the law is unconstitutional.

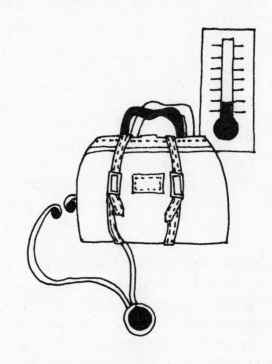

A long-range alternative in those states which have not yet taken any steps to revise their abortion legislation concerns the medical profession. Doctors who want to perform abortions in accordance with the Supreme Court rulings without fear of subsequent prosecution may go to court to challenge their state's laws. Since they do not face the nine-month deadline that makes this an impractical course for pregnant women, and since the Supreme Court has held that physicians have "standing" to bring such suits, they are highly qualified to do so.

Another kind of attempt is being made to challenge abortion statutes. Even as we write, a husband is contesting his wife's right to decide, on her own, to have an abortion; his case is headed for the Supreme Court. In the meantime, perhaps, husbands who want to have a say in their wife's abortion decision should insist she go to Montana or Washington. Both these states have included this provision in their new abortion laws.

There is still a lot of work to be done in the area of abortion-law reform in spite of the 1973 Supreme Court decisions, as the attitude expressed by the Louisiana and South Dakota legislatures should make clear. One has only to think of the entrenched opposition to the Court's 1954 school desegregation ruling to realize that a Supreme Court decision is not a magic wand that once waved will dispel ingrained beliefs.

Abortion is an especially difficult issue to resolve because it provokes such strong religious and moral objections on the part of its opponents, and equally vehement assertions on the part of its proponents. Those who favor noncriminal abortion laws insist that a woman has the right to control her own body and should not be required to give birth to any child she does not want to have, for whatever reason. They feel that no one—and certainly not a state legislature—should be able to prohibit her from making a decision about something that will affect her entire life. The anti-abortion adherents—primarily Roman Catholic—call themselves "right-to-life" groups. Their stand is rooted

in their religious belief that a fetus is a human being in all respects from the moment of conception, and that to destroy it is murder. They insist that the state must not condone the taking of any life. In November 1974 they were bolstered in their stand by

Pope Paul's sweeping statement not only forbidding abortion but also reaffirming the traditional Roman Catholic position against contraception of any kind other than the so-called "rhythm method."

Thus one of the major arguments used in defense of the Texas law held unconstitutional in *Roe v. Wade* was that "life begins at conception and is present throughout pregnancy, and . . . therefore the state has a compelling interest in protecting that life after conception." The Court responded to this argument in Justice Blackmun's majority opinion: "We need not resolve the difficult question of when life begins. When those trained in the respective disciplines of medicine, philosophy, and theology are unable to arrive at any consensus, the judiciary, at this point in the development of man's knowledge, is not in a position to speculate as to the answer."

Under the common law of England, abortion performed before "quickening"—the first recognizable movement of the fetus, which generally occurs after the sixteenth week of pregnancy—was not a crime. Apparently this opinion was based on earlier moral, religious, and civil- and canon-law concepts of when life begins. There was no consensus, however, on the point at which the embryo or fetus became "formed" (recognizably human) or was "animated" (infused with a soul). Christian theology and canon law both fixed the point of animation at forty days for a male and eighty days for a female, but there was no further agreement on the precise time of formation or animation. There *was* agreement, nevertheless, that prior to these points destruction of the fetus was not homicide. Because of continued uncertainty about when animation occurred, quickening became the accepted critical point, was taken up by common-law scholars, and found its way into the received common law of our country.

The first state to enact abortion legislation was Connecticut. In 1821 this state adopted part of England's first criminal abortion statute, Lord Ellenborough's Act of 1803, which related to a woman "quick with child." Abortion before quickening was not a crime in Connecticut until 1860. In 1828 New York enacted legislation that served as a model for early abortion statutes of other states. New York's law barred abortion but made destruction of an unquickened fetus a misdemeanor, of a quickened fetus second-degree manslaughter. Also, this law provided for therapeutic abortion if it "shall have been necessary to preserve the life of such mother, or shall have been advised by two physicians to be necessary for such purpose." By 1840 eight states had statutes on abortion and only after the Civil War did state legislation begin to replace the common law.

Gradually the distinction between a quickened and unquickened fetus began to disappear from abortion laws in the United States, and both the degree of the crime of abortion and the penalties for it increased. This situation prevailed until some states began adopting abortion laws based on the one presented in the American Law Institute's Model Penal Code, proposed in 1961.

The ALI's law provided that a licensed physician could perform an abortion if he "believed there is substantial risk that continuance of the pregnancy would gravely impair the physical or mental health of the mother or that the child would be born with grave physical or mental defect, or that the pregnancy resulted from rape, incest, or other felonious intercourse." It further provided that abortion must be performed in a licensed hospital and the reasons for it must be certified in writing by the attending physician and one colleague. Versions of this law are now on the books in eleven states: Arkansas, California, Colorado, Delaware, Kansas, Maryland, New Mexico, Oregon, South Carolina, Utah, and Virginia. It was Georgia's ALI-based law (which has now been revised) that was declared unconstitutional in *Doe v. Bolton,* in regard to its hospital, certification, and residence requirements. The other sections of these laws do not meet the standards set forth in *Roe v. Wade* because they impose too many conditions relating to the health of the pregnant woman or the fetus or to the manner of conception (rape or incest) before permitting abortion.

Although they are an improvement on laws that absolutely prohibit abortion except to save the mother's life, the ALI-based laws are not much help to a woman who wants an abortion since they do not let her make her own decision. An abortion black market flourished for many years in spite of these "reform" laws. Between a million and a million and a half illegal abortions were performed in the United States each year, resulting in the deaths of between five and ten thousand women, before laws like New York's and Hawaii's were enacted. In recent years, the number of illegal abortions has dropped, but they are still being performed.

With the passage of New York's new law in 1970, the effect of permitting broad grounds for abortion could be assessed for the first time. Far fewer women have died because of abortion-related complications in New York since the passage of the new law. In fact, there are substantially fewer deaths resulting from abortion in New York than there are accompanying full-term deliveries. This is because a woman can get an abortion earlier in her pregnancy, at a time when it is much less dangerous and when the conditions under which the operation is performed are safer. Not to be overlooked is the reality that legal abortions are much less expensive than those available on the black market and thus are more accessible to young and poor women.

Those states with humane abortion laws have shown the way for others, if they will but follow. There are pressures on state legislatures from all sides. In the conservative corner are the "right-to-life" groups, who haven't given up their fight to keep criminal abortion laws on the books and to roll back liberal laws where they have been enacted. In New York, for example, strong anti-abortion forces are actively lobbying for repeal of that state's abortion law.

Furthur, by placing restrictions on how Medicaid funds may be used, Congress as well as some state legislatures are attempting to interfere with a woman's rights to have an abortion if she cannot afford to pay for it. On the national level, Congress is trying to amend the federal Medicaid statute to prohibit federal matching funds from being used to help pay for Medicaid abortions. This legislation is sponsored by James Buckley, the junior senator from New York, perhaps this country's best-known anti-abortion crusader.

On the state level, North Dakota and Indiana have absolutely refused to permit abortions to be paid for under their Medicaid programs. Several other states that have not explicitly barred Medicaid funds from being used for abortions, as Indiana and North Dakota have, nevertheless have made it difficult for Medicaid recipients to be eligible for abortions under the program. This is done by devious procedural requirements, most of which were declared invalid in *Doe v. Bolton,* but which are hard to pinpoint. States in which it is known that these practices have occurred are Alabama, Arkansas, Illinois, Kentucky, Louisiana, Massachusetts, South Carolina, South Dakota, Tennessee, Texas, Vermont, and West Virginia. New York and Utah tried to limit reimbursement for Medicaid abortions to those cases judged to be "therapeutically or medically necessary." This reasoning has been successfully refuted in district courts on grounds established in *Roe v. Wade* and *Doe v. Bolton.*

All these federal and state restraints are vulnerable to multiple challenges on constitutional grounds, but until they are specifically brought to court and ruled on, they will undoubtedly continue to flourish.

Some of those who find it difficult to take a stand for or against abortion want more education about and advocacy of contraceptive measures, for men as well as women. They fear that too many women will see an unlimited right to cheap abortions as just another form of contraception, treating it as casually as they would a general gynecological examination. But no contraceptive device, except the ultimate ones of sterilization and vasectomy, is completely effective, and education is often easier advocated than accomplished. Further, with the frightening prospect of overpopulation throughout the world, many countries that had once refused—on religious grounds—to consider abortion or any other kinds of birth control are changing their attitudes and their laws in an attempt to cope with this problem.

Most abortion-reform proponents simply want what is best for all concerned: for a woman to be able to make and carry out intelligent decisions about a difficult problem that will affect her entire life; for the thousands of unwanted children born every year, many of whom are only burdens on their parents or on the state and who thus bear a terrible burden themselves; for the physicians who in specific cases feel that an abortion is the safest and most compassionate course for a patient but are barred from performing, or even suggesting, it.

In any case, women *will* get abortions whether they are legal or not. A hundred thousand women defied the old New York abortion law every year. A hundred thousand different women would defy it again if it were reinstated. Thousands are defying restrictive laws in those states that still have them. Such laws save neither the lives of unborn children nor of the women who carry them, no matter how vehemently "right-to-life" groups may insist to the contrary. Women, and all those who care about human rights, must not be bound by laws that were passed with no apparent regard for their often terrible consequences.

4
When I Want an Abortion
The Law State by State

Note: Because of the 1973 U.S. Supreme Court rulings in *Roe v. Wade* and *Doe v. Bolton,* only the following states have abortion legislation that is wholly or partially constitutional. The abortion laws of all other states are not included in this section because they are unconstitutional. (For an explanation, see pages 83–85 and 87–88 of the essay on abortion.)

ALASKA

When abortion is legal: At any time before the fetus is viable. An unmarried woman under 18 must have the consent of parents or guardian. [This requirement may be unconstitutional, *Roe v. Wade.*] The operation must be performed by a licensed physician in a hospital or other approved facility. [The hospital requirement is unconstitutional for the first trimester of pregnancy, *Roe v. Wade.*]

Residence requirement: Thirty days. [Unconstitutional, *Doe v. Bolton.*]

GEORGIA

When abortion is legal: During the first or second trimester of pregnancy if the physician, based on his clinical judgment, considers it necessary. After the first trimester, the operation must be performed in a licensed hospital. After the second trimester, abortion may be performed only to save the mother's life or health; two physicians must certify that it is necessary, and it must be approved by a committee of the medical staff of the hospital.

Residence requirement: The woman must be a resident of the state. [Unconstitutional, *Doe v. Bolton.*]

HAWAII

When abortion is legal: At any time before the fetus is viable. The operation must be performed by a licensed physician in a licensed hospital. [The hospital requirement is unconstitutional for the first trimester of pregnancy, *Roe v. Wade.*]

Residence requirement: Ninety days. [Unconstitutional, *Doe v. Bolton.*]

IDAHO

When abortion is legal: During the first or second trimester (approximately the first twenty-five weeks) of pregnancy if the physician, after consulting with the woman, determines it is appropriate *in consideration of such factors as the possibility that the child would be born with a mental or physical defect; the pregnancy resulted from forcible or statutory rape, incest, or other felonious intercourse; and the physical, familial, emotional, and psychological factors in the woman's life (including her age, the potential stigma of unwed motherhood, the psychological harm and stress to all concerned, and the woman's opinion that maternity will force her into a distressful future and the possible need of public assistance).* After the fetus becomes viable, abortion may be performed only to save the life of the mother or if, on birth, the fetus would be unable to survive. [The portion in italics may be unconstitutional as too restrictive for the first two trimesters, *Roe v. Wade.*]

Residence requirement: None.

INDIANA

When abortion is legal: During the first trimester of pregnancy if the woman consents and the operation is performed by a physician in a hospital or licensed facility. [The hospital requirement is unconstitutional for the first trimester of pregnancy, *Roe v. Wade.*] During the second trimester, the abortion must be performed in a hospital. An unmarried woman under 18 must have the consent of parents or guardian unless the abortion is necessary to save her life. After the fetus is viable, abortion may be performed only to save the mother's life or physical health, and the attending physician must certify in writing that it is necessary.

Residence requirement: None.

MONTANA

When abortion is legal: During the first three months of pregnancy if the woman gives her written, "informed" consent. A married woman must have the consent of her husband; an unmarried minor must have the consent of parents or guardian. [These requirements may be unconstitutional, *Roe v. Wade.*] The operation must be performed by a licensed physician. After the first three months, the operation must be performed in a licensed hospital. After the fetus is viable, abortion may be performed only to save the mother's life, and the attending physician must certify in writing that it is necessary, with concurrence from two other physicians.

Residence requirement: None.

NEW YORK

When abortion is legal: During the first twenty-four weeks of pregnancy. Either a licensed physician may perform the abortion or the woman herself may induce a miscarriage on the advice of a physician. After the first twenty-four weeks, abortion may be performed only if a licensed physician believes it is necessary to save the mother's life.

Residence requirement: None.

NORTH CAROLINA

When abortion is legal: During the first twenty weeks of pregnancy. The operation must be performed by a licensed physician in a licensed hospital. [The hospital requirement is unconstitutional for the first trimester of pregnancy, *Roe v. Wade.*] After the first twenty weeks, abortion may be performed only if it is necessary to save the mother's life.

Residence requirement: Thirty days. [Unconstitutional, *Doe v. Bolton.*]

TENNESSEE

When abortion is legal: During first three months of pregnancy if a licensed physician considers it necessary and the woman gives her written consent. The operation must be performed by a licensed physician. After the first three months but before the fetus is viable, the operation must be performed in a licensed hospital. After the fetus is viable, abortion may be performed only to save the mother's life or health.

Residence requirement: The woman must be a resident of the state. [Unconstitutional, *Doe v. Bolton.*]

WASHINGTON

When abortion is legal: During the first four months of pregnancy if the woman gives her consent. A married woman must have the consent of her husband; an unmarried minor must have the consent of parents or guardian. [These requirements may be unconstitutional, *Roe v. Wade.*] The operation must be performed by a licensed physician in an accredited hospital or approved facility unless the physician determines that the pregnancy must be terminated immediately; in that case it may be performed elsewhere. [The hospital requirement is unconstitutional for the first trimester of pregnancy, *Roe v. Wade.*]

Residence requirement: Three months. [Unconstitutional, *Doe v. Bolton.*]

5
When I Want a Divorce

Marital bliss—marital misery: two sides of a single coin. Even way back when the coins were shekels or shark's teeth, society has always had to provide escape routes for those who find themselves unfairly or intolerably mated.

In recent years our divorce rate has been zooming skyward. According to 1974 Census Bureau figures, the American divorce rate has increased as much since 1970 as it did in the ten years from 1960 to 1970. There were thirty-five divorced persons per thousand in 1960; forty-seven per thousand in 1970; and sixty-three per thousand as of March 1974.

Is it true that the entire institution of marriage is really breaking down, as some doomsayers suggest? Or are today's husbands and wives unwilling to put up with the same levels of marital stress that their parents somehow found tolerable and their grandparents accepted as a normal part of the matrimonial condition? Probably the latter. But the fact is that more than a third of U.S. marriages now end in divorce. California's over-all divorce rate is better than 50 per cent annually, and in some sections of this our most advanced and future-shocked state, the rate is 120 per cent, which apparently means that for every five marriages there are six divorces. (This dazzling statistic comes from the all-American bedroom community surrounding Disneyland.)

The laws of each state provide two possible ways to get rid of an unwanted husband or wife: divorce or annulment. A divorce presupposes a valid marriage and ends the marriage. An annulment says the marriage wasn't legal in the first place and therefore does not exist. Thirty-four states and the

District of Columbia have statutory provisions for judicial separation, a halfway measure that permits husband and wife to live apart yet still retain many of the legal rights and obligations of marriage—support duties and prohibitions on remarriage, for example. Sometimes a separation is a prelude to divorce, but just as often it is prolonged indefinitely if no time limit has been set.

In the sixteen states that make no provision for judicial separation, a husband and wife may still decide to live apart and make support agreements between themselves. These agreements, if properly made, will be as enforceable as any valid contract, but the process of separation cannot be sanctioned by a court decision as it can be in those states where it is recognized by law.

Two kinds of behavior during marriage are grounds for divorce. The first encompasses adultery, desertion, conviction of a serious crime (robbery, murder, or rape), nonsupport of a wife by a husband, drunkenness or drug addiction, and "extreme cruelty." Common to all these grounds for divorce is the idea that one spouse is "at fault"—that is, he or she did something which is incompatible with the marriage contract or somehow injured the other partner by his or her behavior. Twenty-five states and the District of Columbia have grounds for divorce that are based exclusively on fault.

The second kind of grounds for divorce include incurable insanity; living apart for a certain period of time; incompatibility (legalese for couples who cannot learn to get on); and in thirteen states—Arizona, California, Colorado, Florida, Hawaii, Iowa,

Kentucky, Michigan, Missouri, Nebraska, Oregon, Texas, Washington—the new, liberal concept of "irreconcilable differences which have caused the irretrievable breakdown of the marriage." Here there is no requirement of fault. That is, one of the spouses does not have to prove that the other is "guilty" of violating the marital vows or, as can often happen, be subjected to similar charges made by the spouse contesting the divorce.

Another group of states recognizes both fault and nonfault grounds. Such grounds as irreconcilable differences, irretrievable breakdown of the marriage, or incompatibility are valid, but so are such fault grounds as adultery and desertion. These states are: Alabama, Alaska, Delaware, Idaho, Indiana, Kansas, Maine, Nevada, New Hampshire, New Mexico, North Dakota, Oklahoma, Texas, and Wyoming.

In states with divorce laws based on fault there are several defenses, each stemming from the theory that only an "innocent" spouse is entitled to a divorce. These defenses are connivance, collusion, condonation, and, the strangest of all, recrimination. If, for example, a husband invites a friend home for the weekend and then fabricates an excuse to leave town himself, hoping that when wife and friend are left alone together nature will take its course—that's connivance. If the husband and wife plan it jointly but don't tell the unsuspecting friend, that's collusion. Either way, no divorce, assuming one of the parties (or a witness) testifies to these facts in court.

Condonation really means forgiveness. Thus, if a wife seeking a divorce can be shown to have forgiven her husband's misbehavior, the divorce will be denied. So, for example, adultery followed by marital sex equals no adultery. If you are planning to charge your husband with adultery, and you think he will actively contest the divorce, be sure you don't get back in bed with him yourself, or at least not until after you get your decree.

Recrimination is a disgraceful concept that is still on the books in a number of states. This defense prohibits a divorce from being granted to a wife even though she has valid

grounds if her husband also has some grounds against her and chooses to prove them. For example, if a wife charges non-support, desertion, or cruelty, and the husband countercharges adultery or theft, the divorce will be denied. This is true in Delaware, Georgia, Idaho, Louisiana, Montana, New Hampshire, New York, West Virginia, and Wyoming. In three other states—Alaska, Arkansas, and Minnesota—recrimination is permitted as a defense only to a charge of adultery. One wonders what baroque puritan mentality first figured out that unhappy

partners must be yoked in everlasting marital doom because neither one is entirely free of blame.

The fault theory of divorce comes down from the time of Henry VIII, when domestic relations were handled by courts that were part of the church. Divorce, leaving both parties free to marry again, was simply out of the question then. One's only hope was annulment, unless the sins of one partner against the other were so grievous that a limited form of separation called "divorce from bed and board" could be obtained. (This is the origin of our modern concept of judicial separation.)

There are certain encouraging signs that the fault theory of divorce is on its way out. It *is* out in those states that have adopted the concept of irreconcilable differences or irretrievable breakdown as the only grounds for ending a marriage. In those states that still have fault divorce laws, the laws create unneccessary problems for both the people involved and the legal system itself. Thus a husband and wife who want to end a marriage are forced to wash their dirty marital linens in public. This may damage the couple psychologically as well as financially. In addition, because the judge, the lawyers, and the divorcing couple often know the charges are being made only to satisfy their state's divorce laws, the legal system itself becomes a mockery, something to be "gotten around." Since this is the only direct experience many people have with the courts, they may come to view the whole legal system as cynically as they do a divorce court.

It is a hopeful sign that the most significant recent divorce-law reforms were first enacted in the nation's two most populous states, New York and California. New York now permits a husband and wife to divorce if they have been voluntarily living apart, with legal papers to prove it, for at least two years. Not much, it might seem, until you consider that until 1967 New York would accept *no* grounds for divorce other than adultery. But the real breakthrough was California's 1970 legislation establishing only two grounds for divorce (or marital dissolution, as it is called there and in other states with similar laws): incurable insanity or irreconcilable differences. The latter beautiful phrase simply means that if two adults do not get along together, for whatever reason, society should not deny them the right to get along apart, nor the right to remarry.

California was the first state to replace outright the archaic and punitive fault theory with the mature, nonmoralistic concept of marital breakdown, and a few other states have followed its example. This theory of divorce recognizes that in most marriages of any duration, the fault probably lies on both sides, and then proceeds on the assumption that fault is immaterial anyway as long as one of the spouses wants to dissolve the marriage.

When a husband and wife with minor children apply for dissolution of their marriage in California, the court may transfer the proceedings to a conciliation court if it appears the children will be adversely affected by the marital breakup and there is any chance for reconciliation. If the couple has no children, either spouse can still request hearings in the conciliation court, which will take the case if it is not overburdened with cases involving children. Dissolution proceedings are suspended for the duration of the hearings, whose purpose is to try for complete reconciliation or at least an amicable settlement. During or after the hearings the court may make any recommendations it feels necessary, but they are effective only for thirty days. Recommendations that the parties consult physicians, psychiatrists, or other specialists need be followed only if both spouses consent. If these efforts fail, the dissolution proceedings are resumed.

Another important difference between traditional divorce laws based on fault and the "no-fault" laws is the rationale on which alimony and marital property are awarded. Under traditional laws these awards often are determined by which of the divorcing spouses is considered the most at fault. Under the new laws, they are based on the relative economic circumstances of the parties without any regard to the cause for dissolution of the marriage.

Alimony is considered a continuation of the support obligation assumed by the husband—and in some cases the wife—at the time of the marriage. (By statute, only the wife is permitted to receive alimony in eighteen states and the District of Columbia; in all others, either spouse is eligible.) These support payments are meant primarily to keep wives from becoming public charges, although in fact it may be the husband who is reduced to a sub-subsistence level. Whether he is or not depends on the basis for awarding alimony, both in terms of whether only the "innocent" wife (or husband) is entitled to *any* alimony and whether the *amount* of alimony awarded is related to economic need and capacity as well as to fault. The "guilty" wife may get nothing; the "guilty" husband may have to pay, and pay, and pay.

Not all states with exclusively fault grounds for divorce consider a spouse's guilt when setting alimony payments; eight of the twenty-six states that have such laws do not. However, even in those states that do consider fault, the amount of the alimony award usually depends on a number of other things besides guilt: the life style to which the couple has become accustomed; the length of the marriage; age; health; child-care responsibilities; financial status; and potential for employment. In four states (Maryland, North Carolina, South Carolina, and Wisconsin), however, a spouse who wins a divorce because of the other's adultery is not obligated to pay, no matter how great the other spouse's need.

If an ex-wife wants to remarry she will usually have to give up her alimony, since it is a continuation of a husband's support obligation. The spouse receiving alimony payments must report them as income; the one making the payments is entitled to claim them as deductions.

In California, alimony has been replaced by "spousal support," which is awarded solely on the basis of need. This corresponds with the replacement of divorce with dissolution proceedings whereby neither spouse is considered the guilty party. If at the time of the dissolution a wife has substantial property of her own or is capable of supporting herself, she will receive either no support or a minimal amount if it is necessary to help her prepare or retrain herself for employment. The period of spousal support has also been re-evaluated. Under the old laws the ex-wife could have received alimony until her death or remarriage; now she gets support only for a specific time, determined by her earning ability and the length of her marriage. Also, if the husband is unable to support himself and his wife has the ability to pay spousal support, she will be ordered to do so by the court.

Under the laws of all states, the amount of alimony remains open to modification by the court. If a previously unemployable wife gets a job, for example, the alimony her ex-husband is paying may be reduced or eliminated altogether. Or, if a woman whose ex-husband could afford to pay next to no alimony at the time of their divorce can prove her need and his increased income, the court will increase the alimony. Even when no alimony is awarded as part of a divorce decree, generally the more affluent spouse is ordered to pay "suit money" (temporary alimony) to the dependent spouse while the suit is pending.

The property settlement is the aspect of divorce that most often requires the assistance of a lawyer and keeps countless lawyers in business. There are two basic approaches to the division of property, depending on whether the couple lives in a community-property or a common-law marital property state (discussed in Chapter 1).

In the community-property states, each spouse is generally entitled to half the community property at the time of the divorce, although there are some variations depending upon the grounds for divorce. In California, however, each spouse is automatically entitled to one-half the property unless such an equal division would be grossly unfair. For example, a woman with four young children, no job, and an ex-husband with a good income will probably get more than half the community property.

The great majority of states—both common law and community property—authorize the courts to divide the property in a divorce action according to what it decides is just. In this way many courts in the common-law states have come up with results comparable to those arrived at in the community-property states. Undoubtedly, though, the most equitable results are achieved under entirely no-fault provisions.

Eighteen states and the District of Columbia allow a divorcing couple to agree by contract on the marital property division and the amount and duration of the support, if any. California, Connecticut, Hawaii, Indiana, Kentucky, Massachussetts, Missouri, and Montana have such statutes. This means the contract must be accepted by the court unless, as one state puts it, the terms are "unconscionable." In Arkansas, Delaware, the District of Columbia, Georgia, Nebraska, Nevada, New Mexico, Oregon, Tennessee, Virginia, and Wyoming contracts are not specifically permitted by statute, but they will be accepted as part of a divorce settlement if they are "fair and equitable."

The custody of minor children (discussed in Chapter 2) is decided in every state on the court's judgment of what will be best for the child; the parents' wishes are part of the court's criteria, as are the child's, if he or she is thought to be mature enough to make a sound decision. So even though there is a presumption in many states that older girls or very young children of either sex should be placed with the mother, this is not stipulated by statute, leaving the court free to make its determination on the basis of other factors it may consider relevant in each case. Child support payments are similarly assigned on the basis of which parent is best able to afford them. Generally it will be the father's duty, as he is usually in the better financial position.

Missouri, Nebraska, Nevada, and Virginia have permitted child custody and support to be included as part of the spouse's alimony and property-division contracts, and Indiana allows such contracts to specify as to the education and religious training of children. But these arrangements are scrutinized very carefully by the court before they are or are not accepted.

Our complex web of overlapping and conflicting state laws has produced the American phenomenon of "migratory divorce." Most states require a year's residence (or at least three to six months, as in a number of states) in the state, and three months in the county, before the court may grant a divorce. The purpose of the residence requirement is to determine which state has the paramount interest in the marital status of the parties.

(In January 1975, residency requirements were declared to be constitutional in a U.S. Supreme Court case—*Sosna v. Iowa*—challenging them. One of the grounds for the decision was that to waive residency periods would cause the state to become a "divorce mill.") Two underpopulated states—Nevada and Idaho—went into the divorce business apparently for purely economic reasons; they require only a six-week residence in the state before granting divorces.

The basic question here is whether a migratory divorce is valid in another state. For example, is a divorce obtained by a woman who leaves her Illinois home for a six-week "residence" in Nevada legal? The Supreme Court has held that a bona fide resident of any state, Nevada and Idaho included, can get a divorce even if the absent spouse never sets foot in that state, providing that sufficient efforts are made to notify him or her that a divorce action is pending, to serve him or her with the appropriate papers, and to provide an opportunity for the other spouse to appear and contest the divorce.

The key words are *bona fide,* and all those who anticipate later trouble from absent spouses—or perhaps only temporarily accommodating spouses who choose not to appear—are well advised to join a country club, rent an apartment, register to vote, buy a car, and do whatever else they can think of to indicate they do not intend to migrate out of the state the moment their divorce is granted. If the absent spouse is properly served and does not appear in court personally or through an attorney, the divorce will be granted by default. But in order to get alimony, property division, or child support and custody, the woman who obtains a default divorce must go to court in the state where her ex-husband is physically located or, in lawyer's jargon, where she can get "personal jurisdiction" over her ex-husband.

A divorced woman's legal problems are not necessarily ended once she gets her final decree. An ex-wife may have difficulty establishing credit. Her income is treated differently by banks, stores, and other lenders from that of a man in comparable economic circumstances. Often there also is what might be called a legal residue from the divorce, no matter how final it may be—that is, a tendency on the part of creditors to judge a divorcee's credit standing on the basis of her ex-husband's, and deny her credit if he has a bad credit rating. If it is ever enacted into law, Title III of the Truth in Lending Act may give some relief to ex-wives—as well as wives and single women—contending with credit discrimination, because it will bar sex discrimination in credit transactions. But it may never become law; after it was passed by the Senate in 1973 it was sent to the House Banking and Currency Committee, and has not been heard of since.

Today it is becoming almost as easy to get divorced as it is to get married. As long as people so often persist in getting married for all the wrong reasons, or before they have matured sufficiently to know what they're letting themselves in for or who they really are, divorce should be as painless as possible. Both partners go through enough emotional trauma during a divorce without having to endure a legal trauma as well.

5
When I Want a Divorce
The Law
State by State

ALABAMA

Grounds for divorce: Irretrievable breakdown of the marriage; complete incompatibility; adultery; abandonment (one year); nonsupport by husband (two years); imprisonment (two years on a sentence of seven or more years); confinement for insanity (five years); cruelty; alcoholism; drug addiction; incurable impotence; legal separation (two years); wife pregnant by another at time of marriage without husband's knowledge; unnatural sexual behavior before or after marriage.

Residence requirement: Six months.

Alimony and property: Fault is one of the bases on which court determines amount and recipient of support unless the divorce is granted on a "no fault" ground. Only the wife is eligible to receive support. There are no statutory provisions for the division of property.

Wife's name: No statute.

Grounds for judicial separation: Same as the grounds for divorce.

Grounds for annulment: None. However, an incestuous marriage can be voided if either spouse is convicted of that crime.

ALASKA

Grounds for divorce: Incompatibility; adultery; willful desertion (one year); willful neglect by husband (one year); conviction for a felony; insanity (eighteen months); cruel and inhuman treatment; alcoholism (one year); drug addiction; impotence; personal indignities.

Residence requirement: One year.

Alimony and property: Fault is not taken into consideration in court's determination of the amount and recipient of support or the division of property. Either spouse is eligible to receive support or property.

Wife's name: Ex-wife may resume her maiden name if the court approves.

Grounds for judicial separation: No statute.

Grounds for annulment: Incest; bigamy. The following grounds are valid unless the marital relationship is continued after the ground no longer exists: mental incapacity at time of marriage; under age and without parental approval; fraud; force or duress.

ARIZONA

Grounds for divorce (dissolution): Irretrievable breakdown of the marriage.

Residence requirement: One year.

Alimony and property: Fault is not taken into consideration in court's determination of the amount and recipient of support or the division of property. Either spouse is eligible to receive support or property. Any community property or joint tenancy property not divided is kept by both spouses as tenants in common.

Wife's name: Ex-wife may resume her maiden name if the court approves.

Grounds for judicial separation: Same as the grounds for divorce.

Grounds for annulment: None. However, incestuous and bigamous marriages, or those where one party was without mental capacity at time of marriage, can be voided.

ARKANSAS

Grounds for divorce: Adultery; desertion (one year); willful nonsupport; conviction for a felony; idiocy or insanity (three years); cruel or barbarous treatment endangering the life of the spouse; alcoholism (one year); impotence at time of marriage; separation (three years); personal indignities; bigamy.

Residence requirement: Two months.

Alimony and property: Fault is one of the bases on which court determines amount and recipient of support and division of property. Only the wife is eligible to receive support and property. Spouses may make a contract stipulating alimony payments and distribution of property; if approved by the court, the contract will be enforceable.

Wife's name: Ex-wife may resume her maiden name if the court approves, providing she does not have custody of couple's minor children.

Grounds for judicial separation: No statute.

Grounds for annulment: Mental incapacity at time of marriage; under age; fraud; force or duress; incest; impotence at time of marriage.

CALIFORNIA

Grounds for divorce (dissolution): Irreconcilable differences; incurable insanity.

Residence requirement: Six months in state, three months in county.

Alimony and property: Fault is not taken into consideration in court's determination of the amount and recipient of support or the division of property. Either spouse is eligible to receive support or property. Community property is divided equally. Spouses may make a contract stipulating support payments and distribution of property; if approved by the court, the contract will be enforceable.

Wife's name: Ex-wife may resume her maiden name if the court approves.

Grounds for judicial separation: Same as the grounds for dissolution.

Grounds for annulment: Bigamy; incurable impotence. The following grounds are valid unless the marital relationship is continued after the ground no longer exists: mental incapacity at time of marriage; under age; fraud; force or duress.

COLORADO

Grounds for divorce (dissolution): Irretrievable breakdown of the marriage.

Residence requirement: Ninety days.

Alimony and property: Fault is not taken into consideration in court's determination of the amount and recipient of support or the division of property. Either spouse is eligible to receive support or property. In the division of property, court may give preference to the spouse who has custody of couple's minor children.

Wife's name: No statute.

Grounds for judicial separation: Same as the grounds for divorce.

Grounds for annulment: Mental incapacity at time of marriage, including that caused by drugs or alcohol; fraud; duress; physical inability to perform sexual intercourse; couple got married on a dare or as a jest. Incestuous and bigamous marriages which were void in the states where they were performed may be declared invalid.

CONNECTICUT

Grounds for divorce: Adultery; willful desertion (one year); absence (seven years); conviction for a crime involving violation of conjugal duty and with a sentence of more than one year; life imprisonment; confinement for insanity (five years); intolerable cruelty; alcoholism; fraud.

Residence requirement: None if grounds for divorce occurred in the state or if plaintiff was a resident of state before marriage and returned with the intention of remaining permanently; otherwise, one year.

Alimony and property: Fault is not taken into consideration in court's determination of the amount and recipient of support or the division of property. Either spouse is eligible to receive support or property. Spouses may make a contract stipulating support payments, distribution of property, and child custody and support; if approved by the court, the contract will be enforceable.

Wife's name: Ex-wife may resume her maiden name if the court approves.

Grounds for judicial separation: Same as the grounds for divorce.

Grounds for annulment: None. However, whenever a marriage is void or voidable for any cause under the laws of Connecticut or of the state where the marriage was performed, the marriage may be declared void.

DELAWARE

Grounds for divorce: Incompatibility (two years); adultery; desertion (one year); nonsupport; imprisonment (two years—or, if the sentence is for an indeterminant time, one year); chronic mental illness or epilepsy (five years); extreme cruelty; alcoholism (two years); separation (eighteen months); bigamy; under age.

Residence requirement: One year.

Alimony and property: Fault is not taken into consideration in court's determination of the amount and recipient of support or the division of property. Support will be granted to the defendant in a divorce case based on incompatibility if he or she can prove dependence on the other spouse. Wife may be granted a reasonable share of husband's real and personal property if the divorce is not granted on grounds of

incompatibility, voluntary separation, or under age. Spouses may make a contract stipulating support payments and distribution of property; if approved by the court, the contract will be enforceable.

Wife's name: No statute.

Grounds for judicial separation: No statute.

Grounds for annulment: Bigamy; incest; incurable impotence. The following grounds are valid unless the marital relationship is continued after the ground no longer exists: under age; fraud; force or duress; insanity.

DISTRICT OF COLUMBIA

Grounds for divorce: Adultery; desertion (one year); conviction for a felony with a sentence of at least two years; separation (one year).

Residence requirement: One year.

Alimony and property: Fault is not taken into consideration in court's determination of the amount and recipient of support or the division of property. Only the wife is eligible to receive support, but either spouse may be awarded property. Spouses may make a contract stipulating support payments and distribution of property; if approved by the court, the contract will be enforceable.

Wife's name: No statute.

Grounds for judicial separation: Same as the grounds for divorce, plus cruelty.

Grounds for annulment: Fraud; force or duress; bigamy; impotence. Mental incapacity at time of marriage is valid unless the marital relationship is continued after the ground no longer exists.

FLORIDA

Grounds for divorce (dissolution): Irretrievable breakdown of the marriage; mental incompetence (three years).

Residence requirement: Six months.

Alimony and property: Fault is not taken into consideration in court's determination of the amount and recipient of support. Either spouse is eligible to receive support. There are no statutory provisions for the division of property.

Wife's name: No statute.

Grounds for judicial separation: No statute.

Grounds for annulment: None.

GEORGIA

Grounds for divorce: Adultery; desertion (one year); conviction for a felony involving immoral behavior with a sentence of at least two years; incurable insanity (two years); mental or physical cruelty; alcoholism; drug addiction; impotence at time of marriage; wife pregnant by another at time of marriage without husband's knowledge; fraud; mental incapacity at time of marriage; force or duress; incest.

Residence requirement: Six months.

Alimony and property: Fault is one of the bases on which court determines amount and recipient of support and division of property. Only the wife is eligible to receive support, but either spouse may be awarded property. Spouses may make a contract stipulating support payments and distribution of property; if approved by the court, the contract will be enforceable.

Wife's name: Ex-wife may resume her maiden name or the name of a former husband if the court approves.

Grounds for judicial separation: No statute.

Grounds for annulment: None. However, if spouses were incompetent or fraudulently induced to marry, an annulment may be granted unless there are children as a result of the marriage.

HAWAII

Grounds for divorce (dissolution): Irretrievable breakdown of the marriage; living apart under a decree of separate maintenance (two years).

Residence requirement: One year in state, three months in county.

Alimony and property: Fault is not taken into consideration in court's determination of the amount and recipient of support or the division of property. Either spouse is eligible to receive support or property. Spouses may make a contract stipulating support payments and distribution of property; if approved by the court, the contract will be enforceable.

Wife's name: No statute.

Grounds for judicial separation: Same as the grounds for divorce. There is a two-year limit on the duration of the separation.

Grounds for annulment: Mental incapacity at time of marriage; under age; fraud; force or duress; bigamy; incest; impotence; either spouse afflicted with any loathsome disease if this is unknown to the other.

IDAHO

Grounds for divorce: Irreconcilable differences; adultery; willful desertion; willful neglect; conviction for a felony; permanent insanity; extreme cruelty (bodily injury or mental suffering); alcoholism; living apart (five years).

Residence requirement: Six weeks.

Alimony and property: Fault is one of the bases on which court determines amount and recipient of support unless the divorce is granted on a "no fault" ground. Only the wife is eligible to receive support. Either party may be awarded community property.

Wife's name: No statute.

Grounds for judicial separation: No statute.

Grounds for annulment: Bigamy; incurable impotence. The following grounds are valid unless the marital relationship is continued after the ground no longer exists: mental incapacity at time of marriage; under age; fraud; force.

ILLINOIS

Grounds for divorce: Adultery; desertion (one year); conviction for a felony; attempt on life of spouse; mental or physical cruelty; alcoholism (two years); drug addiction (two years); impotence; bigamy; venereal disease if communicated to spouse.

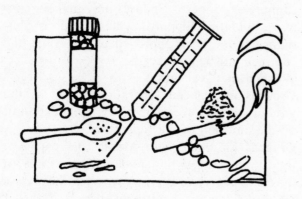

Residence requirement: Six months if grounds occurred in state; otherwise, one year.

Alimony and property: Fault is not taken into consideration in court's determination of the amount and recipient of support or the division of property. Either spouse is eligible to receive support or property.

Wife's name: Ex-wife may resume her maiden name if the court approves.

Grounds for judicial separation: Permitted if "necessary for health and happiness . . . in addition to disregard of the marital obligations."

Grounds for annulment: Annulment may be granted, but grounds are not enumerated by statute.

INDIANA

Grounds for divorce: Irretrievable breakdown of the marriage; adultery; desertion; conviction for a felony after marriage; incurable insanity (two years); impotence at time of marriage.

Residence requirement: Six months in state, three months in county.

Alimony and property: Fault is not taken into consideration in court's determination of the amount and recipient of support or the division of property. Either spouse is eligible to receive support or property, although court may not award support payments unless the spouse is incapacitated, and then only for the duration of the disability. Spouses may make a contract stipulating support payments, distribution of property, and education and religious training of minor children; if approved by the court, the contract will be enforceable.

Wife's name: Ex-wife may resume her maiden name if the court approves.

Grounds for judicial separation: Adultery; husband's desertion or refusal to provide for wife (six months); cruelty; "intolerable recurring strife"; alcoholism; drug addiction; failure to cohabit (six months).

Grounds for annulment: Mental incapacity at time of marriage; under age; fraud; bigamy; incest.

IOWA

Grounds for divorce (dissolution): Irretrievable breakdown of the marriage.

Residence requirement: None if both spouses are residents of state; one year if defendant is not a state resident.

Alimony and property: Fault is not taken into consideration in court's determination of the amount and recipient of support or the division of property. Either spouse is eligible to receive support or property.

Wife's name: No statute.

Grounds for judicial separation: Same as the grounds for divorce.

Grounds for annulment: Mental incapacity at time of marriage; impotence at time of marriage; marriage prohibited by law. Bigamy is valid unless the marital relationship is continued after the first marriage is ended.

KANSAS

Grounds for divorce: Incompatibility; adultery; abandonment (one year); gross neglect of duty; conviction for a felony and imprisonment after marriage; mental illness (three years); extreme cruelty; alcoholism.
Residence requirement: Six months.
Alimony and property: Fault is not taken into consideration in court's determination of the amount and recipient of support or the division of property. Either spouse is eligible to receive support or property.
Wife's name: Ex-wife may resume her maiden name if the court approves.
Grounds for judicial separation: Same as the grounds for divorce.
Grounds for annulment: Fraud; bigamy; impotence at time of marriage; wife pregnant by another at time of marriage without husband's knowledge.

KENTUCKY

Grounds for divorce (dissolution): Irretrievable breakdown of the marriage.
Residence requirement: Six months.
Alimony and property: Fault is not taken into consideration in court's determination of the amount and recipient of support and the division of property. Either spouse is eligible to receive support or property. Spouses may make a contract stipulating support payments and distribution of property; if approved by the court, the contract will be enforceable.
Wife's name: Ex-wife may resume her maiden name or a former husband's name if the court approves.
Grounds for judicial separation: Permitted for "any cause the court deems sufficient."

Grounds for annulment: Mental incapacity at time of marriage, including that caused by drugs or alcohol; fraud; force or duress; physical inability to perform sexual intercourse; marriage prohibited by law.

LOUISIANA

Grounds for divorce: Adultery; conviction for a felony. The following grounds are valid only after a separation and a failure of reconciliation for one year: abandonment; nonsupport; being a fugitive from justice; mental or physical cruelty; attempt on life of spouse; public defamation of spouse.
Residence requirement: None if at least one spouse is domiciled in the state or the grounds occurred there; otherwise, one year.
Alimony and property: Fault is one of the bases on which court determines amount and recipient of support and property. Only the wife is eligible to receive alimony, but either spouse may be awarded property. Community property is divided equally.
Wife's name: No statute.
Grounds for judicial separation: Same as the grounds for divorce.
Grounds for annulment: Duress is valid unless the marital relationship is continued after the ground no longer exists.

MAINE

Grounds for divorce: Irreconcilable differences; adultery; desertion (three years); nonsupport; extreme cruelty; cruel or abusive treatment; alcoholism; drug addiction; impotence.
Residence requirement: None if spouses were married in the state or cohabited there after marriage, the plaintiff resided in the state when the grounds occurred, or the defendant is a resident; otherwise, six months.
Alimony and property: Fault is one of the bases on which court determines amount and recipient of support and division of property unless the divorce is granted on a "no fault" ground. Only

the wife is eligible to receive support, but either spouse may be awarded property.

Wife's name: Ex-wife may resume her maiden name if the court approves.

Grounds for judicial separation: Desertion (one year); living apart for a justifiable reason (one year).

Grounds for annulment: Mental incapacity at time of marriage; bigamy; incest; life imprisonment.

MARYLAND

Grounds for divorce: Adultery; abandonment (one year); imprisonment for at least three years, eighteen months of which must have been served by the time the suit is filed; incurable insanity (three years); impotence at time of marriage; separation (one year); voluntarily living apart (three years).

Residence requirement: None if grounds occurred within the state; otherwise, one year.

Alimony and property: Fault is one of the bases on which court determines amount and recipient of support and division of property. Either spouse is eligible to receive support or property, but support is absolutely barred to a spouse guilty of adultery.

Wife's name: Ex-wife may resume her maiden name if the court approves.

Grounds for judicial separation: Abandonment; desertion; cruelty; "excessively vicious conduct"; living apart without hope of reconciliation.

Grounds for annulment: Incest; bigamy.

MASSACHUSETTS

Grounds for divorce: Adultery; desertion (two years); nonsupport; conviction for a felony with a sentence of at least five years; physical cruelty; alcoholism; drug addiction; impotence.

Residence requirement: None if the couple lived in the state or if the plaintiff is a resident and grounds occurred there; otherwise, two years.

Alimony and property: Fault is not taken into consideration in court's determination of the

amount and recipient of support or the division of property. Either spouse is eligible to receive support or property. Any joint tenancy property not divided is kept by both spouses as tenants in common. Spouses may make a contract stipulating support payments and distribution of property; if approved by the court, the contract will be enforceable.

Wife's name: Ex-wife may resume her maiden name if the court approves.

Grounds for judicial separation: Desertion; husband's failure to support wife; living apart for a justifiable reason.

Grounds for annulment: Mental incapacity at time of marriage; under age; bigamy; incest.

MICHIGAN

Grounds for divorce (dissolution): Irretrievable breakdown of the marriage.

Residence requirement: None if the couple was married in the state and resided there continuously; otherwise, one year.

Alimony and property: Fault is not taken into consideration in court's determination of the amount and recipient of support or the division of property. Either spouse is eligible to receive support or property. Any joint tenancy property not divided is kept by both spouses as tenants in common.

Wife's name: Ex-wife may resume her maiden name or a former husband's name if the court approves.

Grounds for judicial separation: Same as the grounds for divorce.

Grounds for annulment: Mental incapacity at time of marriage; fraud; bigamy; incest. The following grounds are valid unless the marital relationship is continued after the ground no longer exists: under age; force or duress.

MINNESOTA

Grounds for divorce: Adultery; desertion (one year); imprisonment after marriage; insanity (three years); alcoholism (one year); impotence; separation under a decree of limited divorce (five years); separation following a decree of separate maintenance (two years); course of conduct detrimental to the marriage.

Residence requirement: None for adultery; for other grounds, one year.

Alimony and property: Fault is not taken into consideration in court's determination of the amount and recipient of support or the division of property. Either spouse is eligible to receive support or property.

Wife's name: Ex-wife may resume her maiden name if the court approves.

Grounds for judicial separation: No statute.

Grounds for annulment: Mental incapacity at time of marriage; under age; fraud; force; bigamy; incest.

MISSISSIPPI

Grounds for divorce: Adultery; desertion (one year); conviction for a felony; incurable insanity (three years); habitual cruel and inhumane treatment; alcoholism; drug addiction; impotence; wife pregnant by another at time of marriage without husband's knowledge; insanity at time of marriage without other spouse's knowledge; mental incapacity at time of marriage; incest.

Residence requirement: One year.

Alimony and property: Fault is not taken into consideration in court's determination of the amount and recipient of support. Only the wife is eligible to receive support. There are no statutory provisions for division of property, except that joint tenancy is not affected by the divorce.

Wife's name: No statute.

Grounds for judicial separation: No statute.

Grounds for annulment: Mental incapacity at time of marriage; under age; fraud; bigamy; incest; impotence at time of marriage; failure to obtain marriage license; insanity at time of marriage; wife pregnant by another at time of marriage without husband's knowledge.

MISSOURI

Grounds for divorce (dissolution): Irretrievable breakdown of the marriage.

Residence requirement: One spouse must be a resident of the state or a member of the armed forces stationed there for at least ninety days.

Alimony and property: Fault is not taken into consideration in court's determination of the amount and recipient of support or the division of property. Either spouse is eligible to receive support or property. Spouses may make a contract stipulating support payments, distribution of property, and child custody, support, and visitation rights; if approved by the court, the contract will be enforceable.

Wife's name: No statute.

Grounds for judicial separation: No statute.

Grounds for annulment: None. However, incestuous and bigamous marriages, or those where one spouse was without mental capacity at time of marriage or a license was not obtained, are void.

MONTANA

Grounds for divorce: Adultery; willful desertion (one year); willful neglect (one year); conviction for a felony; incurable insanity (five years); extreme physical or mental cruelty, including false charges of unchastity (mental cruelty must continue for one year); alcoholism (one year).

Residence requirement: One year.

Alimony and property: Fault is one of the bases on which court determines amount and recipient of support and division of property. Only the wife is eligible to receive support, but either spouse may be awarded property. Spouses may make a contract stipulating support payments and distribution of property; if approved by the court, the contract will be enforceable.

Wife's name: No statute.

Grounds for judicial separation: Same as the grounds for divorce.

Grounds for annulment: Bigamy; incest; physical inability to perform sexual intercourse. The following grounds are valid unless the marital relationship is continued after the ground no longer exists: lack of mental capacity at time of marriage; under age; fraud; force.

NEBRASKA

Grounds for divorce (dissolution): Irretrievable breakdown of the marriage.

Residence requirement: One year if couple was married in the state and resided there continuously during their marriage.

Alimony and property: Fault is not taken into consideration in court's determination of the amount and recipient of support or the division of property. Either spouse is eligible to receive support or property. Spouses may make a contract stipulating support payments, distribution of property, and child custody and support; if approved by the court, the contract will be enforceable.

Wife's name: No statute.

Grounds for judicial separation: No statute.

Grounds for annulment: Mental illness or retardation at time of marriage; fraud; force; bigamy; impotence at time of marriage; marriage prohibited by law.

NEVADA

Grounds for divorce: Incompatibility; adultery; desertion (one year); nonsupport by husband

when he was capable of providing for wife (one year); conviction for a felony; insanity (two years); extreme cruelty; alcoholism; impotence at time of marriage and continuing to time of divorce; separation (one year).

Residence requirement: Six weeks.

Alimony and property: Fault is not taken into consideration in court's determination of the amount and recipient of support or the division of property. Only the wife is eligible to receive support and part of husband's separate property, but either spouse may be awarded community property. Spouses may make a contract stipulating support payments, distribution of property, and child custody and support; if approved by the court, the contract will be enforceable.

Wife's name: Ex-wife may resume her maiden name if the court approves.

Grounds for judicial separation: No statute.

Grounds for annulment: Bigamy; incest. The following grounds are valid unless the marital relationship is continued after the ground no longer exists: mental incapacity at time of marriage; under age; fraud.

NEW HAMPSHIRE

Grounds for divorce: Irreconcilable differences; adultery; abandonment (two years); nonsupport by husband (two years); refusal to cohabit (two years); wife's absence without husband's consent (two years); wife out of state without husband's consent (ten years); husband becoming a citizen of a foreign country without leaving wife any means of support; imprisonment (at least one year); extreme cruelty; alcoholism; impotence; refusing to live together (six months); joining a religion which believes marital relations are immoral.

Residence requirement: None if both spouses are residents of the state or the plaintiff is a resident and defendant was personally served notice within the state; otherwise, one year.

Alimony and property: Fault is one of the bases on which court determines amount and recipient

of support and division of property unless divorce is granted on a "no fault" ground. Only the wife is eligible to receive support and property.

Wife's name: Wife may resume her maiden name if the court approves.

Grounds for judicial separation: Same as the grounds for divorce.

Grounds for annulment: Being under age is valid unless the marital relationship is continued after the ground no longer exists. Incestuous and bigamous marriages are void.

NEW JERSEY

Grounds for divorce: Adultery; desertion (one year); imprisonment (eighteen months); confinement for mental illness (two years); physical or mental cruelty; alcoholism (one year); drug addiction (one year); separation without prospect of reconciliation (eighteen months); deviant sexual conduct without other spouse's approval.

Residence requirement: None for adultery; for other grounds, one year.

Alimony and property: Fault is one of the bases on which court determines amount and recipient of support and division of property. Either spouse is eligible to receive support or property.

Wife's name: Ex-wife may resume her maiden name if the court approves. Also, the court may rule that the wife may *not* use her ex-husband's name.

Grounds for judicial separation: Same as the grounds for divorce.

Grounds for annulment: Incest; bigamy; impotence at time of marriage without other spouse's knowledge. The following grounds are valid unless the marital relationship is continued after the ground no longer exists: mental incapacity at time of marriage, including that caused by drugs or alcohol; under age; duress; fraud.

NEW MEXICO

Grounds for divorce: Incompatibility; adultery; abandonment; cruel and inhumane treatment.

Residence requirement: Six months.

Alimony and property: Fault is not taken into consideration in court's determination of the amount and recipient of support. Either spouse is eligible to receive support. There are no statutory provisions for the basis on which property is divided because the decree may not include a division of property; proceedings may be instituted later to have it divided, however. Spouses may make a contract stipulating support payments and distribution of property; if approved by the court, the contract will be enforceable.

Wife's name: Ex-wife may resume her maiden name if the court approves.

Grounds for judicial separation: Living apart without hope of reconciliation.

Grounds for annulment: Under age. Incestuous and bigamous marriages are void.

NEW YORK

Grounds for divorce: Adultery; abandonment (one year); imprisonment after marriage (three years); mental or physical cruelty; legal separation (one year).

Residence requirement: None if couple was married in the state, at least one spouse was resident when grounds occurred, and both are residents at time of suit; otherwise, one year or—if neither marriage nor grounds occurred in state—two years.

Alimony and property: Fault is one of the bases on which court determines amount and recipient of support and division of property. Only wife is eligible to receive alimony and property.

Wife's name: No statute.

Grounds for judicial separation: Same as the grounds for divorce, plus husband's failure to support wife.

Grounds for annulment: Mental incapacity at time of marriage; under age; fraud; impotence; insanity (five years).

NORTH CAROLINA

Grounds for divorce: Adultery; desertion; insanity (three years); impotence at time of marriage; separation (one year); wife pregnant by another at time of marriage without husband's knowledge; unnatural or abnormal sex act.

Residence requirement: Six months.

Alimony and property: Fault is one of the bases on which court determines amount and recipient of alimony. Either spouse is eligible to receive support, but it is absolutely barred to a spouse guilty of adultery. There are no statutory provisions for the basis on which property is divided.

Wife's name: Ex-wife may resume her maiden name or a former dead husband's name if the court approves.

Grounds for judicial separation: Abandonment; cruel and barbarous treatment endangering life; "indignities to the person"; alcoholism; drug addiction; one partner "maliciously turning the other out of the home."

Grounds for annulment: Mental incapacity at time of marriage; under age; bigamy; incest; impotence.

NORTH DAKOTA

Grounds for divorce: Irreconcilable differences; adultery; willful desertion; willful neglect; conviction for a felony; insanity (five years); extreme cruelty; alcoholism.

Residence requirement: One year.

Alimony and property: Fault is not taken into consideration in court's determination of the amount and recipient of support or the division of property. Either spouse is eligible to receive support or property.

Wife's name: Ex-wife may resume her maiden name if the court approves.

Grounds for judicial separation: Same as the grounds for divorce.

Grounds for annulment: Bigamy; incest; impotence at time of marriage that seems incurable. The following grounds are valid unless the marital relationship is continued after the ground no longer exists: mental incapacity at time of marriage; under age; fraud; force or duress.

OHIO

Grounds for divorce: Adultery; willful neglect (one year); willful absence (one year); conviction for a felony if imprisoned at time of suit; extreme cruelty; alcoholism (one year); impotence; bigamy; fraud; successful attempt to obtain divorce in another state.

Residence requirement: One year.

Alimony and property: Fault is one of the bases on which court determines amount and recipient of support and division of property. Either spouse is eligible to receive support or property.

Wife's name: Ex-wife may resume her maiden name if the court approves.

Grounds for judicial separation: No statute.

Grounds for annulment: Bigamy; unconsummated marriage. The following grounds are valid unless the marital relationship is continued after the ground no longer exists: mental incapacity at time of marriage; under age; fraud; force or duress. Incestuous marriages are void.

OKLAHOMA

Grounds for divorce: Incompatibility; adultery; abandonment (one year); gross neglect; conviction for a felony if imprisoned at time of suit; insanity (five years); extreme cruelty; alcoholism; impotence; wife pregnant by another at time of marriage; fraud; divorce obtained outside of state but not recognized in state.

Residence requirement: Six months.

Alimony and property: Fault is one of the bases on which court determines amount and recipient of support and division of property unless the divorce is granted on a "no fault" ground. Only the wife is eligible to receive support, but either spouse may be awarded property.

Wife's name: Ex-wife may resume her maiden name if approved by the court, providing her husband was at fault in the divorce.

Grounds for judicial separation: Same as the grounds for divorce.

Grounds for annulment: Mental incapacity at time of marriage and being under age are valid unless the marital relationship is continued after the ground no longer exists. Incestuous and bigamous marriages are void.

OREGON

Grounds for divorce (dissolution): Irretrievable breakdown of the marriage; irreconcilable differences.

Residence requirement: None if couple was married in the state and one spouse is resident there; otherwise, six months.

Alimony and property: Fault is not taken into consideration in court's determination of the amount and recipient of support or the division of property. Either spouse is eligible to receive

support or property. Any joint tenancy property not divided is kept by both spouses as tenants in common. Spouses may make a contract stipulating support payments and distribution of property; if approved by the court, the contract will be enforceable.

Wife's name: Ex-wife may resume her maiden name if the court approves.

Grounds for judicial separation: Same as the grounds for divorce.

Grounds for annulment: Mental incapacity at time of marriage; under age; fraud; bigamy; incest; force or duress.

PENNSYLVANIA

Grounds for divorce: Adultery; desertion (two years); conviction for a felony (two years); insanity (three years); physical cruelty; impotence at time of marriage; inability to procreate at time of marriage; bigamy; fraud; personal indignities; force or coercion; incest.

Residence requirement: One year.

Alimony and property: Fault is one of the bases on which court determines amount and recipient of support, but there are no statutory provisions to grant it except to a wife during a legal separation or to either spouse if the divorce was granted on grounds of insanity and the insane person's estate is not sufficient to provide his or her support. There are no statutory provisions for the basis on which property is divided, but any joint tenancy property not divided is kept by both spouses as tenants in common.

Wife's name: No statute.

Grounds for judicial separation: Adultery; abandonment; cruel and barbarous treatment; being turned out of the home; personal indignities. May be obtained only by the wife.

Grounds for annulment: Mental incapacity at time of marriage; bigamy; incest.

RHODE ISLAND

Grounds for divorce: Adultery; desertion (five years—or less at discretion of court); nonsupport;

life imprisonment if person is considered legally dead; extreme cruelty; alcoholism; drug addiction; voluntarily living apart; bigamy; gross misbehavior; mental incapacity at time of marriage; incest.

Residence requirement: Two years.

Alimony and property: Fault is one of the bases on which court determines amount and recipient of support and division of property. Only the wife is eligible to receive support, but only if she has waived her dower rights, to which she is entitled upon divorce. Either spouse is eligible to receive property.

Wife's name: Ex-wife may resume her maiden name if the court approves.

Grounds for judicial separation: Same as the grounds for divorce.

Grounds for annulment: None. However, incestuous and bigamous marriages, or those where there was mental incapacity at the time of marriage, are void.

SOUTH CAROLINA

Grounds for divorce: Adultery; desertion (one year); physical cruelty; alcoholism; drug addiction; separation (three years).

Residence requirement: One year.

Alimony and property: Fault is one of the bases on which court determines amount and recipient of support. Only the wife is eligible to receive support, but it is absolutely barred to her if she is guilty of adultery. There are no statutory provisions for the basis on which property is divided.

Wife's name: Ex-wife may resume her maiden name if the court approves.

Grounds for judicial separation: No statute.

Grounds for annulment: Mental incapacity at time of marriage; duress; bigamy; marriage not consummated.

SOUTH DAKOTA

Grounds for divorce: Adultery; desertion (one year); willful neglect (one year); conviction for a felony; insanity (five years—or less at discretion of court); physical or mental cruelty; alcoholism (one year).

Residence requirement: None if couple was married in state and plaintiff still resides there; otherwise, one year in state, three months in county.

Alimony and property: Fault is one of the bases on which court determines amount and recipient of support but it is not considered in the division of property. Only the wife is eligible to receive support, but either spouse may be awarded property.

Wife's name: Ex-wife may resume her maiden name if the court approves, providing she does not have custody of couple's minor children.

Grounds for judicial separation: Same as the grounds for divorce.

Grounds for annulment: Under age; bigamy; impotence at time of marriage which appears to be incurable. The following grounds are valid unless the marital relationship is continued after the ground no longer exists: mental incapacity; fraud; force or duress. Incestuous marriages are void.

TENNESSEE

Grounds for divorce: Adultery; abandonment; neglect; cruel and inhuman treatment; indignities.

Residence requirement: One year.

Alimony and property: Fault is one of the bases on which court determines amount and recipient of support but it is not considered in the division of property. Only the wife is eligible to receive support, but either spouse may be awarded property. Spouses may make a contract stipulating support payments and distribution of property; if approved by the court, the contract will be enforceable.

Wife's name: No statute.

Grounds for judicial separation: Same as the grounds for divorce.

Grounds for annulment: Mental incapacity at time of marriage; under age; fraud; force or duress; bigamy; incest.

TEXAS

Grounds for divorce: Irretrievable breakdown of the marriage.

Residence requirement: One year in state, six months in county.

Alimony and property: Fault is not taken into consideration in court's determination of the division of property.

Wife's name: Ex-wife may resume her maiden name if the court approves.

Grounds for judicial separation: No statute.

Grounds for annulment: Under the influence of drugs or alcohol at time of marriage; under age; marriage within six months of a previous divorce. The following grounds are valid unless the marital relationship is continued after the ground no longer exists: lack of mental capacity at time of marriage; fraud; force or duress; impotence at time of marriage. Incestuous and bigamous marriages are void.

UTAH

Grounds for divorce: Adultery; desertion (one year); willful neglect; conviction for a felony; insanity; mental or physical cruelty; alcoholism; impotence at time of marriage; separation (three years).

Residence requirement: Three months.

Alimony and property: Fault is not taken into consideration in court's determination of the amount and recipient of support or the division of property. Either spouse is eligible to receive support or property.

Wife's name: Ex-wife may resume her maiden name if the court approves.

Grounds for judicial separation: Abandonment; desertion; neglect. May be obtained only by the wife.

Grounds for annulment: Mental incapacity at time of marriage; under age; force or duress; incest; marriage not officially solemnized; venereal disease; previous divorce not final.

VERMONT

Grounds for divorce: Adultery; willful desertion; nonsupport; absence for seven years without news; conviction for a felony with a sentence of at least three years; incurable insanity (five years); intolerable severity; separation (six months).

Residence requirement: Six months.

Alimony and property: Fault is not taken into consideration in court's determination of the amount and recipient of support or the division of property. Either spouse is eligible to receive support, but only the wife may be awarded property.

Wife's name: Ex-wife may resume her maiden name or a former husband's name if the court approves.

Grounds for judicial separation: Same as the grounds for divorce.

Grounds for annulment: Mental incapacity at time of marriage; fraud; force; impotence (one year). Being under age is valid unless the marital relationship is continued after the ground no longer exists. Incestuous and bigamous marriages are void.

VIRGINIA

Grounds for divorce: Adultery; abandonment (one year); desertion (one year); imprisonment;

impotence at time of marriage; separation (two years); wife pregnant by another at time of marriage without husband's knowledge; sodomy or buggery; either spouse convicted of a felony before marriage without the other's knowledge; wife a prostitute before marriage without husband's knowledge.

Residence requirement: One year.

Alimony and property: Fault is one of the bases on which court determines amount and recipient of support. Either spouse is eligible to receive

support. There are no statutory provisions for the basis on which property is divided, but any joint tenancy property not divided is kept by both spouses as tenants in common. Spouses may make a contract stipulating support payments, distribution of property, and child custody and support; if approved by the court, the contract will be enforceable.

Wife's name: No statute.

Grounds for judicial separation: Abandonment; desertion; cruelty; fear of bodily harm.

Grounds for annulment: Mental incapacity at time of marriage; under age; fraud; force or duress; incest; impotence; malformation preventing sexual intercourse; marriage not officially solemnized.

WASHINGTON

Grounds for divorce (dissolution): Irretrievable breakdown of the marriage.

Residence requirement: Six months.

Alimony and property: Fault is not taken into consideration in court's determination of the amount and recipient of support or the division of property. Either spouse is eligible to receive support or property.

Wife's name: Ex-wife may resume her maiden name if the court approves.

Grounds for judicial separation: No statute.

Grounds for annulment: Under age; fraud; bigamy; incest.

WEST VIRGINIA

Grounds for divorce: Adultery; desertion (one year); abandonment (one year); insanity (three years); mental or physical cruelty; alcoholism after marriage; drug addiction after marriage; separation (two years).

Residence requirement: None for adultery if defendant can be served notice personally; otherwise, and for other grounds, one year.

Alimony and property: Fault is one of the bases on which court determines amount and recipient of support and division of property. Either spouse is eligible to receive support or property.

Wife's name: Ex-wife may resume her maiden name, providing she does not have custody of couple's minor children.

Grounds for judicial separation: No statute.

Grounds for annulment: The following grounds are valid unless the marital relationship is continued after the ground no longer exists: mental incapacity at time of marriage; under age; fraud;

force or duress; bigamy; incest; impotence; malformation preventing sexual intercourse; wife pregnant by another at time of marriage; venereal disease at time of marriage; conviction for a serious crime before marriage without spouse's knowledge; wife a prostitute before marriage without husband's knowledge; husband known to be immoral before marriage without wife's knowledge.

WISCONSIN

Grounds for divorce: Adultery; desertion (one year); nonsupport; conviction for a felony with a sentence of at least three years; voluntary commitment to a mental institution (one year); mental or physical cruelty; alcoholism (one year); separation (one year); court decree of separate maintenance (one year).

Residence requirement: Six months in state, one month in county.

Alimony and property: Fault is one of the bases on which court determines amount and recipient of support but it is not considered in the division of property. Either spouse is eligible to receive support or property, but support is absolutely barred to a spouse guilty of adultery.

Wife's name: Ex-wife may resume her maiden name or a former husband's name if the court approves, providing she does not have custody of the couple's minor children.

Grounds for judicial separation: Same as the grounds for divorce.

Grounds for annulment: Mental incapacity at time of marriage; under age; fraud; force or duress; bigamy; incest; impotence; inability to perform sexual intercourse; marriage within six months of previous divorce.

WYOMING

Grounds for divorce: Incompatibility; adultery; desertion (one year); nonsupport (one year); vagrancy; conviction for a felony; insanity (two years); mental or physical cruelty; alcoholism; impotence; separation (two years); wife pregnant by another at time of marriage without husband's knowledge.

Residence requirement: Two months.

Alimony and property: Fault is not taken into consideration in court's determination of the amount and recipient of support or the division of property. Only the wife is eligible to receive support and property. Spouses may make a contract stipulating support payments and distribution of property; if approved by the court, the contract will be enforceable.

Wife's name: Ex-wife may resume her maiden name if the court approves.

Grounds for judicial separation: Same as the grounds for divorce.

Grounds for annulment: Mental incapacity at time of marriage; bigamy; incest. The following grounds are valid unless the marital relationship is continued after the ground no longer exists: under age; fraud; force or duress.

6
When I Am Raped

The victim in a rape case is often treated more harshly in the courtroom than the suspect. The law alone is not responsible for this situation, although the rape laws are inadequate in many ways. It is the complex interaction of the laws with two other factors—social attitudes relating to women and to sex, and the rules of evidence in criminal trials (*all* criminal trials, not just rape trials)—that conspires against the woman who is raped.*

Our society has a great deal of ambivalence about rape. At one extreme is the old saying, "Why struggle? Lie back and enjoy it!" At the other extreme is the reality that the laws of fourteen states provide life imprisonment or death as maximum penalties for rape. (In three states—Arkansas, Missis-

sippi, and North Carolina—these are the *only* sentences a convicted rapist may receive.) In between these extremes are some highly questionable assumptions that influence nearly everyone's thinking on the subject.

Many people believe that women are excited by the idea of violent sex and subconsciously invite it; hence they figure the man is not entirely to blame for responding to the supposed invitation. Another widespread assumption is that a woman who is not physically attractive is probably eager for any sexual experience, so the man who rapes her is actually doing her a favor. There is also the notion of the vindictive woman who has been intimate with the accused rapist in the past and has been rejected by him. Now she gets even by charging him with rape. Some other people believe the act of rape is possible only when the victim can be described

*This chapter is about forcible rape *only*. For the law on statutory rape, see Chapter 10.

as a "nice girl." A woman whom they see as promiscuous and not a "nice girl" cannot by definition be a victim of rape.

The implication in all these assumptions is either that the responsibility for the rape lies more with the woman than the man, or else that the rapist is giving his victim something she wants and should not be punished for his generosity.

Our social and moral attitudes affect all aspects of rape, beginning with the motivation of the rapist. They influence the reactions of those persons with whom the rape victim must deal if she decides to report the crime and take legal action. They affect the trial, if there is one.

Rape is an act of aggression that is often motivated chiefly by hatred and fear, feelings that in most people have little to do with sexual gratification. Rapists are dangerously disturbed persons, although they may not appear to be. Often it is the attacker's seeming normalcy that causes his victim to be less sensitive to potential danger and thus less able to avoid entrapment.

A woman's trauma does not end with the personal and physical brutality of the rape itself, even though it leaves her in a state of shock, rage, incoherence, or withdrawal. She may hesitate to tell anyone about her experience, least of all the police. She may have her own doubts. Maybe she shouldn't have been wearing that halter top. Perhaps she should have insisted someone walk with her to the bus stop when she got off work at midnight. *Could* the rape have been at least partly her fault?

If she can bring herself to report the crime (it is believed that three, four, or five times as many rapes are committed than are reported), the rape victim's nightmare is apt to be prolonged. She often must suffer police skepticism and innuendo: "Are you sure you didn't set yourself up for this?" "What were you wearing?" "Why were you in that neighborhood?" "Did he reach a climax? Did *you*?" At best she will have to endure intensive questioning while she is still upset, even if she is asked only the kind of questions that would be asked of the victim in any crime. But waiting a few days to make her report suggests that she was not really upset, and this could be used against her later in court.

A rape victim should be examined by a doctor as soon as possible after the rape—both for her own protection and because the findings may be needed as evidence if there is a trial. Since hospital personnel, especially in emergency wards, are overworked and accustomed to looking after victims of severe physical violence, they often seem brusque and unfeeling to the woman who has been raped. To her it is a deeply traumatic experience; to them it is just another routine examination if she has not been badly injured by her attacker. If she goes to a private doctor instead of to a hospital she risks being turned away by a physician who does not want to take the chance of later becoming involved in a court case.

If a suspect is apprehended and the victim agrees to press charges, the trial will be subject to the rape laws of the state, and to the rules of evidence that apply in all criminal trials. In half the states, the law does not require the victim to present evidence other than her own testimony. In eleven states, other evidence is not required if her testimony is "credible." In fourteen states, additional evidence is required, chiefly medical reports of her physical and emotional state immediately after the rape.

In all states, however, the judge must instruct the jury in a rape trial—as in every trial of a person charged with a sex offense—that the victim's testimony is to be weighed very carefully, on the ground that an accusation of rape is "easy to make but difficult to prove." This emphasis often has

a chilling effect on the case, causing the jurors to be overly suspicious of the victim's allegations. From the victim's point of view, it is not a very auspicious way for the jury to begin its deliberations.

There are three basic issues in a rape trial: Is the defendant the man who attacked the woman? Did she give her consent to the sex act? Did she resist her attacker as much as possible in the circumstances? Because of the nature of rape there are rarely any witnesses, so in the absence of overwhelming evidence

the case comes down to who is more believable—the victim or the accused. The rules of evidence in criminal trials place the "burden of proof" on the prosecution, for whom the victim is the "complaining witness," while the accused—the defendant—is not required to prove anything.

Further, as a protection to the accused, nothing may be said during the trial about any prior arrests he may have had for similar offenses (again, this is true in all criminal trials, not just rape trials) or about his sex life. In all but three states—California, Florida, and Iowa—the rape victim has no such protection; her sex life, however unrelated to the particular case at hand, can be explored during the trial, on the theory that it might be relevant to the issue of her consent or even her credibility as a witness. Because of this discrepancy, it is often possible for a defense attorney to depict the suspect as sexually virtuous in contrast to the apparent immorality of the victim.

The rape laws themselves place an unfair burden on many rape victims if the case is brought to trial. The definition of rape on the books in nearly every state is "the carnal knowledge of a woman forcibly and against her will"—that is to say, the victim was overpowered and did not consent to the sex act. Thus in a trial, a victim must prove two things: not only that her assailant used physical violence to subdue her or seriously threatened to do so, but also that she did not *want* to perform the sex act with him. Either of these arguments alone does not satisfy the law's requirement for a valid charge of rape.

The law does recognize that the victim

need not defend herself if doing so could result in serious injury or death. It also recognizes that a woman unconscious or under the influence of alcohol or drugs is incapable of resisting, and considers this convincing evidence that she did not willingly consent. It acknowledges that an insane or feeble-minded woman is not able to give reasoned consent to sexual intercourse. But this leaves a vast gray area about what is and what is not consent, and what is and is not resistance. It is here that social attitudes and trial procedure can have a great effect on rape cases.

For example, what may have been construed as consent by the rapist may not have been intended as such by the victim. If a woman invites a male neighbor in for coffee or a drink, does that mean she has implicitly given consent to sexual intercourse with that neighbor if that's what *he* assumed? If she tries to fight him off but fails, does that satisfy the law's requirement that she was forced to submit against her will if he didn't actually threaten to harm her? Or is it just another instance, as the defense attorney may insist, that like many women she "really likes a little violence" and it was just part of the game?

No state requires proof that the rapist completed the sex act, only that there was "penetration," however slight. Since "slight penetration" is impossible to verify medically, here too it is a question of the woman's believability, which in large part turns on each juror's subjective assessment of her as a person. This requirement also means that the rape laws do not cover cases of forced sexual contact where there is no penetration

at all but that are just as traumatic to the victim.

Given these ground rules, and because it is crucial to the defendant's case to create doubt about the victim's moral standards in the minds of the jurors, the rape victim can expect hostile, accusatory questions from the defense attorney in an attempt to weaken her credibility. If she was walking on a deserted street after dark, she shouldn't have been there. If she was hitchhiking, she was "asking for it." If she went to the man's apartment, she went *for* something, and that something is what she got. Somehow, the rape was really her fault.

This kind of questioning can be especially damaging if the accused man is someone the victim knows—a casual acquaintance, a man she had dated occasionally or had just met at a singles bar, a rejected boyfriend or an ex-husband. During cross-examination by the defense attorney she may be forced to admit she had at one time been the willing bedmate of the man she is now accusing of rape. Such an admission by itself is enough to make some jurors feel that there is "reasonable doubt" as to the truth of her charges.

In the light of all the traps in the legal process for the rape victim, it is easy to understand why so few women report rapes or want to take the cases to court, and why so few juries convict rapists once they are brought to trial. The laws can probably never deal adequately with rape, given our present attitudes toward both sex and the status of women, but some steps can be taken.

Many believe that treating rape separately—as a sex crime rather than as a form of assault—is not only fundamentally sexist but is discriminatory against both the male defendant and his female victim. It is unfair to the male suspects because sentences for rape convictions are more severe than they are for assault convictions, even aggravated assault. It is unfair to the victims in that they may suffer humiliation in court because of the nature of a "sex offense" trial. Even more important, it is more difficult to prove a rape charge than an assault charge, and that places an added burden on the prosecution in a rape trial.

More states should follow the lead of California and Iowa, where laws have been enacted which specifically prohibit questions about the victim's sex life during a rape trial, except in relation to the accused. Florida has a law stipulating that such questions must be screened in the judge's chambers before being asked in court. This requirement does

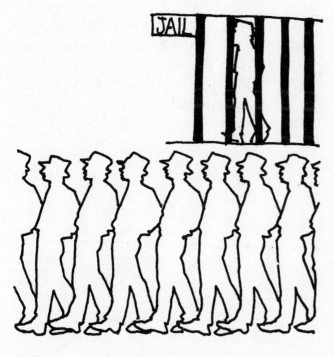

more than help keep testimony within reasonable bounds. The mere fact that such a change is being considered and debated by a state legislature raises public awareness of some of the more complicated aspects of rape.

Penalties for rape should be reduced in those states where they are excessive, especially those with mandatory life sentences or death penalties. Many juries are unwilling to convict a man for rape because the punishment may be more severe than they feel the crime deserves. The conviction rate for rapists is shockingly low—fewer than one out of every ten trials results in a verdict of guilty. While this is due primarily to the difficulty of proving a rape charge, the low conviction rate creates a climate in which the rapist may feel he can act with a minimal fear of the legal consequences.

An aspect of the rape laws that many feminists think should be changed is that a man cannot be charged with raping his wife. This rule goes back to the common-law concept of husband and wife as one person, with the husband's authority predominating. It would be an unusual wife who accused her husband of raping her, no matter how forcefully he performed the sex act with her or how strenuously she resisted, but many persons object to the law's assumption that a married woman should be subject to her husband's will. (A husband *can* be named as a principal in the first degree—which carries the same penalties as the charge of rape itself—in a rape case involving his wife if he encourages or arranges for someone else to rape her. Similarly, a woman may be charged as a principal if she arranges for or helps a man commit rape on another woman.)

Only one state has so far recognized sexual equality for rape victims in its rape laws. In Washington State, either a man or a woman can bring a charge of rape. (Otherwise Washington's rape laws are identical with those of many other states.) In other states, rape cases involving a male victim are covered by sodomy statutes, which are essentially prohibitions on homosexual intercourse. If the Equal Rights Amendment is ratified (see Chapter 11), this change will be automatic in all states' rape laws, but in the meantime Washington is to be commended for its attempt at equality.

Help for the rape victim is now being provided outside of the legal process. Women's groups throughout the country have established rape crisis centers to counsel and reassure rape victims, and to work for legal reforms. A growing number of police departments are setting up special rape units, providing "sensitivity training" sessions to teach their officers to be more understanding, and using women officers, when possible, to interview rape victims. Some hospital staffs are also becoming more aware of the emotional aspects of rape and are making efforts to be more sympathetic, to standardize their tests and questioning of rape victims, and to make follow-up counseling available.

New approaches and reforms, both legal and extra-legal, are essential because in recent years rape has had the highest rate of increase of any violent crime in the United States, even given its disproportionately low rate of reportage. From 1968 to 1972 the number of rapes reported went up 60 per cent; in 1973 alone it leaped another 10 per cent. Some authorities estimate that a woman is raped every eleven minutes.

The rights of the accused must of course be protected, as in any other criminal trial where a person's freedom is at stake. But rape is one crime where the rights of the victim need special consideration. Rape is a psychic as well as a physical assault, a violation of a woman's emotional as well as physical being. How and whether our laws can reflect this deeper trauma is questionable. A society with double sexual standards finds such distinctions hard to make, and the law, after all, only reflects society's attitudes.

6
When I Am Raped
The Law
State by State

NOTE: These laws cover only forcible rape. The laws which govern statutory rape are given in Chapter 10.

ALABAMA

Definition of rape: The carnal knowledge of a woman forcibly and against her will.

Amount of resistance: The victim must have resisted until she was overcome unless she was unconscious.

Other evidence required: Testimony of the victim, if it is credible, is sufficient without other corroboration.

Penalty for rape: Minimum, ten years; maximum, death.

ALASKA

Definition of rape: The carnal knowledge of a woman forcibly and against her will.

Amount of resistance: Proof of the victim's resistance is not necessary.

Other evidence required: Testimony of the victim is sufficient without other corroboration.

Penalty for rape: Minimum, one year; maximum, twenty years.

ARIZONA

Definition of rape: Sexual intercourse with a woman—who is not the wife of the perpetrator—in any of the following circumstances: the woman was incapable because of insanity, whether temporary or permanent, of giving legal consent; her resistance was overcome by force or violence; she was prevented from resisting by threats of great bodily harm which she reasonably believed could be carried out; she was under the influence of alcohol, drugs, or an anesthetic substance administered by the perpetrator without her consent; she was unconscious of the nature of the act, and this was known to the perpetrator; she submitted in the belief that the perpetrator was her husband, and this belief was induced by artifice, pretense, or concealment.

Amount of resistance: The victim must have resisted to the utmost of her ability for as long as possible.

Other evidence required: Testimony of the victim

is sufficient without other corroboration.

Penalty for rape: Minimum, five years; maximum, life imprisonment.

ARKANSAS

Definition of rape: The carnal knowledge of a woman forcibly and against her will.

Amount of resistance: The victim must have resisted unless it would have been futile or she feared great bodily injury.

Other evidence required: Testimony of the victim is sufficient without other corroboration.

Penalty for rape: Life imprisonment or death.

CALIFORNIA

Definition of rape: Sexual intercourse with a woman—who is not the wife of the perpetrator—in any of the following circumstances: the woman was incapable because of insanity, whether temporary or permanent, of giving legal consent; her resistance was overcome by force or violence; she was prevented from resisting by threats of great bodily harm which she reasonably believed could be carried out; she was under the influence of alcohol, drugs, or an anesthetic substance administered by the perpetrator without her consent; she was unconscious of the nature of the act, and this was known to the perpetrator; she submitted in the belief that the perpetrator was her husband, and this belief was induced by artifice, pretense, or concealment.

Amount of resistance: The victim must have resisted enough to demonstrate her unwillingness to yield to the attack.

Other evidence required: Testimony of the victim is sufficient without other corroboration.

Penalty for rape: Minimum, three years; maximum, life imprisonment.

COLORADO

Definition of rape: Sexual intercourse with a woman—who is not the wife of the perpetrator—in any of the following circumstances: the

woman is compelled to submit by force or threat of imminent death, bodily harm, extreme pain, or kidnaping of her or anyone else; she was under the influence of alcohol, drugs, or an anesthetic substance administered by the perpetrator without her consent; she was unconscious; the perpetrator inflicted bodily injury on her or or anyone else while committing the offense. If the victim was a voluntary social companion of the perpetrator and had previously voluntarily engaged in sexual intercourse with him, the rape is a lesser felony than otherwise.

Amount of resistance: The victim must have resisted as much as possible, depending on her age, mental and physical condition, and other circumstances.

Other evidence required: Testimony of the victim is sufficient without corroboration by independent witnesses.

Penalty for rape: Minimum, three years; maximum, life imprisonment.

CONNECTICUT

Definition: Sexual intercourse with a woman by forcible compulsion or when she is physically helpless and incapable of giving consent.

Amount of resistance: The victim must have resisted unless it would have been futile or she feared great bodily injury.

Other evidence required: Testimony of the victim, if it is credible, is sufficient without other corroboration.

Penalty for rape: A prison term at the discretion of the court.

DELAWARE

Definition of rape: Sexual intercourse with a woman forcibly and against her will.

Amount of resistance: The victim must have resisted unless it would have been futile.

Other evidence required: The victim's testimony or circumstantial evidence is sufficient without corroboration by independent witnesses.

Penalty for rape: Life imprisonment; if the jury

recommends mercy, a minimum of three years.

DISTRICT OF COLUMBIA

Definition of rape: The carnal knowledge of a woman forcibly and against her will.

Amount of resistance: The victim must have resisted unless it would have been futile or she feared great bodily injury.

Other evidence required: Corroboration is required, but the degree depends on the case; the testimony of independent witnesses is not necessary.

Penalty for rape: A prison term at the discretion of the court, up to life imprisonment.

FLORIDA

Definition of rape: The carnal knowledge of a woman forcibly and against her will.

Amount of resistance: The victim must have resisted as much as possible depending on the circumstances of the case.

Other evidence required: Testimony of the victim, if it is credible, is sufficient without other corroboration.

Penalty for rape: Death; if the jury recommends mercy, the sentence will be set by the court—up to life imprisonment.

GEORGIA

Definition of rape: The carnal knowledge of a woman forcibly and against her will.

Amount of resistance: The victim need have resisted only slightly.

Other evidence required: Testimony of the victim is sufficient without other corroboration.

Penalty for rape: Minimum, twenty years; maximum, life imprisonment or death.

HAWAII

Definition of rape: The carnal knowledge of a woman forcibly and against her will.

Amount of resistance: The victim must have resisted to the utmost of her ability unless it would have been futile.

Other evidence required: Corroboration is required, but it may be circumstantial.

Penalty for rape: At the discretion of the court, up to life imprisonment.

IDAHO

Definition of rape: Sexual intercourse with a woman—who is not the wife of the perpetrator—in any of the following circumstances: the woman was incapable because of insanity, whether temporary or permanent, of giving legal consent; her resistance was overcome by force or violence; she was prevented from resisting by threats of great bodily harm which she reasonably believed could be carried out; she was unconscious of the nature of the act, and this was known to the perpetrator; she submitted in the belief that the perpetrator was her husband, and this belief was induced by artifice, pretense, or concealment.

Amount of resistance: The victim must have resisted until she was overcome by force or violence.

Other evidence required: Testimony of the victim is sufficient if her character for truth and chastity remain unimpeached; otherwise, the amount of corroboration required depends on the circumstances of the case.

Penalty for rape: Minimum, one year; maximum, life imprisonment.

ILLINOIS

Definition of rape: Sexual intercourse with a woman—who is not the wife of the perpetrator—forcibly and against her will, especially if she was unconscious or so mentally deranged or deficient that she could not give legal consent.

Amount of resistance: The victim must have resisted enough to demonstrate her unwillingness to yield to the attack unless it would have been futile or she feared for her life.

Other evidence required: Corroboration is required, but the degree depends on the case; the testimony of independent witnesses is not necessary.

Penalty for rape: Minimum, four years.

INDIANA

Definition of rape: The carnal knowledge of a woman—who is not the wife of the perpetrator—forcibly and against her will, especially if she is insane, epileptic, idiotic, or feebleminded and the perpetrator knew of this condition.

Amount of resistance: The victim must have resisted as much as possible depending on the circumstances.

Other evidence required: Testimony of the victim is sufficient without other corroboration.

Penalty for rape: Minimum, two years; maximum, twenty-one years.

IOWA

Definition of rape: The carnal knowledge of a woman forcibly and against her will.

Amount of resistance: The victim must have resisted as much as possible depending on the circumstances of the case.

Other evidence required: Corroboration is required but it may be circumstantial; the testimony of independent witnesses is not necessary.

Penalty for rape: Minimum, five years; maximum, life imprisonment.

KANSAS

Definition of rape: Sexual intercourse with a woman—who is not the wife of the perpetrator—against her will in any of the following circumstances: the woman was incapable because of mental deficiency or disease of giving legal consent; her resistance was overcome by force or violence; she was under the influence of alcohol, drugs, or an anesthetic substance administered by the perpetrator without her consent; she was unconscious or physically unable to resist.

Amount of resistance: The victim must have resisted unless she feared personal injury.

Other evidence required: Testimony of the victim is sufficient without other corroboration.

Penalty for rape: A prison term at the discretion of the court and/or up to $10,000 fine.

KENTUCKY

Definition of rape: The carnal knowledge of a woman forcibly and against her will or while she is unconscious.

Amount of resistance: The victim must have resisted unless it would have been futile.

Other evidence required: Testimony of the victim is sufficient without other corroboration.

Penalty for rape: Minimum, ten to twenty years; maximum, life imprisonment or death.

LOUISIANA

Definition of rape: Sexual intercourse with a woman—who is not the wife of the perpetrator (or who is separated from him)—against her will.

Amount of resistance: The victim must have resisted unless it would have been futile.

Other evidence required: Corroboration is required but it may be circumstantial; the testimony of independent witnesses is not necessary.

Penalty for rape: Minimum, one to twenty years; maximum, death.

MAINE

Definition of rape: The carnal knowledge of a woman forcibly and against her will.

Amount of resistance: The victim must have resisted unless it would have been futile or she feared for her life.

Other evidence required: Testimony of the victim—if it is credible—is sufficient without other corroboration.

Penalty for rape: A prison term at the discretion of the court.

MARYLAND

Definition of rape: The carnal knowledge of a woman forcibly and against her will.

Amount of resistance: The victim must have resisted until overcome by force unless she feared great bodily injury.

Other evidence required: Testimony of the victim is sufficient without other corroboration.

Penalty for rape: Minimum, eighteen months to twenty-one years; maximum, life imprisonment or death.

MASSACHUSETTS

Definition of rape: The carnal knowledge of a woman forcibly and against her will.

Amount of resistance: The victim must have resisted enough to demonstrate her unwillingness to yield to the attack.

Other evidence required: Corroboration is required but it may be circumstantial; the testimony of independent witnesses is not necessary.

Penalty for rape: A prison term at the discretion of the court.

MICHIGAN

Definition of rape: The carnal knowledge of a woman forcibly and against her will.

Amount of resistance: The victim must have resisted unless she feared bodily injury.

Other evidence required: Testimony of the victim—if it is credible—is sufficient without other corroboration.

Penalty for rape: A prison term at the discretion of the court, up to life imprisonment.

MINNESOTA

Definition of rape: Sexual intercourse with a woman—who is not the wife of the perpetrator—against her will.

Amount of resistance: The victim must have resisted unless she was unconscious or feared great bodily injury.

Other evidence required: Testimony of the victim is sufficient without other corroboration.

Penalty for rape: Minimum, seven years; maximum, thirty years.

MISSISSIPPI

Definition of rape: The carnal knowledge of a woman by force.

Amount of resistance: The victim must have resisted as much as possible depending on the circumstances.

Other evidence required: Testimony of the victim—if it is credible—is sufficient without other corroboration.

Penalty for rape: Life imprisonment or death.

MISSOURI

Definition of rape: The carnal knowledge of a woman by force.

Amount of resistance: The victim must have resisted unless she feared great bodily injury.

Other evidence required: Testimony of the victim—if it is credible and timely—is sufficient without other corroboration.

Penalty for rape: Minimum, two years; maximum, life imprisonment or death.

MONTANA

Definition of rape: Sexual intercourse with a woman—who is not the wife of the perpetrator—in any of the following circumstances: the woman was incapable because of insanity, whether temporary or permanent, of giving legal consent; her resistance was overcome by force or violence; she was prevented from resisting by threats of immediate and great bodily harm; she was unconscious of the nature of the act, and this was known to the perpetrator; she submitted in the belief that the perpetrator was her husband, and this belief was induced by artifice, pretense, or concealment.

Amount of resistance: The victim must have resisted until overcome by force or fear.

Other evidence required: Corroboration is required but it may be circumstantial.

Penalty for rape: Minimum, two years; maximum, ninety-nine years.

NEBRASKA

Definition of rape: The carnal knowledge of a woman forcibly and against her will.

Amount of resistance: The victim must have resisted unless she was overcome by fear.

Other evidence required: Corroboration is required.

Penalty for rape: Minimum, three years; maximum, twenty years.

NEVADA

Definition of rape: The carnal knowledge of a woman against her will.

Amount of resistance: The victim need not have resisted to the utmost of her ability.

Other evidence required: Corroboration is required but it may be circumstantial.

Penalty for rape: Minimum, five years; maximum, life imprisonment.

NEW HAMPSHIRE

Definition of rape: The carnal knowledge of a woman forcibly and against her will.

Amount of resistance: The victim need not have resisted to the utmost of her ability.

Other evidence required: Corroboration of the victim's testimony may be required, depending on the circumstances of the case.

Penalty for rape: Maximum, thirty years.

NEW JERSEY

Definition of rape: The carnal knowledge of a woman forcibly and against her will or while she is under the influence of drugs.

Amount of resistance: The victim must have resisted enough to demonstrate her unwillingness to yield to the attacker and that he used force.

Other evidence required: Testimony of the victim is sufficient without other corroboration.

Penalty for rape: Maximum, thirty years and/or $5000 fine.

NEW MEXICO

Definition of rape: Sexual intercourse with a woman—who is not the wife of the perpetrator—in any of the following circumstances: the woman was incapable because of mental disability, of which the perpetrator was aware, of giving legal consent; her resistance was forcibly overcome; she was under the influence of alcohol, drugs, or an anesthetic substance administered by the perpetrator without her consent; she was unconscious or physically unable to resist.

Amount of resistance: The victim must have resisted until she was physically overcome.

Other evidence required: Corroboration is required but it may be circumstantial.

Penalty for rape: Minimum, one year; maximum, ninety-nine years.

NEW YORK

Definition of rape: Sexual intercourse with a woman—who is not the wife of the perpetrator—against her will or in the following circumstances: the woman was incapable because of unsoundness of mind of giving legal consent; her resistance was overcome by physical or mental violence; she was prevented from resisting by threats of great bodily harm; she was under the influence of alcohol or drugs administered by the perpetrator without her consent; she was unconscious of the nature of the act, and this was known to the perpetrator.

Amount of resistance: The victim must have resisted unless she was incapable for any of the reasons enumerated above.

Other evidence required: Testimony of the victim is sufficient without other corroboration.

Penalty for rape: Maximum, twenty years.

NORTH CAROLINA

Definition of rape: The carnal knowledge of a woman forcibly and against her will.
Amount of resistance: The victim need not have resisted to the utmost of her ability.
Other evidence required: Corroboration is required.
Penalty for rape: Life imprisonment or death.

NORTH DAKOTA

Definition of rape: Sexual intercourse with a woman—who is not the wife of the perpetrator—in any of the following circumstances: the woman was incapable because of insanity of giving legal consent; her resistance was overcome by force or violence; she was prevented from resisting by threats of great bodily harm which she reasonably believed could be carried out; she was under the influence of alcohol, drugs, or an anesthetic substance administered by the perpetrator without her consent; she was unconscious of the nature of the act, and this was known to the perpetrator; she submitted in the belief that the perpetrator was her husband, and this belief was induced by artifice, pretense, or concealment.
Amount of resistance: The victim must have resisted as much as possible depending on the circumstances.
Other evidence required: Testimony of the victim—if it is credible—may be sufficient without other corroboration.
Penalty for rape: Minimum, one year.

OHIO

Definition of rape: The carnal knowledge of a woman forcibly and against her will.
Amount of resistance: The victim must have resisted as much as possible unless it was futile or she was unconscious.
Other evidence required: Testimony of the victim is sufficient without other corroboration.

Penalty for rape: Minimum, three years; maximum, twenty years.

OKLAHOMA

Definition of rape: Sexual intercourse with a woman—who is not the wife of the perpetrator—in any of the following circumstances: the woman was incapable because of insanity of giving legal consent; her resistance was overcome by force or violence; she was prevented from resisting by threats of great bodily harm; she was under the influence of alcohol, drugs, or an anesthetic substance administered by the perpetrator without her consent; she was unconscious of the act, and this was known to the perpetrator; she submitted in the belief that the perpetrator was her husband, and this belief was induced by fraud.
Amount of resistance: The victim must have resisted as much as possible depending on her age, strength, and the other circumstances.
Other evidence required: Testimony of the victim is sufficient without other corroboration.
Penalty for rape: Minimum, five years; maximum, life imprisonment or death.

OREGON

Definition of rape: Sexual intercourse with a woman forcibly and against her will.
Amount of resistance: The victim must have resisted enough to demonstrate her unwillingness to yield to the attacker and that he used force.
Other evidence required: Testimony of the victim is sufficient without other corroboration.
Penalty for rape: Maximum, twenty years.

PENNSYLVANIA

Definition of rape: The carnal knowledge of a woman forcibly and against her will.
Amount of resistance: The victim must have resisted unless it was futile and would have been unreasonable to do so.
Other evidence required: Testimony of the victim is sufficient without other corroboration.

Penalty for rape: Maximum, twenty years and/or $10,000 fine; if the perpetrator inflicted serious bodily injury on anyone while committing the crime, the sentence is fifteen years to life and $10,000 fine.

RHODE ISLAND

Definition of rape: The carnal knowledge of a woman forcibly and against her will.

Amount of resistance: The victim must have resisted as much as possible unless she feared for her life.

Other evidence required: Testimony of the victim is sufficient without other corroboration.

Penalty for rape: Minimum, ten years; maximum, life imprisonment.

SOUTH CAROLINA

Definition of rape: The carnal knowledge of a woman forcibly and against her will.

Amount of resistance: The victim must have resisted enough to demonstrate her unwillingness to yield to the attack.

Other evidence required: Testimony of the victim is sufficient without other corroboration.

Penalty for rape: Minimum, five years; maximum, forty years or death if the jury recommends it.

SOUTH DAKOTA

Definition of rape: Sexual intercourse with a woman—who is not the wife of the perpetrator—in any of the following circumstances: the woman was incapable because of insanity of giving legal consent; her resistance was overcome by force or violence; she was prevented from resisting by threats of great bodily harm which she reasonably believed could be carried out; she was under the influence of alcohol, drugs, or an anesthetic substance administered by the perpetrator without her consent; she was unconscious of the nature of the act, and this was known to the perpetrator; she submitted in the belief that the perpetrator was her husband, and this belief was induced by artifice, pretense, or concealment.

Amount of resistance: The victim must have resisted enough—depending on her age, strength, and other circumstances—to demonstrate her unwillingness to yield to the attacker.

Other evidence required: Testimony of the victim is sufficient without other corroboration.

Penalty for rape: Minimum, ten years.

TENNESSEE

Definition of rape: The carnal knowledge of a woman forcibly and against her will.

Amount of resistance: The victim must have resisted unless it would have been futile or she feared bodily injury.

Other evidence required: Corroboration is required but it may be circumstantial.

Penalty for rape: Death; if the jury recommends mercy, ten years to life.

TEXAS

Definition of rape: The carnal knowledge of a woman forcibly and against her will or as a result of threat or fraud.

Amount of resistance: The victim must have resisted unless she feared for her life.

Other evidence required: Testimony of the victim, if it is credible, is sufficient without other corroboration.

Penalty for rape: Minimum, five years; maximum, life imprisonment or death.

UTAH

Definition of rape: Sexual intercourse with a woman—who is not the wife of the perpetrator—in any of the following circumstances: the woman was incapable because of insanity of giving legal consent; her resistance was overcome by force or violence; she was prevented from resisting by threats of great bodily harm; she was unconscious of the nature of the act, and this was known to the perpetrator; she submitted in the belief that the perpetrator was her husband, and this belief was induced by artifice, pretense, or concealment.

Amount of resistance: The victim must have resisted to the very utmost of her ability.

Other evidence required: Corroboration is required if the testimony of the victim is not sufficient.

Penalty for rape: Ten years.

VERMONT

Definition of rape: The carnal knowledge of a woman forcibly and against her will.

Amount of resistance: The victim need not have resisted to the utmost of her ability.

Other evidence required: Corroboration is required but it may be circumstantial.

Penalty for rape: Twenty years and/or $2000 fine.

VIRGINIA

Definition of rape: The carnal knowledge of a woman forcibly and against her will.

Amount of resistance: The victim must have resisted as much as possible depending on her strength and the other circumstances.

Other evidence required: Testimony of the victim, if it is credible, is sufficient without corroboration.

Penalty for rape: Minimum, five years; maximum, life imprisonment or death.

WASHINGTON

Definition of rape: Sexual intercourse with a man or a woman—who is not married to the perpetrator—in any of the following circumstances: the victim was incapable because of insanity of giving legal consent; his or her resistance was overcome by force or violence; he or she was prevented from resisting by threats of great bodily harm; he or she was under the influence of alcohol, drugs, or an anesthetic substance administered by the perpetrator without the victim's consent; he or she was unconscious of the nature of the act, and this was known to the perpetrator.

Amount of resistance: The victim must have resisted unless he or she feared great bodily injury.

Other evidence required: Testimony of the victim is sufficient without corroboration.

Penalty for rape: Minimum, five years.

WEST VIRGINIA

Definition of rape: The carnal knowledge of a woman forcibly and against her will.

Amount of resistance: The victim must have resisted enough to demonstrate her unwillingness to yield to the attacker.

Other evidence required: Testimony of the victim is sufficient without corroboration.

Penalty for rape: Life imprisonment; if the jury recommends mercy, ten to twenty years.

WISCONSIN

Definition of rape: Sexual intercourse with a woman—who is not the wife of the perpetrator—forcibly and against her will.

Amount of resistance: The victim must have resisted unless she feared great bodily injury or death.

Other evidence required: Testimony of the victim is sufficient without corroboration.

Penalty for rape: Maximum, thirty years.

WYOMING

Definition of rape: The carnal knowledge of a woman forcibly and against her will.

Amount of resistance: The victim must have resisted unless she feared great bodily injury.

Other evidence required: Testimony of the victim is sufficient without corroboration.

Penalty for rape: Minimum, one year; maximum, life imprisonment.

7
When I Am Widowed

The average American wife is three years younger than her husband and will outlive him by seven years. Thus she can look forward—if that is the phrase—to ten years of widowhood. Chances are not only that she will spend this final decade alone and in increasingly frail health, but that she has been totally unprepared by education or experience to understand her new financial and legal responsibilities. Women do control the wealth in America, but they control it in name only. In reality, women's greater ignorance and inexperience in financial matters means that widowhood makes them far more dependent than men—dependent, that is, on the competence, altruism, honesty, wisdom, and foresight of lawyers, executors, bankers, trustees, family, and friends.

Of course men too are dependent on others' expertise in this area, so the best advice for anyone—male or female—who wants to make realistic and beneficial arrangements in anticipation of death is: get expert advice in dealing with these very complicated matters.

But women are most likely at a greater disadvantage than men because they are more often innocent of regular contact with financial and legal affairs. The bewildered widow who has no idea of her husband's income and holdings, and who is completely unfamiliar with the laws governing her status as a widow, is a commonplace and tragic figure.

Every wife should insist that she know as much as her husband does about their economic status. She should also make sure he has made a will, and know its provisions. She should make a will of her own, which will be a learning process in itself. She should also be informed of any estate plans her husband makes, and should insist on being consulted on these arrangements. The more aware she is, the more intelligently she will be able to handle these affairs herself when she is alone. Further, she will be better able to judge the expert advice she receives from the bankers, executors, and lawyers, and will be able to guide them in their efforts in her behalf.

She should also be familiar with the laws that will affect her if her husband dies. Because this book is aimed primarily at women readers, the laws given at the end of this chapter describe what the widow is entitled to, although all the laws apply equally to widows and widowers (with the exception of the Florida tax law discussed in Chapter 11).

The many details and procedures involved in estate planning are not set by law. The statutes listed deal only very generally with what may be distributed by will. What they do is detail:

• precisely how property is allotted to the surviving spouse and children if there is no will (intestate succession);

• what a wife's rights are to a husband's property regardless of what she would receive under the terms of a will;

• the choices a surviving spouse has if willed less than she, or he, is legally entitled to;

• what support allowance may be paid to a widow while the estate is being settled, and what she may expect as a "probate homestead."

Finally, it must always be remembered that inheritance taxes are governed by statute.

Thus the amount of taxes that must be paid can be greatly affected by advance estate planning and by the terms of a will.

A widow's right to property acquired by either or both spouses during the marriage depends, first, on whether she and her husband lived in a community-property or a common-law state and, second, on the variations in these laws from state to state.

In the eight community-property states (Arizona, California, Idaho, Louisiana, Nevada, New Mexico, Texas, and Washington) a married person's property is divided into two classes: separate and community. Separate property is the property either partner owned before marriage or that he or she received during marriage by gift or inheritance. It also includes the increased value of this property and any proceeds from it as long as neither spouse expended any effort to obtain the increase while they were married. The monetary value of the "effort" is considered to be part of the community property. If a wife establishes a savings account with her own separate funds, for example, the interest earned by the account is her separate property, as would be any income she received from investments of her separate property. It would become community property, however, if her husband made deposits into the savings account or assisted her in investing her funds. Community property is "all other" property acquired during the marriage—in particular, the earnings of both husband and wife. However, separate property that is commingled—in a joint bank account, perhaps—is converted into community property. If the ownership of any of the couple's property is unclear, the law tends to treat it as community property.

When either spouse dies, the survivor automatically owns one-half of the community property. Both wife and husband can make provisions in their wills to leave half the community property to whomever they wish, but cannot will away any part of the other half, which will always go to the surviving spouse. These "halves" are undifferentiated—that is, each spouse owns half of all the property rather than all of half the property. If there is no will and no survivors other than a wife or husband, the entire community property belongs to her or to him.

Usually in community-property states neither husband nor wife has any claim on the separate property of the other at the time of his or her death. Thus either spouse may, by will, leave all of his or her separate property to persons or institutions other than the surviving spouse. But if separate property is not specifically disposed of in a will, state statutes governing "intestate succession" entitle the surviving spouse and children to fixed shares of that property. In California, for example, if a man dies without a will and leaves no children, parents, brothers, sisters, grandchildren, or descendants of dead brothers and sisters, all of his separate property goes to his wife. If he leaves a widow and one surviving child, half his separate property goes to her and the other half to the child. If there is more than one surviving child, only a third of the husband's separate property passes to the widow and the remaining two-thirds is divided equally among the children and the lawful issue (grandchildren) of any children who died before their father. The other community-property states have equally detailed statutes.

In the forty-two states and the District of Columbia that have common-law marital property systems, a widow does not own a half interest in all property acquired during the marriage by both spouses, as she does in the community-property states. In these states, any earnings and property accumulated by either spouse during the marriage are his or her separate property. However, since the property and savings of married couples are usually in the husband's name, the widow's economic protection may depend on that portion of her husband's property to which she is legally entitled regardless of the terms of her husband's will.

The traditional common-law protection for the widow whose husband leaves her only a small part of his separate property—or leaves her none—is called "dower." Dower is a wife's lifetime claim, which she may receive at her husband's death, to a one-third interest in her husband's real property, and sometimes also in his personal property, regardless of the terms of his will. More than half the common-law states have abolished dower rights altogether and others have altered the percentage of the husband's property that constitutes the wife's share. Those states that have abolished dower make provisions for what is called a "nonbarrable forced share" instead, which makes it impossible for a husband to completely disinherit his wife even if he leaves her nothing in his will, or leaves no will. This share varies from state to state.

In both common-law and community-property states, if a husband dies intestate—that is, does not leave a will—a widow's rights depend on the share of her husband's property accorded her under the state's intestate succession laws. These laws will also govern a widow's rights during probate proceedings if her husband's will is contested or challenged by someone who thinks he or she should have been included or, if included, should have received more. During probate the will's authenticity is established and all disputes are resolved; then the husband's estate is formally distributed after taxes, expenses, and creditors' claims are paid. The widow's share varies from state to state but is usually dependent upon whether the husband is survived by certain heirs designated by statute—typically, children and parents, and often grandchildren, brothers, and sisters as well.

In all but four common-law states (Iowa, New Hampshire, Rhode Island, and Vermont) the widow is entitled to *all* of her husband's property when he dies without leaving a will. Arkansas adds the qualification that the couple must have been married for more than three years, and Oklahoma requires the husband's entire estate to have been acquired by the "joint industry" of the spouses. There are many other variations in individual state laws. Florida, for example, grants the widow a share equal to that of each surviving child. Pennsylvania grants the widow half her husband's property if there is one surviving child, one-third if there is more than one surviving child or grandchild, and $20,000 plus half the remainder if there are surviving parents, brothers, or sisters. Virginia and West Virginia grant the widow her dower share of the land and one-third of the personal property if there are surviving children or grandchildren.

If a husband dies intestate or his will does not name an executor, the court may find it necessary to appoint an administrator of his estate. The executor or administrator is charged with collecting any debts owed to the estate and discharging its obligations. If, for example, the husband had a lawsuit against a third person at the time of his death, the executor must see that the case is settled and the proceeds or liabilities are added to or subtracted from the estate. If the husband owed money, the executor or administrator must make sure it is paid out of the estate. All creditors must be notified, usually by publication in a newspaper, that the estate is being settled and given a limited period in which to file their claim. Disputed claims may have to be taken to court, and here again the executor or administrator will see that this is handled properly.

Only after all assets are collected and all debts paid can the estate be distributed. Since this delay can cause financial hardship for the widow and her children, many state statutes provide for a preliminary partial distribution of the estate to the widow. The court, however, must be satisfied that enough assets will remain to meet the claims of creditors and other heirs before it authorizes this distribution.

All states except South Carolina have laws providing for family allowance or support while an estate is being settled. The widow may receive either a lump sum or payments for a specified period of time. (These provisions are based on criteria similar to those used in setting alimony payments, discussed in Chapter 5.) The amounts and time limits vary. Arkansas allows $500 for two months, New York an unstated amount of money for forty days. Wyoming sets no limit on time or money. In between these extremes each state has its own notion of "family support."

Still another protection for widows and their children is the "probate homestead"—a certain portion of the husband's real property (land and buildings) that is set aside for his widow to use as a home even though she may not actually own it. This property is out of the reach of the deceased husband's creditors. Generally a widow may occupy a probate homestead only during her lifetime, but in some states she may be given absolute ownership, which means that she will be able to dispose of it in her own will. In Kansas, for example, one city acre or 160 rural acres or one house trailer is exempt as a probate homestead until the widow dies or the children reach adulthood. In Illinois, New Mexico, Washington, and Wisconsin widows are granted an exemption of $10,000 on their spouses' home from the claim of creditors.

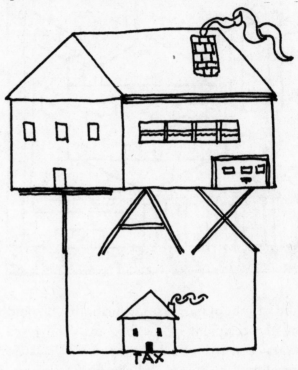

There is no way to avoid paying federal and state taxes on a deceased person's estate unless, perhaps, it is a very small one. The taxes can be extremely high, and tax regulations in this area are very complicated; any married couple should get competent, knowledgeable legal advice before making wills or attempting any estate planning. The larger the estate, of course, the more expert help is needed.

State tax rates depend on the size and composition of the estate, and the laws governing these taxes are different throughout the country. A state may require the payment both of estate taxes, which are levied on the taxable portion of the gross estate and are paid out of the estate before it is distributed,

and of inheritance taxes, which must be paid by the recipient of the bequest. The *gross estate* consists of all the spouse's cash on hand and in savings and checking accounts; life insurance policies (in some cases); real estate; wholly or partly owned businesses; stocks, bonds, and securities; business holdings; outstanding loans made to or by the spouse; pension payments and salary due him or her; and certain gifts and trust arrangements, such as those made within three years of death, or on which the decedent kept the power of revocation and transfer, or on which he or she retained the income during life.

The federal tax rate is based on the size of the *net estate*—that is, after deductions are subtracted. Such deductions include allowances to the surviving spouse and children during probate, the cost of administering the estate, burial expenses, claims against the

estate, and unpaid mortgages. In addition, federal and state income taxes will have to be paid on any income received by the deceased spouse during the last year of his or her life.

If the value of the gross estate is less than $60,000, no federal taxes will have to be paid on it, even though taxes are levied only on the net value of the estate. If it is more than $60,000, a very detailed tax form must be filed within fifteen months of the time of death; a rough estimate has to be filed much sooner—within sixty days. State tax forms must also be filed. They are based on the federal forms, although the time limits for filing vary with the state.

By careful planning ahead of time, many expenses, administrative delays, and tax liabilities can be avoided when a spouse dies. It is always best to make these arrangements with the advice and counsel of an attorney, and this is an absolute necessity if the anticipated estate is worth any significant amount. One thing a spouse may do, for example, is to include what is called a "marital deduction" in his or her will. This permits up to 50 per cent of the gross estate, minus allowed deductions, to go to the surviving spouse tax free, though the estate will eventually be taxed for it.

The establishment of joint bank accounts is another part of advance planning. When a husband and wife have a joint account each has an undivided half interest in any money in the account during the lifetime of both. But as soon as one spouse dies the other automatically owns the whole account, since the dead spouse's claim is simply extinguished. This also holds true for other jointly owned personal property—automobiles, furniture, works of art, and so on. Thus these jointly owned assets are not included as part of the deceased spouse's estate because upon his or her death they are owned solely by the surviving spouse.

In the joint ownership of real property this same rule applies. Any property that husband and wife hold as joint tenants will normally escape probate or any intervention from the courts. Also, there are different tax regulations covering property a surviving husband or wife acquires through probate (by will or intestate succession) and governing any property the spouse owns outright on the death of the other joint tenant. These differences can be important if the property involved is sufficiently valuable.

Anyone named as beneficiary of a life insurance policy may collect on that policy without going through probate. Only if no beneficiary is named—or if the beneficiary is the insured's estate or the policy holder retained the right to change the designated beneficiary—will the proceeds of the policy go into the decedent's estate at death and be subject to administration. This is because a life insurance policy is not treated, for probate purposes, as the property of the insured person but is, rather, a contract between the insured and the insurer in which, in return for the premium paid, the insurer agrees to pay the beneficiary a specified sum of money when the insured person dies.

Trusts and gifts, properly handled, may also be helpful in easing the tax burdens imposed by inheritance. One of the advance plans lawyers often suggest is to have the more affluent spouse—usually, in this case, the husband—transfer designated property or sums of money into a trust during his or her lifetime, naming the other spouse as the beneficiary of the income as well as of the principal. This allows the beneficiary to receive periodic payments before the trust expires, at which time he or she (or possibly another beneficiary, such as the couple's children) receives the balance of the funds if they have not been exhausted by the payments. It is also possible for a spouse to name himself or herself as the trustee with the other as beneficiary. If the trust is irrevocable—that is, if the trustee does not retain the power to terminate it—at the time of his or her death the property held in trust belongs solely to the beneficiary because during life the trustee had relinquished completely any control (ownership) of the trust property.

In establishing such a trust, however, one must be aware of potential tax consequences. If too much money is placed in a trust during the spouse's lifetime, or in any given year, a gift tax may have to be paid. These taxes are levied to make up at least partially for estate taxes that are lost when the property does not go through probate. Under present law, $30,000 worth of gifts exempt from federal gift taxation can be made during a person's lifetime, although individual gifts of $3000 per year can be made to as many people as the donor chooses without being subject to the tax.

In some cases, however, property held in trust—even if the spouse establishes the trust during his or her life rather than in the will—may still be subject to estate taxes, depending on the terms of the trust. This is exactly the kind of complicated estate-planning issue on which the advice of an attorney is essential, because it involves many detailed federal and state laws.

The expense and delay of estate administration has recently been the subject of much criticism. As a result, many states are considering the enactment of new laws based on the proposed Uniform Probate and Administration Act. Among other things, this act provides for relatively rapid settlement of modest estates as well as reducing the cost of administration.

The custody of minor children upon the death of one or both parents is sometimes a problem. If the husband dies leaving a widow, there is usually no question that the custody of any surviving children will go to her, especially if she is also their natural parent, and the same is true if a wife dies first, leaving her husband as a survivor. But because there is always the possibility that parents may die simultaneously, each should name a guardian for their children in their individual wills, just in case. While courts are not bound by such a designation, if it is reasonable it will usually be honored.

Finally, a widow has rights under the federal Social Security Act. If a husband was insured under the act his widow may be entitled to a modest cash payment to help with burial expenses. She may also be eligible for survivors' insurance monthly payments, although she cannot receive them as both the surviving widow of an insured man and an insured worker herself. The amount of her survivor's insurance monthly payments equals 82½ per cent of the benefit her husband would have received had he lived to draw old-age insurance. A widowed mother may also receive 75 per cent of the basic benefit for each of her deceased husband's children until they reach adulthood or until they finish college. The amount of the surviving widow's and children's payments varies according to the length of her husband's employment, his total earnings, and the size of the family, from a minimum of $98.30 to a maximum of $309.40 per month.

In sum, the lawmakers have seen to it that most legal and financial needs of widows are provided for. Thus buttressed by law and shielded by status, the woman alone finally achieves a legal status to be envied by her married sisters.

7
When I Am Widowed
The Law
State by State

ALABAMA

Dower share: Widow is entitled to a life interest in half of all land owned by husband during the marriage. If husband was in debt or left other heirs, widow has a one-third interest. If widow's separate estate or distributive share in her husband's estate is greater than her dower interest, she is not entitled to dower.

If husband left no will: Widow is entitled to entire estate if husband left no children; to half if there is one child; to an equal share with children if there are two to four children; to one-fifth if there are more than four children.

Option to disregard will: Widow may reject the will and take her dower interest plus the share of personal property she would have received if there were no will. However, if the personal property is worth more than $50,000, widow is entitled only to the first $50,000; the rest is distributed according to the will.

Allowances from estate during probate: Widow may be granted $1000 of husband's personal property and $2000 of any salary due to husband; household goods and furnishings, groceries, and clothing for one year.

Homestead exemption: A payment of $6000 or 160 acres is exempt for homestead.

ALASKA

Dower share: Abolished.

If husband left no will: Widow is entitled to entire estate if husband left no other heirs; to $50,000 and half the balance if there are parents or if there are children who are also the widow's children; to half the estate if there are one or more children who are not also the widow's children.

Option to disregard will: Widow may reject the will and take instead one-third of a specially defined estate; if she does so, she need not renounce her share under the will or her share through intestate succession.

Allowances from estate during probate: Widow is granted support payments, for no longer than one year if estate is inadequate to meet claims against it.

Homestead exemption: Land up to $12,000 in value and household goods and furnishings, appliances, and cars up to $3500 in value are exempt for homestead.

ARIZONA

Dower share: None; community-property state.

If husband left no will: Separate property—widow is entitled to all of it if husband left no other heirs; to half the land and all the personal property if there are parents; to one-third of the land and one-third of the personal property if there are children or grandchildren. Community property—widow is entitled to all of it if husband left no children; to a share equal to that of each child if there are children.

Option to disregard will: Widow may not reject the disposition of husband's half of community property.

Allowances from estate during probate: Widow may be granted support payments until estate is settled; $1000 from husband's bank deposits; $2000 of any salary due to husband.

Homestead exemption: Land up to $8000 in value is exempt for homestead.

ARKANSAS

Dower share: Widow is entitled to a life interest in one-third of all land owned by husband during the marriage and to an absolute interest in one-third of all other property he owned at his death.

If husband left no will: Widow is entitled to entire estate if she was married to husband for more than three years and there are no children or grandchildren; to half if they were married less than three years and there are no children or grandchildren; to none if there are children or grandchildren.

Option to disregard will: Widow may reject the will and take her dower share.

Allowances from estate during probate: Widow may be granted property valued at $2000 unless estate is inadequate to meet claims against it—then the amount is $1000; support payments up to $500 for two months; household goods and furnishings; appliances. She may stay in husband's home until her dower share is assigned.

Homestead exemption: A payment of $2500 or—regardless of price—one-quarter acre in the city or eighty acres elsewhere is exempt for homestead.

CALIFORNIA

Dower share: None; community-property state.

If husband left no will: Separate property—widow is entitled to all of it if husband left no other heirs; to half if there is one child or grandchild or if there are parents, brothers, or sisters; to one-third if there is more than one child or grandchild. Community property—widow is entitled to all of it.

Option to disregard will: Widow must choose either to take half of any property which if acquired in California would be community property or to take the amount willed to her.

Allowances from estate during probate: Widow is granted support payments, but for no longer than one year if estate is inadequate to meet claims against it. Expenses for husband's last illness, the funeral, and administration of the estate take precedence over the allowance.

Homestead exemption: A payment of up to $20,000 if widow is the head of the family or over 65, or up to $10,000 if she is not, is exempt for homestead.

COLORADO

Dower share: Abolished.

If husband left no will: Widow is entitled to entire estate if husband left no other heirs; to half if there are children or grandchildren.

Option to disregard will: Widow may reject the will and take half of husband's estate.

Allowances from estate during probate: Widow may be granted $7500 or its equivalent in land (if there are minor children not living with widow, this sum is divided among them according to need); support payments—deducted from the $7500; household furnishings. She may stay in husband's home as long as the court feels it is necessary.

Homestead exemption: A payment of up to $5000 is exempt for homestead.

CONNECTICUT

Dower share: Widow is entitled to a life interest in one-third of all property owned by husband.

If husband left no will: Widow is entitled to entire estate if husband left no other heirs; to $5000 plus half the remainder if there are parents; to one-third if there are children.

Option to disregard will: Widow may reject the will and take her dower share.

Allowances from estate during probate: Widow may be granted support payments until estate is settled. She may stay in husband's home until estate is settled and use the family car.

Homestead exemption: No statute.

DELAWARE

Dower share: Widow is entitled to a life interest in one-third of all land owned by husband during the marriage.

If husband left no will: Widow is entitled to entire estate if husband left no children or grandchildren; to a life interest in half the land and one-third of the personal property if there are children or grandchildren.

Option to disregard will: Widow may reject the will and take her dower share of the land, but she has no such choice regarding the personal property.

Allowances from estate during probate: Widow may be granted up to $1000.

Homestead exemption: No statute.

DISTRICT OF COLUMBIA

Dower share: Widow is entitled to a life interest in one-third of all land owned by husband during the marriage.

If husband left no will: Widow is entitled to entire estate if husband left no other heirs; to half if he left parents, brothers, sisters, nieces, or nephews; to one-third if he left children or grandchildren.

Option to disregard will: Widow may reject the will and take either (1) her dower share of land and the share of personal property she would

receive if there were no will (in this case, she may not take more than half the personal property or more than half the land provided for her in the will) or (2) the share she would receive if there were no will (in this case, she may not take more than half the amount willed).

Allowances from estate during probate: Widow may be granted $2500.

Homestead exemption: No statute.

FLORIDA

Dower share: Widow is entitled to an interest in one-third of all land and one-third of all personal property owned by husband at his death.

If husband left no will: Widow is entitled to entire estate if husband left no children; to a share equal to that of each child if there are children.

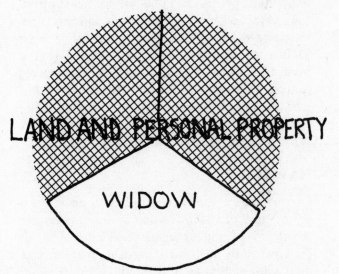

Option to disregard will: Widow may reject the will and take either the share she would receive if there were no will or her dower share.

Allowances from estate during probate: Widow may be granted up to $1200, with the possibility of an additional $3000 if needed; household goods; clothing; farm equipment.

Homestead exemption: A half acre in the city or 160 acres elsewhere is exempt for homestead for widow during her life.

GEORGIA

Dower share: Abolished.

If husband left no will: Widow is entitled to entire estate if husband left no children; to a share equal to that of each child if there are fewer than five children; to one-fifth if there are five or more children.

Option to disregard will: Widow may not reject the will. However, any woman who was entitled to a dower share prior to 1969 may choose between the dower share and the share she would receive if there were no will.

Allowances from estate during probate: Widow may be granted at least $1600 for one year; $1000 from husband's bank deposits; $1000 of any salary due to husband; household furnishings. If the entire estate is less than $1600, widow is entitled to receive it all for her support. If husband made provisions in his will for her support, she must choose between the will and this plan.

Homestead exemption: A payment of at least $1600 is exempt for homestead. Widow may take up to $500 worth of land in the city or fifty acres (plus five for each child under 16) elsewhere and a house and improvements under $200 in value plus specified household goods, food, and livestock instead of the homestead exemption.

HAWAII

Dower share: Widow is entitled to an interest in one-third of all land owned by husband during the marriage and to a one-third interest in all land owned by husband at his death that remains after the estate is administered.

If husband left no will: Widow is entitled to entire estate if husband left no other heirs; to half if there are parents, brothers, sisters, nieces, or nephews; to none if there are children—in this case, she is entitled only to her dower share.

Option to disregard will: Widow may reject the will and take her dower share; if she does not make a choice, she is presumed to prefer the dower share.

Allowances from estate during probate: Widow may be granted support payments if husband was supporting her at the time of his death, but for no longer than one year if estate is inadequate to meet claims against it. She may stay in husband's home and use personal effects for at least sixty days.

Homestead exemption: No statute.

IDAHO

Dower share: None; community-property state.

If husband left no will: Separate property—widow is entitled to all of it if husband left no other heirs; to $50,000 plus half the balance if there are parents or if there are children who are also widow's children; to half if there is one or more child who is not also widow's child. Community property—widow is entitled to all of it.

Option to disregard will: Widow may not reject the will and take the share she would receive if there were no will if it appears that she was omitted intentionally.

Allowances from estate during probate: Widow may be granted up to $6000 until estate is settled.

Homestead exemption: A payment of $10,000 if widow is caring for dependent children, or $4000 if she is not, and up to $3500 worth of household goods and furnishings, appliances, and cars are exempt for homestead.

ILLINOIS

Dower share: Abolished.

If husband left no will: Widow is entitled to entire estate if husband left no children; to one-third if there are children.

Option to disregard will: Widow may reject the will and take half the estate if husband left no children or one-third if there are children.

Allowances from estate during probate: Widow may be granted not less than $5000 for nine months, plus $100 for each dependent child who lives with her, either in money or in goods and personal property that was not specifically allocated in the will.

Homestead exemption: A payment of $10,000 is

exempt for homestead as long as widow lives on it.

INDIANA

Dower share: Abolished.

If husband left no will: Widow is entitled to entire estate if husband left no other heirs; to three-quarters if there are parents; to half if there is one child; to one-third if there is more than one child. However, if widow is childless and husband left children by a previous marriage, she is entitled only to possession for life of one-third of the land although she still receives her full share of the personal property.

Option to disregard will: Widow may reject the will and take one-third of the estate; if she is childless and husband has children from a previous marriage, she may take one-third of the land and one-third of the personal property. If husband left widow less than one-third of the estate in the will, she may keep these bequests and take the balance due her in cash or property.

Allowances from estate during probate: Widow may be granted $3000 until estate is settled, but for no longer than one year, not to exceed $50 a week for herself and $25 a week for each dependent child.

Homestead exemption: No statute.

IOWA

Dower share: Abolished.

If husband left no will: Widow is entitled to $25,000 plus half the remainder if husband left no children; to one-third of all land owned by husband during the marriage plus one-third of the personal property if there are children. If these two latter amounts do not add up to $25,000, she is entitled to additional land and personal property until that amount is reached.

Option to disregard will: Widow may reject the will and take the share she would receive if there were no will, but she may take no more than the share she would receive if husband had left children even if there are no children.

Allowances from estate during probate: Widow may be granted support payments for one year.

Homestead exemption: Widow may use the homestead for life, or she may instead take her share of one-third of the land as if there were no will.

KANSAS

Dower share: Abolished.

If husband left no will: Widow is entitled to entire estate if husband left no children; to half if there are children.

Option to disregard will: Widow may reject the will and take the share she would receive if there were no will, unless she consented—in writing and before witnesses—to the will.

Allowances from estate during probate: Widow may be granted not less than $750 nor more than $3500 for one year; household goods and furnishings; clothing; one car; provisions; fuel.

Homestead exemption: One acre in the city, 160 acres elsewhere, or a house trailer is exempt for homestead until widow dies or children reach adulthood, whichever is later.

KENTUCKY

Dower share: Widow is entitled to a life interest in one-third of all land owned by husband during the marriage and to an absolute interest in half the land and half the personal property he owned at his death.

If husband left no will: Widow is entitled to entire estate if husband left no other heirs; to none if there are children, parents, brothers, sisters, nieces, or nephews—in this case, she is entitled only to her dower share.

Option to disregard will: Widow may reject the will and take her dower share of land plus the share of personal property she would receive if there were no will; in this case, however, the most her share in land may be is an interest in one-third of all land husband owned during the marriage.

Allowances from estate during probate: Widow may be granted $3500 in money or property; $500 from husband's bank deposits.

Homestead exemption: A payment of $1000 is exempt, and widow may keep the homestead as long as she occupies it as her home.

LOUISIANA

Dower share: None; community-property state.

If husband left no will: Separate property—widow is entitled to all of it if husband left no parents or children. However, if widow is destitute and the estate is large, she is entitled to her "marital portion": one-quarter if there are fewer than three children; an equal share with each child if there are more than three children. Community property—widow is entitled to all of it if husband left no children or parents; to half if there are parents; to none if there are children who are not also widow's children. If there are children who are also widow's children, widow has a right to use husband's half of community property during her lifetime unless she remarries.

Option to disregard will: No statute.

Allowances from estate during probate: Widow may be granted $1000 in cash or property; support payments; $2500 from husband's bank deposits; $2500 from his credit union shares; $1000 of any salary due to husband.

Homestead exemption: No statute.

MAINE

Dower share: Abolished.

If husband left no will: Widow is entitled to entire estate if husband left no other heirs; to half if there are parents, brothers, or sisters and to all the remainder if it is not more than $10,000—if it is more than $10,000, she takes the first $10,000 of personal property plus half the remaining personal property and two-thirds of the remaining land; to one-third if there are children.

Option to disregard will: Widow may reject the will and take the share she would receive if there were no will, but she must take the share she would receive if husband left other heirs even if there are none.

Allowances from estate during probate: Widow may be granted support payments; clothing; jewelry. She may stay in husband's home rent-free for ninety days.

Homestead exemption: A payment of $3000 is exempt for homestead until widow remarries or children reach adulthood.

MARYLAND

Dower share: Abolished.

If husband left no will: Widow is entitled to entire estate if husband left no other heirs; to half if there are parents; to $4000 plus half the remainder if there are brothers, sisters, nieces, or nephews; to one-third if there are children.

Option to disregard will: Widow may reject the will and take the share she would receive if there were no will.

Allowances from estate druing probate: Widow may be granted $1000 and $500 for each unmarried dependent child under 18.

Homestead exemption: No statute.

MASSACHUSETTS

Dower share: Widow is entitled to an interest in one-third of all land owned by husband at his death.

If husband left no will: Widow is entitled to entire estate if husband left no other heirs; to $50,000 plus half the remainder if there are other heirs but no children; to one-third if there are children.

Option to disregard will: Widow may reject the will and take $25,000 plus half the remainder of the estate outright if husband left no other heirs or $25,000 plus income for life on the remainder if there are other heirs.

Allowances from estate during probate: Widow may be granted support payments until estate is settled; clothing; jewelry. She may stay in husband's home rent-free for six months.

Homestead exemption: A payment of $10,000 is exempt for homestead until widow dies, remarries, or her youngest child reaches 21, whichever happens last.

MICHIGAN

Dower share: Widow is entitled to a life interest in one-third of all lands owned by husband during the marriage; however, she must file a claim with the registrar of deeds to keep her dower right alive.

If husband left no will: Land—widow is entitled to all of it if husband left no other heirs; to half if there are parents, brothers, sisters, nieces, or nephews; to one-third if there are children. Personal property—widow is entitled to all of it if husband left no other heirs; to the first $3000 plus half the remainder if there are parents, brothers, sisters, nieces, or nephews; to half if there is only one child; to one-third if there is more than one child.

Option to disregard will: Widow may reject the will and take $5000 plus half the personal property she would receive if there were no will and either the entire share of land she would receive if there were no will or her dower share.

Allowances from estate during probate: Widow may be granted support payments until estate is settled, but for no longer than one year if estate is inadequate to meet claims against it. She may stay in husband's home rent-free for one year.

Homestead exemption: Land up to $3500 in value—either one lot in the city or forty acres elsewhere—is exempt for homestead until widow remarries or her children reach adulthood, whichever happens last.

MINNESOTA

Dower share: Abolished.

If husband left no will: Widow is entitled to entire estate if husband left no children; to half the personal property and half of all the land owned by husband during marriage if there is one child; to one-third of both land and personal property if there is more than one child.

Option to disregard will: Widow may reject the will and take the share she would receive if there were no will, but she may take only half—not all—the estate if there are no children.

Allowances from estate during probate: Widow may be granted support payments for eighteen months if estate is adequate to meet all claims against it, for twelve months if it is not; $3000 of any salary due to husband; clothing and household goods and furnishings up to $2000 in value; other personal property up to $1000 in value.

Homestead exemption: A half acre in the city and eighty acres elsewhere are exempt for homestead. If there are no children, the homestead becomes the widow's absolute property; otherwise it is hers only during her lifetime.

MISSISSIPPI

Dower share: Abolished.

If husband left no will: Widow is entitled to entire estate if husband left no children; to a share equal to that of each child if there are children.

Option to disregard will: Widow may reject the will and take the share she would receive if there were no will but she may not take more than half the estate. If she has separate property equal to the share she would take if she disregards the will, she must accept the provisions of the will, and she may not take an amount that would make the sum of her separate property and her share of the husband's estate greater than her intestate share unless her separate estate is less than one-fifth of what she would be entitled to.

Allowances from estate during probate: Widow may be granted support payments for one year; $300 from any salary due to husband.

Homestead exemption: Either 160 acres or $15,000 is exempt for homestead, to be shared equally by widow and children.

MISSOURI

Dower share: Abolished.

If husband left no will: Widow is entitled to entire estate if husband left no other heirs; to half if

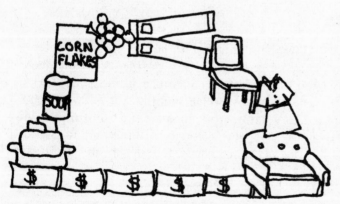

there are children, grandchildren, parents, brothers, sisters, nieces, or nephews.

Option to disregard will: Widow may reject the will and take half the estate if there are no children or one-third if there are children.

Allowances from estate during probate: Widow may be granted support payments for one year; household goods and furnishings; clothing; appliances; implements.

Homestead exemption: A payment which may not exceed half the value of the estate and in no case may be greater than $7500 is exempt for homestead.

MONTANA

Dower share: Widow is entitled to a life interest in one-third of all land owned by husband during the marriage.

If husband left no will: Widow is entitled to entire estate if husband left no children or grandchildren; to half if there is only one child; to one-third if there is more than one child.

Option to disregard will: Widow may reject the will and take the share of personal property she would receive if there were no will and her dower share of the land, but overall she may not take more than two-thirds of the estate.

Allowances from estate during probate: Widow may be granted support payments, but for no longer than one year if estate is inadequate to meet claims against it; household furnishings; clothing. If the entire estate is less than $1500, widow is entitled to receive it all for her support; if it is between $1500 and $3000, the court has discretion whether to give it all to her or not.

Homestead exemption: Widow may use the homestead for life; however, if it is worth more than $2500, she may take only $2500 from the proceeds of its sale.

NEBRASKA

Dower share: Abolished.

If husband left no will: Widow is entitled to entire estate if husband left no other heirs; to half if there is only one child who is also the widow's child or if there are other heirs; to one-third if there is more than one child who is also the widow's child; to one-quarter if there is more than one child who is not also the widow's child.

Option to disregard will: Widow may reject the will and take the share she would receive if there were no will.

Allowances from estate during probate: Widow may be granted support payments until estate is settled; household furnishings; clothing; jewelry; other personal property up to $200 in value. If the entire estate is less than $3000, widow is entitled to receive it all for her support.

Homestead exemption: Two lots in the city or 160 elsewhere, neither exceeding $2000 in value, are exempt for homestead for use by widow during her lifetime.

NEVADA

Dower share: None; community-property state.
If husband left no will: Separate property—widow is entitled to all of it if husband left no other heirs; to half if there is one child or grandchild or if there are parents, brothers, or sisters; to one-third if there is more than one child or grandchild. Community property—widow is entitled to all of it.
Option to disregard will: Widow may not reject the will.
Allowances from estate during probate: Widow may be granted support payments; household goods and furnishings; clothing. She may stay in husband's home. Any of her husband's property that is exempt from creditors may also be set aside for her support; if this is not sufficient, the court may grant additional payments, but for no longer than one year if husband was in debt.
Homestead exemption: Land up to $10,000 in value, without limit as to area, for homestead. If a homestead was chosen and set aside before husband's death, it becomes the widow's absolute property; otherwise, the court may designate a homestead for widow's use during her lifetime.

NEW HAMPSHIRE

Dower share: Abolished.
If husband left no will: Widow is entitled to $10,000, $2000 for each full year of marriage, and half the remainder of the estate if husband left no other heirs; to $10,000 plus half the remainder if there are parents, brothers, or sisters; to one-third if there are children or grandchildren.
Option to disregard will: Widow may reject the will and take the share she would receive if there were no will, but if she makes this choice she is not entitled to the homestead exemption.
Allowances from estate during probate: Widow may be granted support payments. She may stay in husband's home rent-free for forty days.
Homestead exemption: Land up to $1500 in value, without limit as to area, is exempt for homestead for widow's use during her lifetime.

NEW JERSEY

Dower share: Widow is entitled to a life interest in half of all land owned by husband during the marriage.
If husband left no will: Widow is entitled to entire estate if husband left no children; to one-third of the personal property and her dower share of land if there are children.
Option to disregard will: Widow may reject the will and take her dower share of the land, but she has no such choice regarding the personal property.
Allowances from estate during probate: Widow may be granted up to $500.
Homestead exemption: No statute.

NEW MEXICO

Dower share: None: community-property state.
If husband left no will: Separate property—widow is entitled to all of it if husband left no children; to one-quarter if there are children. Community property—widow is entitled to all of it.
Option to disregard will: No statute.
Allowances from estate during probate: Widow

may be granted support payments for six months; withdrawals from husband's bank deposits (amount not specified); $2000 of any salary due to husband.

Homestead exemption: A payment of up to $10,000 is exempt for homestead.

NEW YORK

Dower share: Abolished. However, if widow and her husband were married before September 1, 1930, widow has an interest in one-third of all land owned by husband during the marriage before that date.

If husband left no will: Widow is entitled to entire estate if husband left no other heirs; to $25,000 plus half the remainder if there are parents; to $2000 plus half the remainder if there is one child or grandchild; to $2000 plus one-third of the remainder if there is more than one child or grandchild.

Option to disregard will: Widow may reject a will made between August 21, 1930, and September 1, 1966, and take the share she would receive if there were no will, but she may take no more than half the estate if there are no other heirs and no more than one-third if there are children or grandchildren.

Allowances from estate during probate: Widow may be granted support payments for forty days; personal property up to $1000. She may stay in husband's home rent-free for forty days.

Homestead exemption: Land up to $2000 in value is exempt for homestead if widow lives on it until she dies or the youngest child reaches 21.

NORTH CAROLINA

Dower share: Abolished.

If husband left no will: Widow is entitled to entire estate if husband left no other heirs; to half the land plus the first $10,000 of personal property and half the remainder if there are parents; to half the estate if there is one child or grandchild; to one-third if there is more than one child or grandchild.

Option to disregard will: Widow may not reject the will if it gives her more than half of husband's estate. Otherwise, she may take the share she would receive if there were no will, but she may not take more than half the estate.

Allowances from estate during probate: Widow may be granted $2000 for one year.

Homestead exemption: Land up to $1000 in value, without limitation as to area, is exempt for homestead until the widow remarries or the children reach adulthood, whichever happens last.

NORTH DAKOTA

Dower share: Abolished.

If husband left no will: Widow is entitled to entire estate if husband left no other heirs; to the first $100,000 plus half the remainder if there are brothers and sisters; to the first $50,000 plus half the remainder if there are parents; to half the estate if there are children or grandchildren.

Option to disregard will: No statute.

Allowances from estate druing probate: Widow may be granted up to $5000 until estate is settled, with the possibility of additional funds if needed.

Homestead exemption: Two acres in the city up to $40,000 in value or 160 acres elsewhere are exempt for homestead until widow remarries or dies.

OHIO

Dower share: Widow is entitled to a life interest in one-third of all land owned by husband during the marriage.

If husband left no will: Widow is entitled to entire estate if husband left no other heirs; to three-quarters if there are parents; to half if there is one child; to one-third if there is more than one child or grandchild.

Option to disregard will: Widow may reject the will and take the share she would receive if there were no will, but she may take no more than half the estate.

Allowances from estate during probate: Widow may be granted support payments for one year. She may also select personal property for her support until estate is settled, not to exceed 20 per cent of the value of the estate—a minimum of $500 and a maximum of $2500.

Homestead exemption: Land up to $1000 in value is exempt for homestead as long as widow lives on it and does not remarry. She may choose to receive $500 instead of the homestead exemption.

OKLAHOMA

Dower share: Abolished.

If husband left no will: Widow is entitled to entire estate if husband left no other heirs and the estate was acquired by the joint industry of the widow and her husband; to half if there is one child or grandchild or if there are parents, brothers, or sisters but no children; one-third if there is more than one child or grandchild. If husband was married previously and the estate was not acquired during his marriage to the widow, she is entitled to a share equal to that of each child.

Option to disregard will: Widow may reject the will and take the share she would receive if there were no will only if she would receive more that way.

Allowances from estate during probate: Widow may be granted support payments until estate is settled.

Homestead exemption: A quarter of an acre without regard to value or one acre up to $5000 in value in the city or 160 acres elsewhere is exempt for homestead for widow's use during her life.

OREGON

Dower share: Abolished.

If husband left no will: Widow is entitled to entire estate if there are no children or grandchildren; to half if there are children or grandchildren.

Option to disregard will: Widow may reject the will and take a quarter share of husband's estate, but the share will be reduced by the value of any property she receives outright.

Allowances from estate during probate: Widow may be granted support payments if she petitions the court for them, although temporary support will be provided until the hearing is held. She may stay in husband's home for one year.

Homestead exemption: One city block or 160 acres elsewhere, neither to exceed $7500 in value, is exempt for homestead.

PENNSYLVANIA

Dower share: Abolished.

If husband left no will: Widow is entitled to entire estate if husband left no other heirs; to $20,000 plus half the remainder if there are parents, brothers, or sisters; to half if there is one child; to one-third if there is more than one child or grandchild.

Option to disregard will: Widow may reject the will and take the share she would receive if there were no will, but she may not take more than one-third of the estate if there are children or grandchildren or more than half in any case.

Allowances from estate during probate: Widow may be granted $1500 until estate is settled.

Homestead exemption: No statute.

RHODE ISLAND

Dower share: Widow is entitled to a life interest in one-third of all land owned by husband during the marriage.

If husband left no will: Widow is entitled to an interest for life in all the land husband owned at his death, to absolute ownership of land up to $25,000 in value, and to $50,000 worth of personal property plus half the remainder if husband left no children or grandchildren; to her dower share in land and half the personal property if there are children or grandchildren.

Option to disregard will: Widow may reject the will and take her dower share of the land, but she has no such choice regarding the personal property.

Allowances from estate during probate: Widow may be granted support payments for six months.

Homestead exemption: No statute.

SOUTH CAROLINA

Dower share: Widow is entitled to either a life interest in one-third of all land owned by husband during the marriage or an absolute interest in one-sixth of this land. However, if husband leaves no will and widow chooses to take her share of the estate as outlined in that circumstance, she is barred from taking her dower share.

If husband left no will: Widow is entitled to entire estate if husband left no other heirs; to half if there is one child or there are parents, brothers, sisters, nieces, or nephews; to one-third if there is more than one child.

Option to disregard will: Widow may reject the will and take her dower share of the land, but she has no such choice regarding personal property.

Allowances from estate during probate: No statute.

Homestead exemption: Land up to $1000 in value is exempt for homestead.

SOUTH DAKOTA

Dower share: Abolished.

If husband left no will: Widow is entitled to entire estate if husband left no other heirs; to $100,000 plus half the remainder if there are parents, brothers, or sisters; to half if there is one child or grandchild; to one-third if there is more than one child or grandchild.

Option to disregard will: No statute.

Allowances from estate during probate: Widow may be granted $1500 (or $2500 if the estate consists entirely of personal property), with the possibility of additional funds if needed.

Homestead exemption: One acre in the city, 160 acres elsewhere, or $15,000 from the sale of husband's home is exempt for homestead for widow's use during her life.

TENNESSEE

Dower share: Widow is entitled to a life interest in one-third of all land owned by husband at his death.

If husband left no will: Widow is entitled to entire estate if husband left no other heirs; to her dower share of the land and a child's share of the personal property if there are children.

Option to disregard will: Widow may reject the will and take her dower share of the land and one-third of the personal property if husband left one or two children; her dower share of the land and a child's share of the personal property if there are more than two children.

Allowances from estate during probate: Widow may be granted support payments. She may have up to $500 of any salary due to husband, but it will be deducted from the support payments.

Homestead exemption: Land up to $1000 in value is exempt for homestead for widow's use during her life.

TEXAS

Dower share: None; community-property state.

If husband left no will: Separate property—widow is entitled to all of it if husband left no other heirs; to half if there are parents, brothers, or sisters; to a life interest in one-third of the land and an absolute interest in one-third of the personal property if there are children. Community property—widow is entitled to all of it if husband left no children or grandchildren; to half if there are children or grandchildren.

Option to disregard will: Widow may reject the will only if it attempts to dispose of more than husband's half of the community property. If she does reject the will, she must take her half share of the community property.

Allowances from estate during probate: Widow may be granted support payments for one year if her own property is not sufficient for support.

Homestead exemption: Land in the city up to $10,000 in value or 200 acres elsewhere is exempt for homestead. Widow may choose to take a $5000 payment instead of the homestead exemption.

UTAH

Dower share: Abolished.

If husband left no will: Widow is entitled to entire estate if husband left no other heirs; to $100,000 plus half the remainder if there are parents, brothers, sisters, nieces, or nephews; to half if there is one child or grandchild; to one-third if there is more than one child or grandchild.

Option to disregard will: Widow may not reject the will in regard to personal property, but she may take a one-third interest in all land owned

by husband during the marriage instead of the will's bequest.

Allowances from estate during probate: Widow may be granted support payments until estate is settled, but for no longer than one year if estate is inadequate to meet all the claims against it. She may stay in husband's house unless directed otherwise by the court, but only for a year if estate is in debt.

Homestead exemption: Land up to $4000 in value, plus $1500 for widow and $600 for each child, is exempt for homestead.

VERMONT

Dower share: Widow is entitled to an interest in one-third of all land owned by husband at his death. She is entitled to an interest in half this land if husband left one child.

If husband left no will: Widow is entitled to $25,000 plus half the remainder of the estate if husband left no other heirs; to half the land if there is one child who is also widow's child; to one-third of the land and one-third of the personal property if there is more than one child.

Option to disregard will: Widow may reject the will and take her dower share.

Allowances from estate during probate: Widow may be granted support payments until estate is settled, but for no longer than eight months if estate is inadequate to meet claims against it.

Homestead exemption: Land up to $5000 in value is exempt for homestead. If a homestead has not already been designated for widow, the court may do so.

VIRGINIA

Dower share: Widow is entitled to an absolute interest in one-third of all land husband owned during the marriage.

If husband left no will: Widow is entitled to entire estate if husband left no children or grandchildren; to her dower share of the land and one-third of the personal property if there are children or grandchildren.

Option to disregard will: Widow may reject the will and take her dower share of the land and half the personal property if husband left no children, or her dower share of the land and one-third of the personal property if there are children.

Allowances from estate during probate: Widow may be granted support payments until estate is settled. She may stay in husband's home until dower share has been assigned.

Homestead exemption: Land up to $2000 in value is exempt for homestead until widow remarries or dies. However, she loses the homestead exemption if she takes her dower share.

WASHINGTON

Dower share: None; community-property state.

If husband left no will: Separate property—widow is entitled to all of it if husband left no other heirs; to three-quarters if there are parents, brothers, or sisters; to half if there are children. Community property—widow is entitled to all of it if husband left no other heirs; to half if there are parents or children.

Option to disregard will: Widow may reject the will only if it attempts to dispose of more than husband's half of the community property. If she does reject the will, she must take her half share of the community property.

Allowances from estate during probate: Widow may be granted support payments until estate is settled.

Homestead exemption: Land up to $10,000 in value is exempt for homestead.

WEST VIRGINIA

Dower share: Widow is entitled to a life interest in one-third of all land husband owned during the marriage.

If husband left no will: Widow is entitled to entire estate if husband left no children or grandchildren; to her dower share of the land and one-third of the personal property if there are children or grandchildren.

Option to disregard will: Widow may reject the will and take the share she would receive if there were no will.

Allowances from estate during probate: Widow may be granted $200. She may stay in husband's home until dower share has been assigned.

Homestead exemption: Land up to $1000 in value is exempt for homestead for use by the family. This exemption passes to the minor children rather than the widow.

WISCONSIN

Dower share: Abolished.

If husband left no will: Widow is entitled to entire estate if husband left no children; to $25,000 plus half the remainder if there is one child who is also the widow's child; to $25,000 plus one-third of the remainder if there is more than one child who is also the widow's child; to half the estate if there is one child who is not the widow's child; to one-third if there is more than one child who is not the widow's child.

Option to disregard will: Widow may reject the will and take one-third of husband's estate, but the share will be reduced by the value of any property she receives outright, specifically the homestead exemption. This option is not allowed if husband and wife had signed an agreement on another settlement or if widow receives more than half of certain property from the estate.

Allowances from estate during probate: Widow may be granted support payments until estate is settled if she applies to probate court for them.

Homestead exemption: Land up to $10,000 in value is exempt for homestead.

WYOMING

Dower share: Abolished.

If husband left no will: Widow is entitled to entire estate if husband left no other heirs; to $20,000 plus three-quarters of the remainder if there are parents, brothers, sisters, nieces, or nephews; to half if there are children.

Option to disregard will: Widow may reject the will and take half the estate if there are no children or one-quarter of the estate if there are children who are not also widow's children.

Allowances from estate during probate: Widow may be granted support payments until estate is settled.

Homestead exemption: Land up to $4000 in value is exempt for homestead.

8
When I Go to Work

Married or single, widowed or divorced, with or without children, more women are working outside the home today than ever before. Most work because they have to. But the underlying attitude in the laws covering the rights of working women has been that they work chiefly because they *want to,* or to earn extra family income for special luxuries.

Until recently the law has tended to consider working women as dilettantes, as "unserious" wage earners, as marginal employees, and as incapable of doing as much or as well—and therefore of earning as much—as men. Paradoxically, the law also has considered women as frail creatures in need of special protection against long hours, heavy work, night work, and so on. The results of these two false assumptions—that women workers don't need their jobs as much as men do, and that women on the job need

special protections—have combined to create widespread discrepancies between men and women in salaries, job opportunities, and prospects for advancement in employment.

With the advent of the women's liberation movement, however, consistent pressure has been put on legislators and business leaders to narrow the gap between women and men in the work force. These efforts have raised the national consciousness on the issue, and some progress has been made, both in terms of job opportunities for women and equalization of pay standards.

Even so, women are still seriously undervalued in terms of their earning power in the marketplace. Between 1957 and 1972 women's median earnings *dropped* 5.9 per cent compared with the earnings of men. In 1972 women earned $5903, men $10,202, and the median income of women who had completed four years of college was $8736—just $100 more than the median income of men who had finished only one year of high school.

Insight into the status of working women in the United States requires a brief look at a series of Supreme Court rulings going back to 1908. At that time the Court held unconstitutional many minimum-wage, maximum-hour, control-of-working-condition laws on the ground that such legislation interfered with the employee's as well as the employer's "freedom of contract," a right then considered constitutionally protected by the due process clause of the Fifth and Fourteenth amendments.

In 1908, in the famous case of *Muller v. Oregon,* the Supreme Court upheld the constitutionality of a state law that prohibited employment of women in factories or laundries for more than ten hours a day. The Court declined to follow one of its leading "freedom of contract" cases—*Lochner v. New York* (1905), which held unconstitutional a state law prohibiting more than sixty hours a week and more than ten hours a day working in a bakery—on the ground that a state had a stronger interest in regulating the hours of work of women than of men. The Court emphasized the physical differences between women and men, and stated that "history discloses the fact that woman has always been dependent upon man."

More recently, in *Goesaert v. Cleary* (1948), the Supreme Court upheld a state bartender-licensing rule that prohibited a woman from being licensed unless she was the wife or daughter of the owner of the establishment where she was to be employed.

The premise on which this decision was based was that women, unlike men, must be protected from working in surroundings that might be detrimental to their morals.

The attitudes toward sex discrimination displayed in *Muller, Goesaert,* and similar cases are gradually disappearing. Today there is an emerging recognition of the similarity between discrimination against women and discrimination against racial minorities, although the constitutional status of bias on sexual grounds has yet to be clearly resolved (see Chapter 11).

Some progress has also been made in fair-employment legislation. To take advantage of these laws, however, means learning to cope with the serpentine, overlapping, and often baffling complexities of the federal minimum-wage law; the Equal Pay Act; Title VII of the 1964 Civil Rights Act; several presidential executive orders; and various court decisions.

In the field of equal-employment opportunities and practices, national legislation is more comprehensive, and carries greater weight, than the many state laws modeled on federal statutes. That is, a woman who seeks relief for what she feels is discriminatory treatment on her job usually does so on the basis of federal guidelines and laws, resorting to her state's laws only if they will be especially helpful to her case.

If a woman believes she is being discriminated against, she should get legal assistance to understand how to proceed and how to evaluate her work situation. It cannot be said too often that this is an extremely complicated field. Law schools devote major portions of labor-law courses to learning how to interpret and bring lawsuits under Title VII of the Civil Rights Act, for example. It is also possible that instead of bringing an individual action, a woman may be able to join with others who have similar grievances in a class-action suit, something she would not be aware of if she were trying to handle everything on her own.

To complicate matters still further, all the criteria regulating fair-employment practices, minimum wages, and equality of pay are subject to exemptions. There may even be exceptions to the exemptions, depending on the circumstances. It is not entirely adequate, for example, to say that the minimum wage in a given state is $2.00 without citing every instance of what category of worker is affected by that law. This is also true of the provisions of the federal minimum-wage law; a listing in detail of which industries and employees are covered runs to hundreds of pages. In this limited discussion, it is pos-

sible to present only a broad outline of the provisions and coverage of the most important legislation.

Wage standards are governed by the federal Minimum Wage Act, which generally covers all employees in federal, state, and local government and in private business. Not included are executive, administrative, and professional employees, domestic and migrant workers, apprentices and trainees (in some cases), and part-time or temporary employees. All the included categories are further defined by whether the business engaged in is seasonal, interstate or intrastate, and whether it employs a certain number of people or does a specified dollar volume of business annually. There are precise tests to be applied in each category to determine whether an employer must pay the federal minimum wage. Similar criteria and tests apply to state minimum-wage laws in those states that have enacted them.

The federal minimum wage for eligible employees was raised from $1.60 to $2.10 an hour as of January 1975. It is scheduled to be raised again in January 1976, to $2.30 an hour. Not all states have minimum-wage laws, and of the twenty-eight that do, none has set a rate that is higher than the federal minimum.

Discrimination in the payment of wages is governed by the federal Equal Pay Act and is administered by the Wage and Hours Division of the U.S. Department of Labor. This act covers the same groups of workers as the minimum-wage law, with the addition of executive, administrative, and professional employees and labor unions. As is true in regard to minimum-wage legislation, there are many exemptions in all categories of employment and types of businesses covered by the Equal Pay Act, as well as special tests to clarify coverage.

Once an employee has determined whether he or she is covered under the provisions of the Equal Pay Act, it is still not a simple matter to figure out whether he or—more often—she is being discriminated against on the basis of sex. First, to make a claim of unequal wages a woman must show that her job is equal to that performed by her higher-paid male counterpart. "Equal work" means that the job requires equal skill, effort, and responsibility, and is performed under similar working conditions. Male workers can get higher wages than women doing the same work only on the basis of seniority, merit, quantity or quality of production, or any other factor not based solely on the sex of the lower-paid worker. If women are paid less than men for performing the same work, an employer cannot comply with the Equal Pay Act simply by reducing the pay of the male worker. Compliance requires *raising* the pay of the women workers to that of their male counterparts.

This aspect of the law was judicially clarified and enforced by a 1970 Supreme Court decision, *Schulz v. Wheaton Glass Co.*, which held that women performing work "substantially" equal to that of men should receive equal pay. Between 1964 and mid-1972, firms paying women less than men performing the same job were forced to repay almost $44.5 million to nearly 198,000 employees. More recently—in June 1974—Corning Glass Works was required to pay a million dollars in back salary as a result of another similar Supreme Court case that upheld the claims of women employees who had been receiving a lower base rate for daytime work than men performing the same jobs on another shift.

A woman has two remedies if she feels she is being underpaid in violation of the Equal Pay Act. She can file a written request with her local office of the Wage and Hours Division of the Department of Labor, which—after an investigation—may bring a suit on her behalf to recover the illegally underpaid wages. Or she can bring her own private lawsuit, by which she may recover twice the amount of underpaid wages, plus attorney's fees and the costs of the suit. The latter course is likely to be more expedient and more personally satisfying, but it is closed to women who cannot afford to gamble on getting back money paid out for legal fees.

Whichever alternative she chooses, however, she should get expert legal advice before proceeding. Many women's groups have legal counseling services, and are especially interested in sex discrimination in employ-

ment. Local chapters of the National Organization for Women or the American Civil Liberties Union should be able to give assistance and advice. Finally, there are feminist groups in the law schools of the larger universities which sometimes take an interest in such cases.

The Equal Pay Act also prohibits unions from causing or allowing employers to pay unequal wages to women doing the same work as men. Unions, like employers, can be fined up to $10,000 and their officers imprisoned for six months for willful violations of the act. Unlike employers, however, unions do not appear subject to claims for back pay through either the Labor Department or private lawsuits.

An even more important federal law for women's employment rights is Title VII of the 1964 Civil Rights Act. It covers, with some exceptions, private businesses with more than fifteen employees; federal, state, and local government workers; employment agencies; and labor organizations. (A description of how to file a discrimination suit under the provisions of Title VII is given on page 164.)

The extensive use of the sex provisions of Title VII indicates that equal-employment protection for women cannot be provided adequately by the Equal Pay Act, which covers only inequality of wages. Since the enactment of Title VII, the Equal Employment Opportunity Commission (EEOC), which is the federal agency responsible for administering Title VII, has reported that between 20 and 25 per cent of its cases are concerned with charges of sex discrimination.

For over ten years, however, the effectiveness of Title VII was inferior to that of the Equal Pay Act because the EEOC had power only to investigate and negotiate sex-discrimination disputes between employers and employees. It was unable to file charges on behalf of employees, who had to initiate court action themselves. The Equal Employment Opportunity Act of 1972 did away with that discrepancy by giving the EEOC enforcement power.

Title VII makes it unlawful for employers, employment agencies, and labor unions to discriminate in hiring, job classification, promotion, wages, fringe benefits, discharge, or any other "terms, conditions, and privileges" of employment. In its "Guidelines on Discrimination Because of Sex" (which may be ordered from the Equal Employment Opportunity Commission, Washington, D.C.), the EEOC specifically bars hiring based on stereotyped characterizations of the sexes; classifications labeled "men's jobs" or "women's jobs"; advertising under male or female headings; automatically terminating the employment of pregnant women; refusal to hire married women; differences in retirement age between men and women; and discrepancies between the sexes in such matters as sick leave and pay, vacation time and pay, classes given on company time, and payment while on jury duty.

But not all discrimination in employment is outlawed by Title VII. Discrimination is permitted in cases where sex is "a bona fide occupational qualification reasonably necessary to the normal operation of that particular business or enterprise." The precise meaning of the "bona fide occupational qualification" provision of the act is yet to be worked out fully by the courts.

So far, the EEOC interprets it narrowly, and has specified some practices it does *not* consider to be valid in judging bona fide occupational qualifications: (a) sex-based assumptions of comparative employment characteristics of men versus women, such as hiring based on the premise that the turnover rate of women is higher than for men; (b) stereotyped ideas about the sexes, such as "women work well with their hands" and should be placed in such positions while men are "thinkers" and should be placed in executive jobs; (c) refusal to hire women because of the preferences of co-workers, employers, clients, or customers; (d) deciding to hire anyone on the basis of his or her sex except for such jobs as actor, model, and restroom attendant. In one federal court case—*Rosenfeld v. Southern Pacific Railroad Co.* (1971) —the point was made that the only two jobs in which sex is a bona fide qualification are sperm donor and wet nurse!

The EEOC has also ruled that "separate lines of progression" based on sex are illegal. Thus policies that make it impossible for secretaries to move into the executive side of a business but do not place the same restrictions on mailboys violate Title VII. Title VII also prohibits discrimination against married women, holding they should receive the same benefits and consideration as married male employees do.

Another area in which Title VII bars discrimination concerns the child-care responsibilities of employed mothers versus employed fathers, but it took a Supreme Court decision—in *Phillips v. Martin Marietta Corporation* (1971)—to settle the issue, at least partially. In that case, Mrs. Ida Phillips sued Marietta, claiming that her rights under Title VII has been violated because she had been denied employment solely on the ground that she was the mother of pre-school-age children, although men with children of the same age were employed by the company. Before the case reached the Supreme Court, the EEOC had ruled that Marietta had violated Title VII, but two lower federal courts had disagreed, holding that Mrs. Phillips had been turned down not because she was a woman, but because she was a woman *with children of pre-school age*. When the Supreme Court got the case, it agreed with the Title VII ruling—that separate hiring policies for women and men with pre-school-age children are not automatically permitted.

The decision, however, was not a "definitive" one. Eight of the nine justices suggested that "such conflicting family obligations," if they proved to be more relevant to a woman's job performance than to a man's, *could* justify separate treatment under Title VII's bona fide occupational qualification provisions. Justice Thurgood Marshall, the Court's lone black member and only dissenter on this point, suggested that his colleagues had "fallen into the trap of assuming that the act permits ancient canards about the proper role of women to be a basis for discrimination."

Discrimination based upon sex is outlawed in Title VII whether directed against men or women. Thus men have recourse to Title VII's remedies if they feel they have been denied jobs or job-related benefits because of sex. The EEOC ruled, for example, that

Title VII is violated when an airline refuses to hire men as flight attendants because one's sex is not a bona fide qualification for such a job. It has also ruled that an employer cannot refuse to hire a male solely because his hair is shoulder-length unless the same restriction is applied to women employees.

One of the most difficult problems raised by the bona fide occupational qualification provisions of Title VII is the relationship between those provisions and a variety of state protective labor laws that apply only to women, such as requiring seats at work, regular rest periods, and minimum wages for female but not male employees. Some states prohibit employers from requiring or permitting women employees to work more than a designated number of hours per day or week, or to lift objects weighing more than a designated number of pounds.

The EEOC has divided protective laws into two categories: those providing women with distinct benefits, such as minimum-wage laws, and others, such as hours-limitation laws, that in the EEOC's opinion impose a burden on women by depriving them of the right to earn overtime pay or by keeping them out of jobs requiring overtime work. Over a half-dozen state hours-limitation laws have been challenged by women workers. Almost unanimously, the courts have invalidated these state laws as conflicting with the Title VII prohibition against sex discrimination in employment.

If the Supreme Court follows these decisions, it will be an important victory not only for the individual complainants in the cases but for all women employees—and perhaps eventually for male employees as well. Women will then be able to earn overtime pay on an equal basis with men, and their employers will no longer be able to invoke "protective" state laws to deny women jobs requiring occasional overtime work. This would create some new problems, however. For one thing, those women workers who are neither able to nor want to work overtime will have lost the genuine protection afforded by hours-limitation laws. For another, if these laws are extended to men—which most men would not object to with respect to minimum wages, rest periods, and seats at work—many male workers would resent interference with a right they have come to regard as their own: the opportunity to work overtime.

Regardless of the ultimate outcome of the court challenges to hours-limitation and similar protective laws for women only, new state and federal laws have been suggested that would embody the principle of voluntary overtime for everyone. These laws would permit both men and women to work a designated number of hours in excess of an established norm but would prohibit employers from discharging any employee for his or her refusal to work overtime.

Aside from protective labor laws governing employment conditions for women, many states have laws absolutely prohibiting women from working in certain occupations, most frequently mining, professional wrestling, or bartending. Many of these laws are being challenged as violating Title VII or on constitutional (equal protection) grounds, and some—for example, bartending restric-

tions— have been struck down in some states. Undoubtedly many more will be.

With its guidelines and rulings on individual complaints, the EEOC has begun to build a substantial body of legal doctrine in the employment sex-discrimination area. The courts have differed with the EEOC on some issues, but the general contours of American employment-discrimination law are beginning to emerge.

Anyone who thinks she has grounds to institute a suit on the basis of the provisions of Title VII should write or visit her regional office of the Equal Employment Opportunity Commission. The EEOC will determine if she is included in Title VII's coverage. If she is, she will fill out a form charging the company she works for with discrimination and giving the details of her case. The EEOC will then investigate and, if it finds the charge to be accurate, take the necessary steps to try to get the company to stop the practice. This is a complicated and time-consuming process, made even slower because the EEOC always has a backlog of cases.

If these efforts fail to gain compliance, the person who made the charge may want to take her case to court. Again, as is true when challenging discrimination in wages on the basis of the Equal Pay Act, it would be helpful to have support from a legal or paralegal group interested in sex discrimination in employment. This help would be absolutely essential if one were to take a case to court.

In addition to legislation and court cases, there are two federal executive orders pertinent to sex discrimination. One is Executive Order 11478, which prohibits discrimination on grounds of race, color, religion, national origin, and sex in all federal agencies; it is administered by the U.S. Civil Service Commission. The other is Executive Order 11246, which has the same prohibitions for all federal contractors and subcontractors—or at least all those who have a federal contract of $10,000 or more. This order is administered by the Office for Federal Contract Compliance (OFCC), which has issued "Sex Discrimination Guidelines" similar to those issued by the Equal Employment Opportunity Commission in behalf of Title VII.

Executive Order No. 4, issued in January 1970, requires all federal contractors with fifty or more employees and a contract of $50,000 or more not only to abide by the OFCC guidelines, but also to take "affirmative action" in setting goals and timetables for hiring minorities in job categories where they have been "underutilized." Revised Order No. 4, issued in December 1971, adds women to the minorities covered in the original order.

Revised Order No. 4 also sets forth standards to be used in determining whether enough women are being hired: the amount of female employment in the labor area surrounding the enterprise, the female proportion of the total work force in the immediate area, the general availability of women with the necessary skills, the availability of women eligible for promotion within the contractor's organization, the existence of training institutions capable of teaching persons the necessary skills, and the degree of training which the contractor is reasonably able to undertake as a means of making all job classifications available to women.

These orders are especially effective because noncompliance—or lack of affirmative action—by covered contractors and subcontractors may lead to suspension or cancellation of their federal contracts. This frightening prospect often motivates a firm to compliance where appealing to a supposed sense of fair play and human dignity fails. Federal officials, however, must try to obtain cooperation through mediation, conciliation, and persuasion before any penalties are invoked.

This is often a time-consuming and frustrating process.

A woman who works for a business or in an occupation not covered by Title VII, the Equal Pay Act, or an executive order may still have recourse to state equal-pay or anti-sex-discrimination laws. Many of these laws are modeled on the federal statutes, but they are just as complex and difficult to understand as the federal laws. A helpful book for the reader who wants a more complete picture of this very complicated field than can be given here is *The Rights of Women,* by Susan C. Ross (available in paperback). It is part of a series of handbooks produced under the aegis of the American Civil Liberties Union.

Equal employment is the most rapidly changing area of the law that affects women. The Equal Employment Opportunity Commission is one branch of the federal government that is moving in a positive direction. Lawsuits to correct long-standing inequalities are proliferating. They involve many millions of dollars of government-contract funds, especially to the big universities working on federal scientific and defense projects, as well as private business capital in some of this country's largest corporations.

Passage of the Equal Rights Amendment will strengthen the efforts of those working to end sexual discrimination in employment (see Chapter 11). But even if the amendment is finally ratified by the required number of states, it will not cause all sex discrimination to disappear as if by magic. It will still be up to women themselves to know their rights and to insist that their rights not be denied them.

8
When I Go to Work
The Law
State by State

ALABAMA

Occupations barred to women: Mining.
Equal pay laws: None.
Fair employment practices laws: None.
Minimum wage laws: None.
Maximum hours laws for women: None.

ALASKA

Occupations barred to women: None.
Equal pay laws: Yes.
Fair employment practices laws: Employers and labor unions may not discriminate because of sex—unless it is a bona fide occupational qualification—in hiring, compensation, union membership, or expulsion of members.
Minimum wage laws: Yes, but no rate specified by statute.
Maximum hours laws for women: None.

ARIZONA

Occupations barred to women: Mining, quarrying, work on coal breakers.
Equal pay laws: Yes.
Fair employment practices laws: Employers, employment agencies, and labor unions may not discriminate because of sex in hiring, firing, other terms, conditions, and privileges of employment, job placement and categorization, advertising relating to employment, union membership, or expulsion of members.
Minimum wage laws: None.
Maximum hours laws for women: None.

ARKANSAS

Occupations barred to women: Mining.
Equal pay laws: Yes.
Fair employment practices laws: None.
Minimum wage laws: Yes—$1.20 an hour.
Maximum hours laws for women: For most jobs, 8 hours a day, 48 hours a week (or longer at time and a half overtime). Some industries and executive or managerial employees are exempt.

CALIFORNIA

Occupations barred to women: None.
Equal pay laws: Yes.

Fair employment practices laws: Employers, employment agencies, and labor unions may not discriminate because of sex in hiring, compensation, other terms, conditions, and privileges of employment, advertising relating to employment, union membership, or training programs.

Minimum wage laws: None.

Maximum hours laws for women: 8 hours a day, 48 hours a week, in manufacturing, mechanical, and mercantile establishments, laundries, cleaners, hotels, apartments, hospitals, beauty and barber shops, amusement places, restaurants, cafeterias, telegraph and telephone offices, and as elevator operators in express and transportation companies.

COLORADO

Occupations barred to women: None.

Equal pay laws: Yes.

Fair employment practices laws: Employers and labor unions may not discriminate because of sex in hiring, firing, compensation, promotion, advertising relating to employment, or union membership.

Minimum wage laws: None.

Maximum hours laws for women: None.

CONNECTICUT

Occupations barred to women: None.

Equal pay laws: Yes.

Fair employment practices laws: Employers, employment agencies, and labor unions may not discriminate because of sex in hiring, firing, compensation, other terms, conditions, and privileges of employment, job placement, or union membership.

Minimum wage laws: None.

Maximum hours laws for women: 9 hours a day. 48 hours a week, in manufacturing and mechanical establishments; 8 hours a day, 6 days a week, in mercantile establishments; 9 hours a day, 6 days a week, in restaurants, barber shops, amusement places, shoeshine parlors, bowling alleys, billiard rooms, and photography galleries; 40 hours a week as entertainers.

DELAWARE

Occupations barred to women: None.

Equal pay laws: Yes.

Fair employment practices laws: Employers, employment agencies, and labor unions may not discriminate because of sex—unless it is a bona fide occupational qualification—in hiring, firing, compensation, other terms, conditions, and privileges of employment, job placement, union membership, training programs, or apprenticeships.

Minimum wage laws: Yes—$1.60 an hour.

Maximum hours laws for women: None.

DISTRICT OF COLUMBIA

Occupations barred to women: None.

Equal pay laws: None.

Fair employment practices laws: None.

Minimum wage laws: Yes, but no rate specified by statute.

Maximum hours laws for women: 8 hours a day, 48 hours a week, in manufacturing, mechanical, and mercantile establishments, laundries, hotels, restaurants, or express and transportation companies.

FLORIDA

Occupations barred to women: None.

Equal pay laws: Yes.

Fair employment practices laws: None.

Minimum wage laws: None.

Maximum hours laws for women: None.

GEORGIA

Occupations barred to women: None.

Equal pay laws: Yes.

Fair employment practices laws: None.

Minimum wage laws: Yes—$1.25 an hour.

Maximum hours laws for women: None.

HAWAII

Occupations barred to women: None.

Equal pay laws: Yes.

Fair employment practices laws: Employers, employment agencies, and labor unions may not discriminate because of sex in hiring, firing, compensation, other terms, conditions, and privileges of employment, job categorization, advertising relating to employment, union membership, or apprenticeships.

Minimum wage laws: Yes—$1.60 an hour.

Maximum hours laws for women: None.

IDAHO

Occupations barred to women: None.

Equal pay laws: Yes.

Fair employment practices laws: Employers, employment agencies, and labor unions may not discriminate because of sex in hiring, firing, compensation, other terms, conditions, and privileges of employment, job placement, advertising relating to employment, union membership, or classification of members.

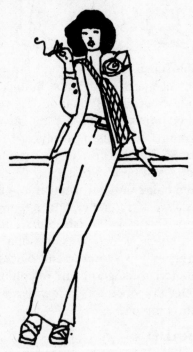

Minimum wage laws: Yes—$1.60 an hour.

Maximum hours laws for women: 8 hours a day, 48 hours a week (or longer at time and a half overtime), in mechanical and mercantile establishments, laundries, hotels, restaurants, telegraph and telephone offices, and express and transportation companies.

ILLINOIS

Occupations barred to women: Manual labor in mines. In addition, local communities have the power to prohibit any woman who is not herself a liquor licensee or the wife of a licensee from drawing, pouring, or mixing alcoholic beverages as an employee of the establishment.

Equal pay laws: Yes.

Fair employment practices laws: Employers, employment agencies, and labor unions may not discriminate because of sex in hiring, tenure, other terms and conditions of employment, job placement and referrals, union membership, classification of members, or apprenticeships.

Minimum wage laws: Yes—$1.75 an hour.

Maximum hours laws for women: 8 hours a day, 48 hours a week, in mechanical and mercantile establishments, factories, laundries, hotels, restaurants, barber and beauty shops, amusement places, telephone and telegraph offices, express and transportation companies, public utilities, common carriers, and public or private institutions.

INDIANA

Occupations barred to women: Mining.

Equal pay laws: Yes.

Fair employment practices laws: A civil rights commission has been established to investigate charges of sex discrimination in employment, to issue cease and desist orders, and to order any affirmative action such as restoration of back pay.

Minimum wage laws: Yes—$1.25 an hour.

Maximum hours laws for women: None.

IOWA

Occuptaions barred to women: None.

Equal pay laws: None.

Fair employment practices laws: Employers, employment agencies, and labor unions may not discriminate because of sex in hiring, firing, job categorization, advertising relating to employment, and union membership.

Minimum wage laws: None.

Maximum hours laws for women: None.

KANSAS

Occupations barred to women: None.

Equal pay laws: Yes.

Fair employment practices laws: Employers, employment agencies, and labor unions may not discriminate because of sex in hiring, firing, compensation, other terms, conditions, and privileges of employment, job categorization, union membership, training programs, or apprenticeships.

Minimum wage laws: None.

Maximum hours laws for women: The commissioner may establish a standard of wages, hours, and conditions of labor for women, minors, trainees, and apprentices.

KENTUCKY

Occupations barred to women: May work only as waitresses, cashiers, or ushers in connection with the sale of alcoholic beverages in taverns, bars, restaurants, and other such establishments.

Equal pay laws: Yes.

Fair employment practices laws: Employers, employment agencies, and labor unions may not discriminate because of sex in employment, job categorization, advertising relating to employment, union membership, training programs, or apprenticeships.

Minimum wage laws: Yes, but no rate specified by statute.

Maximum hours laws for women: 10 hours a day, 60 hours a week, in laundries, bakeries, factories, workshops, stores, mercantile, manufacturing, and mechanical establishments, hotels, restaurants, and telephone and telegraph offices.

LOUISIANA

Occupations barred to women: None.

Equal pay laws: None.

Fair employment practices laws: None.

Minimum wage laws: None.

Maximum hours laws for women: 8 hours a day, 48 hours a week, in manufacturing, mechanical, and mercantile establishments, laundries, hotels, theaters, restaurants, telegraph and telephone offices, transportation companies, and as elevator operators.

MAINE

Occupations barred to women: None.
Equal pay laws: Yes.
Fair employment practices laws: There are such laws, but they do not include discrimination because of sex in their provisions.
Minimum wage laws: Yes—$2.00 an hour.
Maximum hours laws for women: 9 hours a day, 54 hours a week, in workshops, nursing homes, beauty shops, hotels, amusement places, restaurants, dairies, bakeries, laundries, telegraph and telephone offices, and express and transportation companies; 50 hours a week in factories and mercantile, manufacturing, and mechanical establishments.

MARYLAND

Occupations barred to women: None.
Equal pay laws: Yes.
Fair employment practices laws: Employers, employment agencies, and labor unions may not discriminate because of sex in hiring, firing, compensation, other terms, conditions, and privileges of employment, job referrals, advertising relating to employment, union membership, training programs, or apprenticeships.
Minimum wage laws: Yes—$1.60 an hour.
Maximum hours laws for women: None—but no employee in factories manufacturing yarns and fabrics may work more than 10 hours a day.

MASSACHUSETTS

Occupations barred to women: None.
Equal pay laws: Yes.
Fair employment practices laws: Employers, employment agencies, and labor unions may not discriminate because of sex in hiring, firing,

compensation, other terms, conditions, and privileges of employment, job categorization, advertising relating to employment, or union membership.
Minimum wage laws: Yes—same as federal minimum ($2.10 an hour).
Maximum hours laws for women: 9 hours a day, 48 hours a week (although there are many exceptions), applies to most women except professional, executive, administrative, or supervisory personnel and personal secretaries. However, the courts have held this law inapplicable when it limits the rights of women to overtime on the same basis as men in positions that are covered by the federal Fair Employment Practices Act.

MICHIGAN

Occupations barred to women: Any job that is disproportionate to a woman's strength or which is located in a place detrimental to health, morals, or potential capacity for motherhood.
Equal pay laws: Yes.
Fair employment practices laws: Employers, employment agencies, and labor unions may not discriminate because of sex in hiring, promotion, tenure, other terms, conditions, and privileges of employment, job placement and categorization, advertising relating to employment, union membership, or classification of members.
Minimum wage laws: Yes—$1.60 an hour.
Maximum hours laws for women: None.

MINNESOTA

Occupations barred to women: Moving molds into and out of ovens in foundries.
Equal pay laws: Yes.
Fair employment practices laws: Employers, employment agencies, and labor unions may not discriminate because of sex in hiring, firing, compensation, promotion, other terms, conditions, and privileges of employment, job placement and categorization, advertising relating to employment, union membership, benefits of membership, or classification of members.

Minimum wage laws: None.
Maximum hours laws for women: 54 hours a week in public housekeeping, manufacturing, mercantile, and mechanical establishments, laundries, and as telephone operators in towns with populations over 1500.

MISSISSIPPI

Occupations barred to women: None.
Equal pay laws: None.
Fair employment practices laws: None.
Minimum wage laws: None.
Maximum hours laws for women: 10 hours a day, 60 hours a week, in all employment except domestic service.

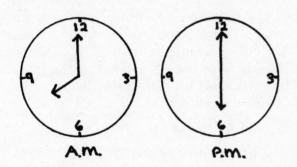

MISSOURI

Occupations barred to women: Mining, certain work around machinery.
Equal pay laws: Yes.
Fair employment practices laws: Employers, employment agencies, and labor unions may not discriminate because of sex in hiring, firing, compensation, other terms, conditions, and privileges of employment, job placement and categorization, advertising relating to employment, union membership, classification of members, or training programs.
Minimum wage laws: None.

Maximum hours laws for women: None.

MONTANA

Occupations barred to women: None.
Equal pay laws: Yes.
Fair employment practices laws: Employers may not discriminate because of sex in hiring, firing, compensation, or other terms, conditions, and privileges of employment.
Minimum wage laws: None.
Maximum hours laws for women: 8 hours a day in manufacturing, mercantile, and mechanical establishments, telephone and telegraph offices, foundries, hotels, and restaurants.

NEBRASKA

Occupations barred to women: None.
Equal pay laws: Yes.
Fair employment practices laws: Employers, employment agencies, and labor unions may not discriminate because of sex in hiring, firing, compensation, other terms, conditions, and privileges of employment, job placement and categorization, union membership, or classification of members.
Minimum wage laws: None.
Maximum hours laws for women: None.

NEVADA

Occupations barred to women: County liquor boards have the power to prohibit women from selling or dispensing liquor.
Equal pay laws: Yes.
Fair employment practices laws: Employers, employment agencies, and labor unions may not discriminate because of sex in hiring, firing, compensation, other terms, conditions, and privileges of employment, job placement and categorization, union membership, classification of members, or training programs.
Minimum wage laws: Yes—$2.00 an hour.
Maximum hours laws for women: 8 hours per 13-hour period, 48 hours a week, except for executives or supervisors who agree to longer hours.

NEW HAMPSHIRE

Occupations barred to women: None.
Equal pay laws: Yes.
Fair employment practices laws: Employers, employment agencies, and labor unions may not discriminate because of sex in hiring, firing, compensation, other terms, conditions, and privileges of employment, advertising relating to employment, or union membership.
Minimum wage laws: Yes—same as the federal minimum ($2.10 an hour).
Maximum hours laws for women: 10 hours a day, 48 hours a week, in mechanical and manual jobs in manufacturing establishments; 10¼ hours a day, 54 hours a week, in any other manual or mechanical jobs, except for household and domestic workers, laboratory technicians, nurses, and employment in hotels and cabins (including dining facilities), boarding-houses, telephone and telegraph offices, farming, and canneries handling perishables.

NEW JERSEY

Occupations barred to women: None.
Equal pay laws: Yes.
Fair employment practices laws: Employers, employment agencies, and labor unions may not discriminate because of sex or marital status in hiring, firing, compensation, promotion, other terms, conditions, and privileges of employment, job placement and referrals, advertising relating to employment, union membership, expulsion of members, or training programs.
Minimum wage laws: Yes—$1.75 an hour.
Maximum hours laws for women: None.

NEW MEXICO

Occupations barred to women: None.
Equal pay laws: None.
Fair employment practices laws: Employers, employment agencies, and labor unions may not discriminate because of sex in hiring, firing, compensation, promotion, job placement and categorization, advertising relating to employment, or union membership.
Minimum wage laws: Yes—$1.60 an hour.
Maximum hours laws for women: 8 hours a day, 40 hours a week, unless there is a written agreement for additional time, which shall be paid at time and a half overtime.

NEW YORK

Occupations barred to women: May not work in basements of mercantile establishments or restaurants unless permission is obtained from the industrial commissioner.
Equal pay laws: Yes.
Fair employment practices laws: Employers, employment agencies, and labor unions may not discriminate because of sex in hiring, firing, compensation, fringe benefits, job placement and categorization, advertising relating to employment, union membership, classification of members, or training programs.
Minimum wage laws: Yes—$1.85 an hour.
Maximum hours laws for women: 8 hours a day, 48 hours a week, for women under 21.

NORTH CAROLINA

Occupations barred to women: None.
Equal pay laws: None.
Fair employment practices laws: None.
Minimum wage laws: Yes—$1.80 an hour.
Maximum hours laws for women: 9 hours a day, 48 hours a week.

NORTH DAKOTA

Occupations barred to women: May not work in any job in surroundings detrimental to health or morals.
Equal pay laws: Yes.
Fair employment practices laws: None.
Minimum wage laws: None.
Maximum hours laws for women: None.

OHIO

Occupations barred to women: Mining; selling, mixing, or dispensing alcoholic beverages in es-

tablishments that cater exclusively to male customers.
Equal pay laws: Yes.
Fair employment practices laws: None.
Minimum wage laws: None.
Maximum hours laws for women: 8 hours a day, 48 hours a week.

OKLAHOMA

Occupations barred to women: May not be employed under conditions detrimental to health or morals.
Equal pay laws: Yes.
Fair employment practices laws: Employers, employment agencies, and labor unions may not discriminate because of sex in hiring, firing, compensation, other terms, conditions, and privileges of employment, job placement and categorization, advertising relating to employment, union membership, classification of members, or training programs.
Minimum wage laws: None.
Maximum hours laws for women: 9 hours a day, 54 hours a week.

OREGON

Occupations barred to women: None.
Equal pay laws: Yes.

Fair employment practices laws: Employers, employment agencies, and labor unions may not discriminate because of sex in hiring, firing, compensation, promotion, other terms, conditions, and privileges of employment, advertising relating to employment, or union membership.
Minimum wage laws: Yes—$1.75 an hour.
Maximum hours laws for women: 10 hours a day, 48 hours a week.

PENNSYLVANIA

Occupations barred to women: May not be employed in any occupation that is dangerous to life or limb or injurious to health or morals.
Equal pay laws: Yes.
Fair employment practices laws: Employers, employment agencies, and labor unions may not discriminate because of sex in hiring, firing, compensation, other terms, conditions, and privileges of employment, job placement and categorization, advertising relating to employment, union membership, or classification of members.
Minimum wage laws: Yes—$1.45 an hour.
Maximum hours laws for women: 10 hours a day, 48 hours a week.

RHODE ISLAND

Occupations barred to women: None.
Equal pay laws: Yes.
Fair employment practices laws: Employers, employment agencies, and labor unions may not discriminate because of sex in hiring, compensation, tenure, other terms, conditions, and privileges of employment, job placement and categorization, advertising relating to employment, union membership, or classification of members.
Minimum wage laws: Yes—$1.60 an hour.
Maximum hours laws for women: 9 hours a day, 48 hours a week.

SOUTH CAROLINA

Occupations barred to women: None.
Equal pay laws: None.
Fair employment practices laws: None.

Minimum wage laws: None.
Maximum hours laws for women: 8 hours a day, 40 hours a week, but only in certain industries.

SOUTH DAKOTA

Occupations barred to women: None.
Equal pay laws: Yes.
Fair employment practices laws: Employers, employment agencies, and labor unions may not discriminate because of sex in hiring, compensation, tenure, other terms, conditions, and privileges of employment, job placement, advertising relating to employment, union membership, training programs, or apprenticeships.
Minimum wage laws: Yes—$1.60 an hour.
Maximum hours laws for women: None.

TENNESSEE

Occupations barred to women: None.
Equal pay laws: None.
Fair employment practices laws: None.
Minimum wage laws: None.
Maximum hours laws for women: 10 hours a day, 50 hours a week.

TEXAS

Occupations barred to women: None.
Equal pay laws: None.
Fair employment practices laws: None.
Minimum wage laws: Yes—$1.40 an hour.
Maximum hours laws for women: None.

UTAH

Occupations barred to women: Work in smelters and mines if found by the industrial commission to be detrimental to health and safety.
Equal pay laws: Yes.
Fair employment practices laws: Employers, employment agencies, and labor unions may not discriminate because of sex in hiring, firing, compensation, promotion, job placement and referrals, advertising relating to employment, union membership, or training programs.

Minimum wage laws: None.
Maximum hours laws for women: None.

VERMONT

Occupations barred to women: None.
Equal pay laws: None.
Fair employment practices laws: Employers, employment agencies, and labor unions may not discriminate because of sex in compensation, job categorization, advertising relating to employment, union membership, or classification of members.
Minimum wage laws: Yes—$1.60 an hour.
Maximum hours laws for women: None.

VIRGINIA

Occupations barred to women: None.
Equal pay laws: None.
Fair employment practices laws: None.
Minimum wage laws: None.
Maximum hours laws for women: 9 hours a day, 48 hours a week.

WASHINGTON

Occupations barred to women: None.
Equal pay laws: Yes.
Fair employment practices laws: None, but a law has been enacted stating that women may pursue any calling open to men.
Minimum wage laws: Yes—$2.00 an hour.
Maximum hours laws for women: 8 hours a day.

WEST VIRGINIA

Occupations barred to women: Director of the Department of Mines.
Equal pay laws: Yes.
Fair employment practices laws: None.
Minimum wage laws: None.
Maximum hours laws for women: 48 hours a week.

WISCONSIN

Occupations barred to women: None.
Equal pay laws: None.
Fair employment practices laws: Employers, employment agencies, and labor unions may not discriminate because of sex in hiring, firing, compensation, other terms, conditions, and privileges of employment, job placement, or union membership.
Minimum wage laws: None.
Maximum hours laws for women: None.

WYOMING

Occupations barred to women: None.
Equal pay laws: Yes.
Fair employment practices laws: Employers, employment agencies, and labor unions may not discriminate because of sex in hiring, firing, compensation, promotion, job placement, or union membership.
Minimum wage laws: Yes—$1.50 an hour.
Maximum hours laws for women: 8 hours a day,

9
When I Commit a Crime

Crime is in one sense an equal-opportunity occupation; no one is barred from participation on grounds of race, religion, age, or sex. A woman is as capable as a man of committing murder, manslaughter, mayhem, burglary, larceny, robbery, arson, and so on. It is true that more men commit crimes than women do, and that only about one inmate out of twenty in correctional institutions is female. It is also true that women are more likely to commit embezzlement, forgery, and fraud rather than more aggressive crimes such as auto theft, burglary, robbery, and assault. Only one out of every six murders is the work of a woman.

But the rate at which women are being arrested for violent crimes is increasing much faster than it is for men. From 1960 to 1972, arrests for serious crimes rose 81 per cent for men and 256 per cent for women. Violent crimes committed by boys increased by 203 per cent; the rate for girls was an astronomical 388 per cent.

Some observers see a relationship between these statistics and the broader implications of the women's liberation movement, but Dr. Eleanor Emmens Maccoby, Professor of Psychology at Stanford University, the outstanding expert on male-female sex differences, states in her new book, *The Psychology of Sex Differences:*

Males are more aggressive than females. A sex difference in aggression has been observed in all cultures in which aggressive behavior has been observed. Boys are more aggressive physically and verbally. They engage in mock-fighting and aggressive fantasies as well as direct forms of aggression more frequently than girls. The sex difference manifests itself as soon as social play begins, at age two or two and a half. From an early age, the primary victims of male aggression are other males, not females.

Although both sexes become less aggressive with age, boys and men remain more aggressive through the college years. Little information is available for older adults.

Certain crimes, by their very nature, are difficult for a woman to take an active part in—rape, for example. Yet even here a woman may be charged as a principal in the first degree if she aids a man in his scheme to rape another woman, or if she is voluntarily present while another person is being raped. The penalties for a woman found guilty of this charge can be as severe as they are for the rapist himself.

The only crime for which more women than men are consistently arrested is prostitution. Some estimates place the female-to-male arrest ratio at forty to one. While prostitution may be engaged in by men with men or by women with women, the crime is almost invariably defined in terms of a male-female relationship. For example, prostitution is variously described in law as: "The practice of a female in offering her body to an indiscriminate intercourse with men for money or its equivalent," "indiscriminate sexual intercourse with males for compensation," and "common lewdness of a woman for gain."

A prostitute's customers may sometimes be prosecuted for secondary crimes—criminal fornication, lewdness, solicitation, trespassing, or association with a prostitute. But even where such laws exist, courts usually protect the prostitute's patron. Studies indicate that these secondary laws are invoked less to punish the man than to force him to cooperate with the authorities by testifying against the prostitute. Arrest and conviction of men for these crimes is rare, and a much milder sentence is commonly imposed than for prostitution.

Recent efforts in New York to prosecute the customers of prostitutes proved futile because of the difficulties in gathering evidence, thereby making it impossible to build solid cases against the men. The police in Washington, D.C., began a campaign against the predominantly suburban clientele of urban prostitutes during the summer of 1970, but the resulting clamor by men was so overwhelming that the program was dropped within a month. Though everyone recognizes that without customer demand prostitution would not exist, it seems clear that the prostitution laws—and the discriminatory way in which they are enforced—will not be changed until they are successfully challenged on constitutional grounds.

But if crime is an equal-opportunity occupation, punishment sometimes is not. More often judges give harsher penalties to men than they do to women who commit the same crime. Yet there are some instances of longer prison sentences being given to women than to men guilty of the same crime. Recent federal court decisions in Connecticut, New Jersey, and Pennsylvania have reversed unequal sentences because they violate the constitutional guarantee of equal protection under the law. When an unequal sentence is imposed, however, it is often due less to a specific law mandating a different penalty for men and women than to the discretion of the judge who is handing out the sentence. The variations in sentencing may be well within the limits set by law.

In well over half the states a wife cannot be found guilty of certain minor crimes if she performs them in her husband's presence or with his knowledge. Here the law assumes that he coerced her and that she is not to be held responsible for her inability to resist his influence. As was pointed out in Chapter 1, this distinction is a vestige of the old common-law concept of husband and wife as one person, that one person being the husband. Such laws are a prime target for reform. They smack of the same paternalism which underlies "protective" labor laws (see Chapter 8).

Utah is the one state that still recognizes another kind of discrimination in the operation of criminal law, which is called the "unwritten law defense." This statute permits a man to kill "in the heat of passion" to prevent "rape or defilement" of a wife, daughter, sister, or mother. It has been interpreted by court decisions to be a valid defense for a husband who kills a man he finds committing adultery with his wife. This defense may not be used, however, by a wife who kills the "other woman" under identical circumstances. Texas and New Mexico have recently repealed similar statutes. This law is now being challenged in California courts in the Inez Garcia rape case.

In the field of criminal law, discrimination in America is less likely to be sexual than it is racial and economic. Nonetheless, a basic familiarity with our criminal procedures is essential to understanding how our society works.

The major efforts of courts and legislatures in the field of criminal law and procedure are directed toward two goals. One is the safeguarding of the general public against criminal and other antisocial activities. The other is the preservation of constitutional rights and guarantees of persons who are or might be accused and convicted of crimes.

The reasons for the first goal are self-evident: society could not survive if people were free to kill, rape, assault, and steal from one another at will. Indeed, one of the major functions of government is to offer protection from such dangers. The reasons for the second goal—the preservation of the constitutional rights of all persons—may not be as readily apparent. Many critics of our judicial system accuse it of being too lenient, of coddling criminals and disregarding the rights of "law-abiding citizens." These champions of "law and order" forget that constitutional safeguards protect everyone, including those accused and convicted of crimes. The law not only provides that a person is innocent until proven guilty; it also allows a convicted person to retain certain constitutional rights, though *which* rights is a constant source of litigation.

Both from experience and from a sense of history, the Founding Fathers were keenly aware of the vulnerability of ordinary men and women to government abuse. The rack and screw, "confessions" coerced out of the innocent as well as the guilty, unannounced searches and seizures by governmental authorities, and the absence of any right to be represented by counsel when accused of crime were excesses familiar to our colonial leaders. To protect against such abuse in the new nation, specific safeguards were written into the Constitution and the Bill of Rights.

These safeguards impose the duty of "law and order" upon those who administer the criminal law as well as those who are subject to it. Government thus has a constitutional as well as moral obligation to set an example to the rest of society. When government and law-enforcement officials fail in that duty, the injury to the legal order is severe indeed. For these reasons, the Supreme Court has—at least until recently—frequently reversed criminal convictions and required retrials if unconstitutionally obtained evidence has been used. Such convictions are the result of lawless activity on the part of law-enforcement officials. The Warren Court in particular upheld the principle that it is better for a guilty person to go free, if it is impossible to prove guilt without unconstitutional evidence, than for an innocent person to be convicted.

Freed of constitutional restraints in their activities, law-enforcement officials would of course have an easier job. But the price to human liberty is too great. Experience has demonstrated that when police are not allowed to rely on legally questionable methods, they tend to develop more efficient ways to prevent, detect, and investigate crime.

Restraints on law enforcement stem principally from the Bill of Rights. The Fourth Amendment prohibits unreasonable searches and seizures. The Fifth Amendment creates the privilege against compulsory self-incrimination, requires grand jury indictment in certain classes of cases, and says that no person shall be "subject for the same offense to be twice put in jeopardy of life or limb." The Sixth Amendment guarantees the right to a speedy and public trial by an impartial jury, provides that the accused shall be permitted to know the nature of the charges and to confront the accuser, and guarantees the right to counsel. The Eighth Amendment prohibits excessive bail, unrea-

sonable fines, and cruel and unusual punishments. All of these specific provisions of the Bill of Rights were originally designed as protections against the federal government, but now also apply in state criminal proceedings in accordance with the due process clause of the Fourteenth Amendment. In addition, many state constitutions have provisions similar to all or some of those found in the Bill of Rights.

The Fourth Amendment's prohibition against unreasonable searches and seizures is one of the most important constitutional guarantees, whether or not one is likely to be accused of a crime. It guarantees privacy and freedom from arbitrary, unpredictable government intrusions. It also prevents random or "dragnet" searches for persons or property. In conjunction with the Fifth Amendment's self-incrimination privilege and the Sixth's guarantee of a speedy public trial, it prevents officials from engaging in police-state practices.

There are two sets of problems in interpreting and applying the Fourth Amendment's protection. The first is to determine what are the circumstances that justify an arrest; when an arrest or search can be made without obtaining a search warrant; and what, who, or how much can be legally seized or searched. The second is to determine how to keep law-enforcement officials from engaging in unconstitutional searches and seizures. The famous 1961 Supreme Court case of *Mapp v. Ohio* held that evidence procured by state officers through an illegal search or seizure could not be used in a state court, thus extending to the states the federal rule that barred illegally obtained evidence in

federal court prosecutions. Further, evidence may not be used if it could only have been secured on the basis of earlier illegal evidence. For example, if the police search someone's home without first getting the required search warrant and as a result discover evidence of another crime, this evidence is considered "tainted" and cannot be used in court.

The present Supreme Court has rendered several decisions that limit the scope of the Fourth Amendment. Consider two 1973 decisions. Both involved suspects arrested on traffic violations who were then subsequently searched and found to possess drugs (marijuana in one case, heroin in the other). The Court held the searches constitutional even though there was no probable cause to believe that either traffic violator possessed drugs. Therefore the drugs were admissible as evidence in subsequent drug (felony) prosecutions of the traffic violators. As a result, the police have blanket authority to search—without a warrant—the person and property of anyone lawfully arrested for any crime, however minor. Any evidence obtained from such a search may be used in court no matter how unrelated it is to the charge on which he or she was arrested.

The two most important aspects of the Fifth Amendment privilege against self-incrimination are, first, that persons accused of a crime cannot be required to testify in their own criminal prosecutions, though they may testify on their own behalf if they want to. Second, even if a person is called as a witness in proceedings where someone else is the accused, he or she may refuse to testify at all or, more particularly, may refuse to answer specific questions if answering might tend to be incriminating.

In 1966, in the renowned *Miranda* decision, the Supreme Court ruled that statements of a person in custody are not admissible in the criminal prosecution if the defendant had not been informed of the right to remain silent, the right of the prosecution to use any statement of the accused against him or her, the right to have an attorney present at the interrogation, and the right to have a court-appointed attorney if the accused could not afford to hire an attorney. The *Miranda* decision protects the accused person who, because of ignorance, fear, or poverty, would not know of her or his constitutional right to remain silent.

A very special case was found with which to test the scope of the *Miranda* decision. A man arrested—and subsequently convicted—on a rape charge was advised of his right to remain silent and his right to counsel, but not of his right to *free* counsel. He appealed his conviction on the grounds that his Fifth Amendment rights as spelled out in *Miranda* had been violated. In June 1974 the Supreme Court upheld the conviction, noting that the *Miranda* decision was to be viewed as only a "guideline" rather than as an absolute command. This would seem to open the door for a renewal of all the abuses the *Miranda* ruling was to counteract in the first place.

The Sixth Amendment's right-to-counsel guarantee was originally meant to give persons accused of crime the right to be represented by a lawyer—a right not always available under English law. The amendment did not require that counsel be appointed at public expense if the accused person was too poor to hire an attorney. However, the guarantee of counsel was interpreted by the Supreme Court as requiring the appointment of free counsel, when necessary, in federal court prosecutions. Then, in 1963, in the case of *Gideon v. Wainwright,* the Court held that the right to court-appointed counsel extends to defendants prosecuted in state courts as well. Finally, in 1972, the Court ruled that the Sixth Amendment right to counsel applies to all criminal defendants.

The Eighth Amendment's prohibition of cruel and unusual punishment has only recently received important consideration. The problem has been to determine both what is "punishment" and whether it is "cruel and unusual." The Court has held, for instance, that the Eighth Amendment prohibits a state from executing a prisoner who has become insane after imprisonment; it has also ruled that convicting someone on the ground that he or she is a narcotics addict constitutes "cruel and unusual punishment." By contrast, the Court has upheld a state law that makes it a crime to be under the influence of alcohol in public.

In the very important and controversial case of *Furman v. Georgia,* the Supreme Court held (in 1972) that the death penalty is a cruel and unusual punishment. However, since there was not one opinion to which a majority of the justices subscribed, the precise basis of the decision is unclear. Depending on which opinion in *Furman* is followed, laws recently enacted in almost half the states that impose the death penalty for a limited group of specified crimes may or may not violate the Eighth Amendment. Clarification will have to await a case in which the Supreme Court decisively answers the question of whether capital punishment is in and of itself, regardless of how it is meted out, "cruel and unusual punishment."

To those who care about our constitutional guarantees of due process and fairness for all, there are disturbing trends in the criminal-justice field. Although the Burger Court has made a number of "liberal" rulings, the bulk of its decisions on criminal-procedure cases indicate a pro-law-enforcement, anti-criminal-defendant attitude, as exemplified in the 1973 Fourth Amendment cases and 1974 post-*Miranda* decision discussed in this chapter. If this trend is not reversed, our constitutional guarantees in the area of criminal justice may gradually be eroded into nonexistence.

9
When I Commit a Crime
The Law
State by State

ALABAMA

Coercion by husband: The law holds that a wife is not responsible for committing certain crimes in her husband's presence, nor is she responsible if he threatened or commanded her to commit them.

Conspiracy between spouses: A husband and wife cannot be guilty of conspiring with each other.

Testimony against wife: A husband may not be compelled to testify for or against his wife in a criminal proceeding if he chooses not to.

ALASKA

Coercion by husband: The law holds that a wife is not responsible for committing certain crimes in her husband's presence because he is presumed to have forced her to commit them.

Conspiracy between spouses: A husband and wife cannot be guilty of conspiring with each other.

Testimony against wife: A husband may not testify against his wife in a criminal proceeding without her consent, and he may not reveal any confidential communication between him and his wife during the marriage.

ARIZONA

Coercion by husband: The law holds that a wife is not responsible for committing misdemeanors if her husband threatened or commanded her to commit them, but she is responsible for any felonies she commits.

Conspiracy between spouses: A husband and wife cannot be guilty of conspiring with each other.

Testimony against wife: A husband may not testify against his wife in a criminal proceeding without her consent unless she is charged with a crime against him or with bigamy, adultery, seduction, or crimes against nature.

ARKANSAS

Coercion by husband: The law holds that a wife is not responsible for committing certain crimes if her husband threatened or commanded her to commit them as long as the husband is prosecuted as a principal and receives the punishment the wife would have received.

Conspiracy between spouses: A husband and wife cannot be guilty of conspiring with each other.

Testimony against wife: A husband may not testify against his wife in a criminal proceeding

unless he is charging her with injury to him or his property.

CALIFORNIA

Coercion by husband: The law holds that a wife is not responsible for committing misdemeanors if her husband threatened or commanded her to commit them, but she is responsible for any felonies she commits.

Conspiracy between spouses: A husband and wife cannot be guilty of conspiring with each other.

Testimony against wife: A husband may not testify against his wife without her consent and he may not be compelled to testify if he chooses not to unless she is charged with a crime against him or their children or with bigamy, adultery, or abandonment.

COLORADO

Coercion by husband: The law holds that a wife is not responsible for committing certain crimes if her husband threatened or commanded her to commit them unless the crime is punishable by death.

Conspiracy between spouses: A husband and wife

may validly be prosecuted for conspiring with each other.

Testimony against wife: A husband may not testify against his wife in a criminal proceeding without her consent unless she is charged with a crime against him.

CONNECTICUT

Coercion by husband: The law holds that a wife is not responsible for committing certain crimes in her husband's presence because he is presumed to have forced her to commit them.

Conspiracy between spouses: A husband and wife cannot be guilty of conspiring with each other.

Testimony against wife: A husband may not be compelled to testify against his wife in a criminal proceeding unless she has been charged with a crime against him or their children or with a crime involving her own immoral conduct.

DELAWARE

Coercion by husband: The law holds that a wife is not responsible for committing certain crimes in her husband's presence because he is presumed to have forced her to commit them.

Conspiracy between spouses: A husband and wife cannot be guilty of conspiring with each other, but both can be charged with conspiracy if a third person joins with them in committing the crime.

Testimony against wife: A husband may testify for or against his wife in a criminal proceeding, but he may not reveal any confidential communication between him and his wife during the marriage.

DISTRICT OF COLUMBIA

Coercion by husband: The law holds that a wife is not responsible for committing certain crimes in her husband's presence because he is presumed to have forced her to commit them.

Conspiracy between spouses: A husband and wife may validly be prosecuted for conspiring with each other.

Testimony against wife: A husband may not be compelled to testify for or against his wife if he chooses not to, and he may not reveal any confidential communication between him and his wife during the marriage.

FLORIDA

Coercion by husband: The law holds that a wife is not responsible for committing certain crimes in her husband's presence, nor is she responsible if he threatened or commanded her to commit them.

Conspiracy between spouses: A husband and wife cannot be guilty of conspiring with each other.

Testimony against wife: A husband may testify against his wife in a criminal proceeding, but he may not reveal any confidential communication between him and his wife during the marriage.

GEORGIA

Coercion by husband: There is no legal presumption that a wife is not responsible for a crime committed in her husband's presence, but if he actually threatened or commanded her to commit it she will be excused.

Conspiracy between spouses: A husband and wife cannot be guilty of conspiring with each other.

Testimony by husband: A husband may not testify against his wife in a criminal proceeding except in certain special cases or unless she is charged with a crime against him, and in any case he may not reveal any confidential communication between him and his wife during the marriage.

HAWAII

Coercion by husband: The law holds that a wife is not responsible for committing certain crimes in her husband's presence because he is presumed to have forced her to commit them.

Conspiracy between spouses: A husband and wife cannot be guilty of conspiring with each other.

Testimony against wife: A husband may not be compelled to testify against his wife in a criminal proceeding.

IDAHO

Coercion by husband: There is no legal presumption that a wife is not responsible for a crime committed in her husband's presence, but if he actually threatened or commanded her to commit it she will be excused unless the crime is punishable by death.

Conspiracy between spouses: A husband and wife cannot be guilty of conspiring with each other.

Testimony against wife: A husband may not testify for or against his wife in a criminal proceeding without both his and her consent unless she is charged with a crime of violence against him.

ILLINOIS

Coercion by husband: There is no legal presumption that a wife is not responsible for a crime committed in her husband's presence, but if he actually threatened or commanded her to commit it she may be excused.

Conspiracy between spouses: A husband and wife may validly be prosecuted for conspiring with each other.

Testimony against wife: A husband may testify for or against his wife in a criminal proceeding, but he may not reveal any confidential communication between him and his wife during the marriage. However, if she is charged with a crime of theft or injury against her husband or their children, he may testify even to private conversations between them.

INDIANA

Coercion by husband: The law holds that a wife is not responsible for committing certain crimes in her husband's presence, nor is she responsible if he threatened or commanded her to commit them.

Conspiracy between spouses: A husband and wife cannot be guilty of conspiring with each other.

Testimony against wife: A husband may not testify against his wife in a criminal proceeding as to any confidential communications between him and his wife during the marriage unless she is charged with failure to support their children.

IOWA

Coercion by husband: There is no legal presumption that a wife is not responsible for a crime committed in her husband's presence, but if he actually threatened or commanded her to commit it she will be excused.

Conspiracy between spouses: A husband and wife cannot be guilty of conspiring with each other.

Testimony against wife: A husband may not testify against his wife in a criminal proceeding unless she is charged with a crime against him.

KANSAS

Coercion by husband: There is no legal presumption that a wife is not responsible for a crime committed in her husband's presence, but if he actually threatened or commanded her to commit it she will be excused.

Conspiracy between spouses: A husband and wife cannot be guilty of conspiring with each other.

Testimony against wife: A husband may not testify against his wife in a criminal proceeding without her consent as to any confidential communication between them during the marriage unless she is charged with a crime against him or their children or the crime involves the marriage, including desertion.

KENTUCKY

Coercion by husband: There is no legal presumption that a wife is not responsible for a crime committed in her husband's presence, but if he actually threatened or commanded her to commit it she may be excused.

Conspiracy between spouses: A husband and wife cannot be guilty of conspiring with each other.

Testimony against wife: A husband may not be compelled to testify against his wife if he chooses not to, and he may not reveal any confidential communication between him and his wife during the marriage.

LOUISIANA

Coercion by husband: The law holds that a wife is not responsible for committing certain crimes in her husband's presence, nor is she responsible if he threatened or commanded her to commit them.

Conspiracy between spouses: A husband and wife cannot be guilty of conspiring with each other.

Testimony against wife: A husband may not be compelled to testify against his wife if he chooses not to, and he may not reveal any confidential communication between him and his wife during the marriage.

MAINE

Coercion by husband: The law holds that a wife is not responsible for committing certain crimes in her husband's presence, nor is she responsible if he threatened or commanded her to commit them.

Conspiracy between spouses: A husband and wife cannot be guilty of conspiring with each other.

Testimony against wife: A husband may testify against his wife in a criminal proceeding, but he may not reveal any confidential communication between him and his wife during the marriage.

MARYLAND

Coercion by husband: There is no legal presumption that a wife is not responsible for a crime committed in her husband's presence.

Conspiracy between spouses: A husband and wife cannot be guilty of conspiring with each other.

Testimony against wife: A husband may not be compelled to testify against his wife in a criminal proceeding unless she is charged with a crime against any of their children who are under 18, and he may not reveal any confidential communication between him and his wife during the marriage.

MASSACHUSETTS

Coercion by husband: The law holds that a wife is not responsible for committing certain crimes in her husband's presence, nor is she responsible if he threatened or commanded her to commit them.

Conspiracy between spouses: A husband and wife cannot be guilty of conspiring with each other.

Testimony against wife: A husband may not be compelled to testify against his wife in a criminal

proceeding if he chooses not to, and he may not reveal any confidential communication between him and his wife unless she is charged with nonsupport.

MICHIGAN

Coercion by husband: There is no legal presumption that a wife is not responsible for a crime committed in her husband's presence.

Conspiracy between spouses: A husband and wife cannot be guilty of conspiring with each other.

Testimony against wife: A husband may not testify for or against his wife in a criminal proceeding without her consent unless she is charged with a personal crime against him or their children or with bigamy or adultery.

MINNESOTA

Coercion by husband: There is no legal presumption that a wife is not responsible for a crime

Jones X132578   Jones X132578

committed in her husband's presence.

Conspiracy between spouses: A husband and wife cannot be guilty of conspiring with each other.

Testimony against wife: A husband may not testify against his wife in a criminal proceeding—either during the marriage or after it—without her consent unless she is charged with a crime against him or their children or with homicide or attempted homicide.

MISSISSIPPI

Coercion by husband: The law holds that a wife

is not responsible for committing certain crimes in her husband's presence because he is presumed to have forced her to commit them.

Conspiracy between spouses: A husband and wife cannot be guilty of conspiring with each other, but both can be charged if a third person joined with them in committing the crime.

Testimony against wife: A husband may not testify against his wife in a criminal proceeding without her consent unless she is charged with desertion, nonsupport, or contributing to the delinquency of their children.

MISSOURI

Coercion by husband: The law holds that a wife is not responsible for committing certain crimes in her husband's presence, nor is she responsible if he threatened or commanded her to commit them.

Conspiracy between spouses: A husband and wife cannot be guilty of conspiring with each other.

Testimony against wife: A husband may not be compelled to testify against his wife if he chooses not to, nor may he be compelled to reveal any confidential communication between him and his wife during the marriage.

MONTANA

Coercion by husband: The law holds that a wife is not responsible for committing misdemeanors if her husband threatened or commanded her to commit them, but she is responsible for any felonies she commits.

Conspiracy between spouses: A husband and wife cannot be guilty of conspiring with each other.

Testimony against wife: A husband may not testify for or against his wife in a criminal proceeding without her consent, and he may not reveal any confidential communication between him and his wife during the marriage.

NEBRASKA

Coercion by husband: There is no legal presumption that a wife is not responsible for a crime committed in her husband's presence.

Conspiracy between spouses: A husband and wife cannot be guilty of conspiring with each other.

Testimony against wife: A husband may not testify against his wife in a criminal proceeding unless she is charged with a crime against him or with abandonment or bigamy.

NEVADA

Coercion by husband: The law holds that a wife is not responsible for committing certain crimes if her husband threatened or commanded her to commit them unless the crime is punishable by death.

Conspiracy between spouses: A husband and wife cannot be guilty of conspiring with each other.

Testimony against wife: A husband may not testify against his wife in a criminal proceeding without her consent unless she is charged with a crime against him or their child or with bigamy or adultery.

NEW HAMPSHIRE

Coercion by husband: The law holds that a wife is not responsible for committing certain crimes in her husband's presence because he is presumed to have forced her to commit them.

Conspiracy between spouses: A husband and wife cannot be guilty of conspiring with each other.

Testimony against wife: A husband may testify against his wife, but he may not reveal any confidential communication between him and his wife during the marriage. However, if she is charged with child abuse or neglect he may testify even to private conversations between them.

NEW JERSEY

Coercion by husband: There is no legal presumption that a wife is not responsible for a crime committed in her husband's presence, but if he actually threatened or commanded her to commit it she will be excused.

Conspiracy between spouses: A husband and wife

cannot be guilty of conspiring with each other. **Testimony against wife:** A husband may not testify for or against his wife in a criminal proceeding without both his and her consent unless the wife is charged with a crime against him or their children, the husband is the complainant, or the testimony will prove the validity of the marriage.

NEW MEXICO

Coercion by husband: There is no legal presumption that a wife is not responsible for a crime committed in her husband's presence.

Conspiracy between spouses: A husband and wife cannot be guilty of conspiring with each other.

Testimony against wife: No statute.

NEW YORK

Coercion by husband: There is no legal presumption that a wife is not responsible for a crime committed in her husband's presence.

Conspiracy between spouses: A husband and wife cannot be guilty of conspiring with each other.

Testimony against wife: A husband may not testify as to any confidential communication between him and his wife during the marriage without the wife's consent. If she is charged with adultery, the husband may not testify except to prove the marriage.

NORTH CAROLINA

Coercion by husband: The law holds that a wife is not responsible for committing certain crimes in her husband's presence, nor is she responsible if he threatened or commanded her to commit them.

Conspiracy between spouses: A husband and wife may validly be prosecuted for conspiring with each other.

Testimony against wife: A husband may not be compelled to testify against his wife in a criminal proceeding unless she is charged with assault against him, with bigamy or criminal cohabitation, or if the testimony will prove the validity of the marriage or of a divorce or annulment.

NORTH DAKOTA

Coercion by husband: The law holds that a wife is not responsible for committing certain crimes in her husband's presence because he is presumed to have forced her to commit them.

Coercion between spouses: A husband and wife cannot be guilty of conspiring with each other.

Testimony against wife: A husband may not testify for or against his wife in a criminal proceeding without her consent.

OHIO

Coercion by husband: There is no legal presumption that a wife is not responsible for a crime committed in her husband's presence, but if he actually threatened or commanded her to commit it she will be excused.

Conspiracy between spouses: A husband and wife cannot be guilty of conspiring with each other.

Testimony against wife: A husband may not testify against his wife in a criminal proceeding as to any confidential communication between them during the marriage unless this communication was heard by a third person.

OKLAHOMA

Coercion by husband: The law holds that a wife is not responsible for committing certain crimes in her husband's presence, nor is she responsible if he threatened or commanded her to commit them.

Conspiracy between spouses: A husband and wife cannot be guilty of conspiring with each other, but both may be charged with conspiracy if a third person joined them in committing the crime.

Testimony against wife: A husband may not testify against his wife in a criminal proceeding unless she is charged with a crime against him or a minor child in their custody.

OREGON

Coercion by husband: There is no legal presumption that a wife is not responsible for a crime committed in her husband's presence, but if he actually threatened or commanded her to commit it she will be excused.

Conspiracy between spouses: A husband and wife cannot be guilty of conspiring with each other.

Testimony against wife: A husband may not testify against his wife in a criminal proceeding without her consent unless she is charged with a crime against him or a minor child in their custody.

PENNSYLVANIA

Coercion by husband: The law holds that a wife is not responsible for committing certain crimes in her husband's presence because he is presumed to have forced her to commit them.

Conspiracy between spouses: A husband and wife cannot be guilty of conspiring with each other, but both may be charged with conspiracy if a third person joined them in committing the crime.

Testimony against wife: A husband may not testify against his wife in a criminal proceeding unless she is charged with threatened or actual bodily harm to him or to any child in their care.

RHODE ISLAND

Coercion by husband: The law holds that a wife is not responsible for committing certain crimes in her husband's presence because he is presumed to have forced her to commit them.

Conspiracy between spouses: A husband and wife cannot be guilty of conspiring with each other.

Testimony against wife: A husband may not testify against his wife in a criminal proceeding as to any confidential communication between him and his wife during the marriage unless she is charged with pandering.

SOUTH CAROLINA

Coercion by husband: The law holds that a wife is not responsible for committing certain crimes in her husband's presence, nor is she responsible if he threatened or commanded her to commit them.

Conspiracy between spouses: A husband and wife cannot be guilty of conspiring with each other.

Testimony against wife: A husband may testify against his wife, but he may not reveal any confidential communication between him and his wife during the marriage.

SOUTH DAKOTA

Coercion by husband: The law holds that a wife is not responsible for committing certain crimes in her husband's presence, nor is she responsible if he threatened or commanded her to commit them.

Conspiracy between spouses: A husband and wife cannot be guilty of conspiring with each other.

Testimony against wife: A husband may not testify against his wife without her consent unless she is charged with physical injury to him or to a minor, or unless the charge involves her moral reputation.

TENNESSEE

Coercion by husband: There is no legal presumption that a wife is not responsible for a crime committed in her husband's presence.

Conspiracy between spouses: A husband and wife cannot be guilty of conspiring with each other.

Testimony against wife: A husband may testify for or against his wife in a civil proceeding, but he may not reveal any confidential communication between him and his wife during the marriage.

TEXAS

Coercion by husband: There is no legal presumption that a wife is not responsible for a crime committed in her husband's presence; if he actually threatened or commanded her to commit it, however, she will not be excused but her sentence will be reduced.

Conspiracy between spouses: A husband and wife may validly be prosecuted for conspiring with each other.

Testimony against wife: A husband may testify against his wife, but he may not reveal any confidential communication between him and her during the marriage.

UTAH

Coercion by husband: There is no legal presumption that a wife is not responsible for a crime committed in her husband's presence, but if he actually threatened or commanded her to commit it she will be excused.

Conspiracy between spouses: A husband and wife cannot be guilty of conspiring with each other.

Testimony against wife: A husband may not testify against his wife without her consent unless she is charged with criminal violence against him or with pandering.

VERMONT

Coercion by husband: The law holds that a wife is not responsible for committing certain crimes in her husband's presence because he is presumed to have forced her to commit them.

Conspiracy between spouses: A husband and wife cannot be guilty of conspiring with each other.

Testimony against wife: A husband may testify against his wife, but he may not reveal any con-fidential communication between him and her during the marriage.

VIRGINIA

Coercion by husband: There is no legal presumption that a wife is not responsible for a crime committed in her husband's presence, but if he actually threatened or commanded her to commit it she may be excused.

Conspiracy between spouses: A husband and wife cannot be guilty of conspiring with each other.

Testimony against wife: A husband may not be compelled to testify against his wife in a criminal proceeding without both his and her consent unless she is charged with a crime against him or any of their children under 19 or with having forged her husband's name.

WASHINGTON

Coercion by husband: The law holds that a wife is not responsible for committing certain crimes in her husband's presence because he is presumed to have forced her to commit them.

Conspiracy between spouses: A husband and wife cannot be guilty of conspiring with each other.

Testimony against wife: A husband may not testify against his wife in a criminal proceeding unless she is accused of committing a crime against him or a minor child in her custody.

WEST VIRGINIA

Coercion by husband: The law holds that a wife is not responsible for committing certain crimes in her husband's presence, nor is she responsible if he threatened or commanded her to commit them.

Conspiracy between spouses: A husband and wife cannot be guilty of conspiring with each other.

Testimony against wife: A husband may not testify against his wife in a criminal proceeding unless she is charged with a crime against him, one of their children, or the father, mother, sister, or brother of either spouse. He may not reveal any confidential communication between him and his wife during the marriage without his wife's permission.

WISCONSIN

Coercion by husband: There is no legal presumption that a wife is not responsible for a crime committed in her husband's presence, but if he actually threatened or commanded her to commit it she may be excused.

Conspiracy between spouses: A husband and wife cannot be guilty of conspiring with each other, but both may be charged with conspiracy if a third person joins them in the crime.

Testimony against wife: A husband may testify against his wife but he may not reveal any confidential communication between him and his wife during the marriage unless both husband and wife were parties to the action, there was personal violence toward either of them, one acted as the agent to the other, there was pandering or prostitution, or there was violence to a minor child by one or the other.

WYOMING

Coercion by husband: The law holds that a wife is not responsible for committing certain crimes in her husband's presence because he is presumed to have forced her to commit them.

Conspiracy between spouses: A husband and wife cannot be guilty of conspiring with each other.

Testimony against wife: A husband may testify for his wife in a criminal proceeding but he may testify against her only if she is charged with a crime against him.

10
When Am I Old Enough?

Coming of age in the United States can be compared with a camel getting up—it happens in several stages and keeps going on for quite a while. It may not be as sudden and as sharply delineated a process as it is in many cultures, but what it lacks in ritual it more than makes up for in complexity.

Perhaps in a previous age or a simpler society young people matured at about the same time and were given the legal or customary rights and duties of adults. When a woman was old enough to bear children she knew all she needed to know about keeping a home and caring for a family. A young man, by the time he was in his mid-teens, knew enough about hunting, fishing, and fighting to be a provider and deal effectively with his society. But as "civilization" evolved, it also convinced itself that a young man mature enough to fight in wars, or a young woman mature enough to bear children, is still too immature to deal with the complexities of business or the vagaries of politics.

As a result, the law acknowledges a time gap between physical and mental maturity. Most states have set statutory minimum ages for entering into legally recognized marriage and other contracts, and—on a young woman's part—engaging in sex without exposing her partner to criminal penalties. Many of the laws relating to the rights of minors make no distinction between female and male, but the laws are just as binding on a young woman as on a young man.

Minimum ages vary from state to state, and so do the penalties for disregarding them. When we inherited our common law from England, part of the legacy was a set of age limits that have become irrelevant to contemporary society. Over the years new legislation has attempted to protect both young people in particular and society in general.

The most important contract many people make during their lifetime is marriage. At one time girls might be married off as soon as they reached puberty. Although the practice of child marriage has long since fallen out of favor, there are still vestiges of it in our laws. Nine states and the District of Columbia permit women to marry earlier than men without parental consent, and thirty-three states and the District of Columbia have set a lower age for women than men to marry *with* their parents' approval.

Only Mississippi still requires both men and women to wait until they are twenty-one to marry without parental consent. But in seven other states and the District of Columbia, men must be twenty-one but women need be only eighteen years old, and in Alaska the man must be nineteen and the woman eighteen. The age at which both sexes can marry without their parents' approval—usually eighteen—is the same in all other states.

In twenty-one states and the District of Columbia, the age at which teenagers may marry with parental consent is sixteen for women and eighteen for men; there is also a lower age for women than for men in eleven other states. The age is the same for both sexes in fifteen states, and in California, Massachusetts, Montana, and New Hampshire parental consent alone is not enough—there must be a court order authorizing the marriage. In Alabama, New York, South Carolina, and Utah girls (but not boys) of fourteen may marry if they have

parental approval, and Kansas allows a girl as young as twelve to marry if it's all right with her parents. It is ironic that these states do not permit twelve- or fourteen-year-olds to buy or drive cars, hold regular jobs, or vote but do permit them to contract to be married till death do them part.

The reason most young people are allowed to make binding marriage contracts is that the law recognizes that teenagers can and do become parents. Because society feels a responsibility to the offspring of these child-parents, in many states teenagers—whatever their age—are permitted to marry if they have or are expecting a child. Another group of states has set an absolute minimum age—usually either eighteen or sixteen for boys, and sixteen or fourteen for girls—at which teenagers can marry whether they are prospective parents or not. A third set of states allows the court to examine individual circumstances before granting anyone below a certain age permission to marry.

Some of our traditional assumptions about the ages when people can make a reasoned choice of a partner-for-life need to be re-examined. The divorce rate among those who marry in their mid-teens is extremely high. The presumption that a fifteen- or sixteen-year-old girl is emotionally mature enough to make what is supposed to be a lifelong commitment is debatable, and the fact that she may be pregnant makes it no less so. Laws allowing marriage to insure the legitimacy of a child often exact a toll in human misery that far outweighs the "morality" of the situation. These laws should be reconsidered in light of alternative ways to protect the child from the legal disadvantages and social stigma of illegitimacy.

A trend away from early marriages seems to be developing. Although young people are dating at an earlier age and are sexually freer than at any other time in our history, since 1960 there has been an increase of from 28 to 39 per cent in the number of women in their early twenties who remain single. The rate is slower for men of the same age, but it too is rising—from 53 to 57 per cent. Since more young people are choosing to live together either instead of marrying at all or as a prelude to marriage, perhaps state legislators will seriously begin to question the assumptions on which laws regulating marriage are based. Dr. Margaret Mead and others have suggested two types of legal marriages. The first would be marriage-for-companionship. This "marriage" would not be contracted for life and would be childless. The second type would be a contract between mature adults for the purpose of having and raising children, and it would be expected to last, at least while the children are growing up.

Under common law, the right to make contracts was restricted to adult men and, in special circumstances, unmarried adult women. The underlying premise was that contracts should be made only between persons of similar intelligence and maturity. A married woman was not allowed to make contracts on her own because she was presumed to be inferior to her husband and had no separate legal status. Since the passage of the Married Women's Property Acts in the nineteenth century, however, married women may contract on the same basis as all other adults. (See essay and laws in Chapter 1.) Common law also held that a contract between an adult and a minor would bind the minor only as long as the minor wished to be bound.

Binding contracts are still permitted only between adults, but thirty-seven states have lowered the common-law age of majority (the age at which one legally assumes the obligations and responsibilities of adulthood) from twenty-one to eighteen. Other variations from the traditional age are found in Hawaii, which has set the age of majority at twenty, and in Alaska, Nebraska, and Wyoming, where it is nineteen. In fact, adulthood is conferred at twenty-one in only seven states (Alabama, Colorado, Mississippi, Missouri, New York, Pennsylvania, and South Carolina) and the District of Columbia—with two partial exceptions.

The exceptions are the two states which still make a distinction based on sex as to the age at which minors reach adulthood: Arkansas and Utah require men to be twenty-one while women must only be eighteen. Utah's law is being challenged in a case that will be decided by the U.S. Supreme Court in its 1974–75 session. If the discrepancy is held to be unconstitutional, all the laws discussed in this chapter in which different ages are set for males and females will have to be re-examined. Passage of the Equal Rights Amendment (see Chapter 11) would also affect such laws.

Most states allow married minors to contract as adults. Once married, the minor is regarded as having taken on the rights and duties of an adult, at least those essential to carry out financial obligations. State laws vary, however, on whether a minor spouse can join an adult spouse in making contracts or selling land, although the rule seems to be that both spouses will be bound by such contracts.

The common-law rule that minors could break contracts did not apply to buying the so-called "necessities of life." This exception was permitted because it was feared that a destitute minor might starve if he or she was refused credit from merchants who knew the child would not be legally obligated to pay for the goods. Therefore, a minor who has neither parents nor guardians who are able to provide for his or her welfare is legally permitted to be bound by a contract to purchase the necessary items.

This rule appears sound until one attempts to define what is "necessary." The endeavor is further complicated by the fact that at common law the phrase "suitable to his station in life" was often added. There have been many attempts to define what items are essential. Food, clothing, and medical care clearly are. Sometimes education and items necessary for the support of the minor's family are included. However, such seeming necessities as dental work and housing have sometimes been excluded along with such seeming luxuries as cars and expensive university educations, so clearly a great deal is left to the discretion of the deciding judge. Further, if there is an adult who should and could be providing life's necessities, the minor's contract is binding on that responsible adult and not on the minor.

Most states have followed the common-law rule in requiring a minor to return whatever he or she has received under a contract before it may be broken, but the rules differ among the states. In a few, the minor must return everything or its equivalent value with interest before he or she can be released from the contract; in others, this applies only if the contract was made by a minor between eighteen and twenty-one years of age. Some states hold that the minor must return only that portion of the goods still in his or her possession. A final group of states sets no restrictions at all in this matter.

In banking, state laws are fairly uniform with regard to contracts made by young persons. Most states allow minors of any age to maintain their own bank deposits and to draw on them with checks just as an adult would. Credit unions and savings and loan associations often allow minors to hold stocks or be members on the same terms as adults. Some states, however prohibit these organizations from having members who are under fourteen or fifteen or prohibit minors from being officers. Also, minors of fifteen or over may contract for life or accident insurance in most states. In such instances insured minors will then be held to settlements just as though they were adults.

Another growing exception to the common-law rule allows persons over sixteen or eighteen to contract as adults for the purpose of obtaining loans for higher education. Some states require parents of minors to sign also, but more are allowing teenagers to make these contracts on their own. Minors who cannot obtain their parents' signatures and lack substantial assets of their own will have a hard time getting such loans, of course, whether the law allows them to or not.

What happens if a minor lies about his or her age to induce an adult to make a contract? Usually the court will consider the specific circumstances before deciding whether or not the contract is binding on the minor. A mature-looking twenty-year-old with false identification would normally be bound by a contract to purchase a car, for example. But if a sixteen-year-old who was obviously under age signed a contract for a car and lied about his or her age, the court would probably rule that the seller was aware of the lie. In this case, the minor could break the contract and, upon return of the car, would not be liable for any more payments.

While the law applies to everyone, sometimes it creates hardships for certain groups. If it does, statutory provisions are often made to ease the hardship, as is true in the case of minors who need to be able to contract as adults. Thus most states have a special procedure called "emancipation." If a minor goes into court and demonstrates that he or she should be allowed to deal with the business world on equal terms, the court can empower the minor to operate as an adult. Some states say the minor must be at least eighteen to be emancipated; others set no minimum age. The law bends, too, to accommodate practical necessities. In California, for example, the land of movie stars, a minor's entertainment contract must be approved by a court. Once approved it cannot be broken simply because it was made by a minor.

It must be remembered that any other contracts a minor makes are unenforceable, or void, only until he or she reaches the age of majority. Before that time the contract may be broken without penalty ex-

cept for the special cases mentioned above. Some states allow a grace period after reaching adulthood during which a minor can still break contracts. But a minor paying on an installment purchase, for example, who continues making the payments after becoming an adult will then be bound by that contract.

In all states there is an age below which girls may not consent to engage in sex. If a girl is beneath that age, her partner may be charged with the serious crime of statutory rape. It does not matter that she may have agreed to the sex act, or even that she instigated it. Statutory rape, which is distinct from forcible rape (discussed in Chapter 6), is solely a matter of the age of the participants. Since young women lie about their age as often as older women, this is one example of a law that discriminates against males, not females.

The aims of these statutes are to preserve the chastity of young girls and to prevent them from agreeing to a seduction out of curiosity. The law says that a girl who is under age is not capable of consenting to the sex act since she is not able to appreciate its social, physical, and legal consequences. Hence the responsibility is the male's.

Most states set the age of consent at sixteen or eighteen. In some, it is necessary to establish that the victim was a virgin before statutory rape can be charged. In others, such as Missouri, virginity is not an issue. In one noteworthy Missouri case, some young men were convicted of rape despite the fact that the female victim was a young prostitute and the male defendants were described by the court as "callow youths of otherwise blameless lives."

Sentences are heavy for grown men who are convicted of seducing young girls, but the penalties are usually lighter for boys who engage in sex with girls of about their own age. In some states, if the male is the same age as his female victim he cannot be prosecuted for statutory rape, and in Maryland a male who is not yet eighteen cannot be charged with statutory rape at all. Elsewhere, the man's age correlates to the age of his victim—the younger she is, the lower will be the age at which he may be guilty of statutory rape.

Few states regard the seduction of a young man by an older woman as a crime. The woman could be charged with contributing to the delinquency of a minor, but the penalties for this are much less severe than for statutory rape. This is a reflection of society's

double standard of sexual morality, and of the greater value society traditionally places on the chastity of girls than that of boys. But the "double standard" works two ways.

A man had best beware if he has any doubt about the age of a girl with whom he contemplates sexual relations. Ignorance of her age is generally no defense. If a twelve-year-old girl looks twenty the male is just as guilty as if she looked ten.

Until only a few years ago, the age at which persons could vote in state and national elections was twenty-one. In June 1970, Congress enacted a law that would have changed the age to eighteen in all state as well as federal elections. Later that year, the Supreme Court held that the law was constitutional only for national elections, because Congress had no power to set age qualifications for voting in the states. The Twenty-sixth Amendment to the Constitution, enacted and ratified in mid-1971, settled the issue by permitting anyone eighteen or older to vote in state as well as national elections.

Despite the ratification of the eighteen-year-old voting-rights amendment, there is still a question as to the status of some young persons who are working or attending school away from home. Since a person who is not of age is regarded as being a resident of the same place as his or her parents, an eighteen-year-old may be deprived of the right to vote if his or her parents live in one of the states that has not lowered the age of majority to eighteen. This will be the case if the courts hold that the minor's residence is not in the state where he or she is actually living or going to school and do not permit him or her to receive an absentee ballot.

The question is now being litigated in the courts. In some jurisdictions, the courts have already decided that eighteen-year-olds are capable of establishing their own domiciles. Only time will tell whether the vote will be a reality for all eighteen-year-olds who wish to exercise that right.

The laws pertaining to the rights of minors raise interesting questions about our sexual and social assumptions. Do females mature earlier than males, and should they therefore be considered more adult and less in need of parental consent when making contracts or deciding to marry? Is it more important for girls than boys to be "chaste"? Why should girls, but not boys, be considered incapable of making decisions about whether to engage in sex legally before a certain age? Why in some instances does the law see the female as emotionally and intellectually more mature than the male but deny—in its conception of statutory rape—that she has the emotional maturity to decide how she will use her own body? It is obvious that the laws in this area could stand much rethinking.

10
When Am I Old Enough?
The Law
State by State

ALABAMA

Marriage: Without parents' consent—males, 21; females, 18. With parents' consent—males, 17; females, 14.

Contracts: Everyone over 21 may contract as an adult. Minors may make binding contracts only for the necessities of life.

Age of consent: A male over 16 who has sexual relations with a female under 16 may be charged with statutory rape.

Age of majority: All minors come of age at 21, at 18 upon marriage, or by court order.

ALASKA

Marriage: Without parents' consent—males, 19; females, 18. With parents' consent—males, 18; females, 16; there are provisions for waiver in case of pregnancy.

Contracts: Everyone over 19 may contract as an adult. Minors may make binding contracts only for the necessities of life. Minor wives may contract as adults.

Age of consent: A male over 16 who has sexual relations with a female under 16 may be charged with statutory rape whether or not she consented.

Age of majority: All minors come of age at 19 or upon marriage for women.

ARIZONA

Marriage: Without parents' consent—males and females, 18. With parents' consent—males, 18; females, 16; there are provisions for waiver in case of pregnancy.

Contracts: Everyone over 18 may contract as an adult. Minors may make binding contracts in the following areas: necessities of life; insurance (over 15); loans for higher education; medical treatment; hospital care; treatment for venereal disease and drug abuse; medical care for female rape victims (over 12). Minor veterans and their minor spouses may contract as adults.

Age of consent: A male who has sexual relations with a female under 18 may be charged with statutory rape.

Age of majority: All minors come of age at 18.

ARKANSAS

Marriage: Without parents' consent—males, 21; females, 18. With parents' consent—males, 17; females, 16; there are provisions for waiver in case of pregnancy.

Contracts: Males over 21 and females over 18 may contract as adults; these ages may be lowered by court order to 18 for males and 16 for females. Minors may make binding contracts in the following areas: necessities of life; loans for higher education; stock investments (males, 18; females, 16). If a minor disaffirms a contract, all money or property received because of it must be returned.

Age of consent: A male who has sexual relations with a female under 16 may be charged with statutory rape whether or not she consented.

Age of majority: Women come of age at 18, men at 21; or by court order for women at 16, men at 18.

CALIFORNIA

Marriage: Without parents' consent—male and female, 18. With parents' consent—parental consent alone is not sufficient; court approval is also required.

Contracts: Everyone over 18 may contract as an adult. Minors may make binding contracts in the following areas: necessities of life; life or disability insurance (over 16); medical or dental treatment; professional acting, entertainment, or sports (with court approval). Minor veterans may buy homes or farms. Any other contracts made by a minor are not binding unless they are reaffirmed when he or she reaches adulthood or within a reasonable time thereafter.

Age of consent: A male who has sexual relations with a female under 18 may be charged with statutory rape.

Age of majority: All minors come of age at 18.

COLORADO

Marriage: Without parents' consent—males and females, 18. With parents' consent—males and females, 16; under this age court approval is required.

Contracts: Everyone over 18 may contract as an adult. Minors may make binding contracts in the following areas: veterans' benefits; insurance (over 16). Any other contracts made by a minor are not binding unless they are reaffirmed when he or she reaches adulthood.

Age of consent: A male who has sexual relations with a female under 16 who is at least two years younger than he is may be charged with statutory rape.

Age of majority: All minors come of age at 21.

CONNECTICUT

Marriage: Without parents' consent—males and females, 18. With parents' consent—males and females, 16; under this age court approval is required.

Contracts: Everyone over 18 may contract as an adult. Minors may make binding contracts in the following areas: necessities of life; veterans' benefits; insurance (over 15).

Age of consent: A male over 18 who has sexual relations with a female under 16 may be charged with statutory rape.

Age of majority: All minors come of age at 18.

DELAWARE

Marriage: Without parents' consent—males and females, 18. With parents' consent—males, 18; females, 16; there are provisions for waiver in case of pregnancy.

Contracts: Everyone over 18 may contract as an adult. Minors may make binding contracts in the following areas: necessities of life; medical care in an emergency.

Age of consent: A male who has sexual relations with a female under 18 may be charged with statutory rape whether or not she consented.

Age of majority: All minors come of age at 18.

DISTRICT OF COLUMBIA

Marriage: Without parents' consent—males, 21;

females, 18. With parents' consent—males, 18; females, 16.

Contracts: Everyone over 21 may contract as an adult. Minors may make binding contracts in the following areas: veterans' benefits; life, health, or accident insurance (over 15); loans for higher education. A minor wife (over 18) may release rights to her husband's property. Any other contracts made by a minor are not binding unless they are reaffirmed when he or she reaches adulthood.

Age of consent: A male who has sexual relations with a female under 16 may be charged with statutory rape.

Age of majority: All minors come of age at 21.

FLORIDA

Marriage: Without parents' consent—males and females, 18. With parents' consent—males, 18; females, 16; there are provisions for waiver in case of pregnancy.

Contracts: Everyone over 18 may contract as an adult. Minors may make binding contracts in the following areas: veterans' benefits; loans for higher education (over 16); membership in credit unions. Married minors may contract as adults, even if they are subsequently divorced.

Age of consent: Either a male or a female who has sexual relations with a previously chaste unmarried member of the opposite sex who is under 18 may be charged with statutory rape.

Age of majority: All minors come of age at 18 or upon marriage.

GEORGIA

Marriage: Without parents' consent—males and females, 18. With parents' consent—males, 18; females 16; there are provisions for waiver in case of pregnancy.

Contracts: Everyone over 18 may contract as an adult. Minors may make binding contracts in the following areas: necessities of life; veterans' benefits; insurance (over 15). Married minors may contract for loans, make mortgages, and settle claims as adults. Minor widows or widow-ers take their share of spouses' estates as adults. Disabled minor veterans may contract as adults.

Age of consent: A male who has sexual relations with a female under 14 may be charged with statutory rape.

Age of majority: All minors come of age at 18.

HAWAII

Marriage: Without parents' consent—males and females, 16. With parents' consent—males and females, 15.

Contracts: Everyone over 18 may contract as an adult. Minors may make binding contracts in the following areas: veterans' benefits; life or disability insurance. Any other contracts made by a minor are not binding unless they are reaffirmed when he or she reaches adulthood or within a reasonable time thereafter.

Age of consent: A male who has sexual relations with a female under 16 may be charged with statutory rape whether or not she consented.

Age of majority: All minors come of age at 20.

IDAHO

Marriage: Without parents' consent—males and females, 18. With parents' consent—males and females, 16; under this age court approval is required.

Contracts: Everyone over 18 may contract as an adult. Minors may make binding contracts in the following areas: necessities of life; insurance (over 15); giving consent for the adoption of his or her child.

Age of consent: A male who has sexual relations with a female under 18 may be charged with statutory rape whether or not she consented.

Age of majority: All minors come of age at 18.

ILLINOIS

Marriage: Without parents' consent—males, 21; females, 18. With parents' consent—males, 18; females, 16; there are provisions for waiver in case of pregnancy.

Contracts: Everyone over 18 may contract as an adult. Minors may make binding contracts in the following areas: health, accident, and life insurance (over 15); loans for higher education; membership in credit unions and savings and loan associations; medical treatment; treatment for venereal disease, drug abuse, or pregnancy. Any other contracts made by a minor are not binding unless they are reaffirmed when he or she reaches adulthood.

Age of consent: A male over 17 who has sexual relations with a female under 16 may be charged with statutory rape unless he was mistaken as to her age or she was a prostitute or previously married.

Age of majority: All minors come of age at 18.

INDIANA

Marriage: Without parents' consent—males and females, 18. With parents' consent—males and females, 17; there are provisions for waiver in case of pregnancy.

Contracts Everyone over 18 may contract as an adult. Minors may make binding contracts in the following areas: necessities of life; life, health, or accident insurance (over 16); loans for higher education; treatment for venereal disease; blood donation. A minor may contract to sell property if his or her adult spouse joins in the contract and it is approved by the court.

Age of consent: A male who has sexual relations with a female under 16 may be charged with statutory rape.

Age of majority: All minors come of age at 18.

IOWA

Marriage: Without parents' consent—males and females, 18. With parents' consent—males, 18; females, 16; there are provisions for waiver in case of pregnancy.

Contracts: Everyone over 18 may contract as an adult. Minors may make binding contracts in the following areas: necessities of life; veterans' benefits; bank accounts; blood donation. Married minors may contract as adults. Any other contracts made by a minor are not binding unless they are reaffirmed when he or she reaches

adulthood. If a minor disaffirms a contract, all remaining money or property received because of it must be returned. Contracts made by a minor are binding if he or she is engaged in business or misrepresents his or her age in making them.

Age of consent: A male who has sexual relations with a female under 16, or a male over 25 who has sexual relations with a female under 17, may be charged with statutory rape.

Age of majority: All minors come of age at 18 or upon marriage.

KANSAS

Marriage: Without parents' consent—males and females, 18. With parents' consent—males, 14; females, 12.

Contracts: Everyone over 18 may contract as an adult. This age may be lowered by court order. Minors may make binding contracts in the following areas: necessities of life; insurance (with written approval of parent or guardian). Any other contracts made by a minor are not binding unless they are reaffirmed when he or she reaches adulthood or within a reasonable time thereafter. If a minor disaffirms a contract, all remaining money or property received because of it must be returned. Contracts made by a minor are binding if he or she is engaged in business or misrepresents his or her age in making them.

Age of consent: A male who has sexual relations with a female under 16 may be charged with statutory rape.

Age of majority: All minors come of age at 18.

KENTUCKY

Marriage: Without parents' consent—males and females, 18. With parents' consent—males, 18; females, 16; there are provisions for waiver in case of pregnancy.

Contracts: Everyone over 18 may contract as an adult. Minors may make binding contracts in the following areas: necessities of life; veterans' benefits; insurance (over 15); loans for higher education.

Age of consent: Either a male or a female who has sexual relations with a member of the opposite sex who is under 18 may be charged with statutory rape. However, if the male offender is between 17 and 21, the female offender is between 18 and 21, or the younger person was previously unchaste, the penalty is much lighter than it would be otherwise.

Age of majority: All minors come of age at 18.

LOUISIANA

Marriage: Without parents' consent—males and females, 18. With parents' consent—males, 18; females, 16; under these ages court approval is required.

Contracts: Everyone over 18 may contract as an adult. This age may be lowered by court order to permit minors to contract in specified situations. Minors may make binding contracts in the following areas: life, health, and accident insurance (over 15); bank accounts; credit union membership. Married minors may contract as adults in some situations. Contracts made by a minor are binding if he or she is engaged in business.

Age of consent: A male over 17 who has sexual relations with a female under 17 may be charged with statutory rape.

Age of majority: All minors come of age at 18 or upon marriage.

MAINE

Marriage: Without parents' consent—males and females, 18. With parents' consent—males and females, 16; under this age court approval is required.

Contracts: Everyone over 18 may contract as an adult. Minors may make binding contracts in the following areas: necessities of life; veterans' benefits; life insurance (over 15); loans for higher education (over 16); credit union membership (without voting privileges); property in their

possession. Married minors may make binding contracts in managing and selling property.

Age of consent: A male over 18 who has sexual relations with a female under 16, or a male of any age who has sexual relations with a female under 14, may be charged with statutory rape.

Age of majority: All minors come of age at 18.

MARYLAND

Marriage: Without parents' consent—males and females, 18. With parents' consent—males and females, 16; there are provisions for waiver in case of pregnancy.

Contracts: Everyone over 18 may contract as an adult. Minors may make binding contracts in the following areas: necessities of life; veterans' benefits; insurance (over 15); loans for higher education; treatment of venereal disease, pregnancy, and mental or emotional disorders (the latter over 16); blood donation. Married minors may consent to medical treatment; a minor wife (over 16) may join her adult husband in selling property they own jointly. Any other contracts made by a minor are not binding unless they are reaffirmed when he or she reaches adulthood.

Age of consent: A male who has sexual relations with a female under 16 may be charged with statutory rape whether or not she consented. However, if the female is over 14 and the male is under 18 the act is not criminal.

Age of majority: All minors come of age at 18.

MASSACHUSETTS

Marriage: Without parents' consent—males and females, 18. With parents' consent—parental consent alone is not sufficient; court approval is also required.

Contracts: Everyone over 18 may contract as an adult. Minors may make binding contracts in the following areas: life insurance (over 15); automobile liability insurance (over 16); bank accounts; membership in credit unions and savings and loan associations; treatment for drug addiction (over 12).

Age of consent: A male who has sexual relations with a female under 16 may be charged with statutory rape.

Age of majority: All minors come of age at 18.

MICHIGAN

Marriage: Without parents' consent—males and females, 18. With parents' consent—males, 18; females, 16; there are provisions for waiver in case of pregnancy.

Contracts: Everyone over 18 may contract as an adult. Minors may make binding contracts in the following areas: necessities of life; life insurance (over 16). Married minors may contract as adults. Any other contracts made by a minor are not binding unless they are reaffirmed when he or she reaches adulthood. If a minor disaffirms a contract, all remaining money or property received because of it must be returned. Contracts made by a minor are binding if he or she misrepresents his or her age in making them.

Age of consent: A male who has sexual relations with a female under 16 may be charged with statutory rape.

Age of majority: All minors come of age at 18 or during active duty in the armed forces, by court order, by a written release from the parents, or by being abandoned by parents.

MINNESOTA

Marriage: Without parents' consent—males and females, 18. With parents' consent—males, 18; females, 16 and court approval.

Contracts: Everyone over 18 may contract as an adult. Minors may make binding contracts in the following areas: necessities of life; veterans' benefits; bank accounts; membership in credit unions; treatment for venereal disease, pregnancy, and drug or alcohol abuse; blood donation. A minor spouse may join an adult spouse in selling land. Any other contracts made by a minor are not binding unless they are reaffirmed when he or she reaches adulthood.

Age of consent: A male who has sexual relations

with a female under 18 may be charged with statutory rape.

Age of majority: All minors come of age at 18 or upon marriage.

MISSISSIPPI

Marriage: Without parents' consent—males and females, 21. With parents' consent—males, 17; females, 15; under these ages court approval is required.

Contracts: Everyone over 21 may contract as an adult. Minors may make binding contracts in the following areas: necessities of life; health, accident, and life insurance (over 15). Married minors (over 18) may make binding contracts concerning real property in their possession. Any other contracts made by a minor are not binding unless they are reaffirmed when he or she reaches adulthood.

Age of consent: A male over 18 who has sexual relations with a previously chaste female under 18 may be charged with statutory rape whether or not she consented.

Age of majority: All minors come of age at 21.

MISSOURI

Marriage: Without parents' consent—males, 21; females, 18. With parents' consent—males and females, 15; under this age court approval is required.

Contracts: Everyone over 21 may contract as an adult. Minors may make binding contracts in the following areas: necessities of life; veterans' benefits; loans for higher education; bank accounts; membership in credit unions and savings and loan associations; treatment for venereal disease, pregnancy, and drug abuse; blood donation. Any other contracts made by a minor are not binding unless they are reaffirmed when he or she reaches adulthood. If a minor disaffirms a contract, all remaining money or property received because of it must be returned.

Age of consent: A male who has sexual relations

with a female under 16, or a male over 17 who has sexual relations with a previously chaste female between 16 and 18, may be charged with statutory rape whether or not she consented.

Age of majority: All minors come of age at 21.

MONTANA

Marriage: Without parents' consent—males and females, 18. With parents' consent—parental consent alone is not sufficient; court approval is also required.

Contracts: Everyone over 18 may contract as an adult. Minors may make binding contracts in the following areas: necessities of life; veterans' benefits; loans for higher education; bank accounts; membership in building and loan associations; treatment for venereal disease, pregnancy, and—in an emergency—mental or emotional disorders. Married minors may consent to health care. Any other contracts made by a minor are not binding unless they are reaffirmed when he or she reaches adulthood or within a reasonable time thereafter. If a minor disaffirms a contract, all money or property received because of it must be returned.

Age of consent: A male who has sexual relations with a female under 18 may be charged with statutory rape.

Age of majority: All minors come of age at 18 or upon marriage.

NEBRASKA

Marriage: Without parents' consent—males and females, 19. With parents' consent—males, 18; females, 16; there are provisions for waiver in case of pregnancy.

Contracts: Everyone over 19 may contract as an adult. Minors may make binding contracts in the following areas: necessities of life; veterans' benefits; life or disability insurance and annuities; bank accounts; membership in credit unions and savings and loan associations; treatment for venereal disease. Any other contracts made by a minor are not binding unless they are reaffirmed when he or she reaches adulthood.

Age of consent: A male over 18 who has sexual relations with a female under 18 may be charged with statutory rape unless she is over 15 and was previously unchaste.

Age of majority: All minors come of age at 19 or upon marriage.

NEVADA

Marriage: Without parents' consent—males and females, 18. With parents' consent—males, 18; females, 16; under these ages court approval is required.

Contracts: Everyone over 18 may contract as an adult. Minors may make binding contracts in the following areas: necessities of life; veterans' benefits; insurance (with parents' approval); bank accounts; membership in credit unions or savings and loan associations (with parents' approval); mining claims. Any other contracts made by a minor are not binding unless they are reaffirmed when he or she reaches adulthood.

Age of consent: A male over 18 who has sexual relations with a female under 16 may be charged with statutory rape.

Age of majority: All minors come of age at 18.

NEW HAMPSHIRE

Marriage: Without parents' consent—males and females, 18. With parents' consent—parental consent alone is not sufficient; court approval is also required.

Contracts: Everyone over 18 may contract as an adult. Minors may make binding contracts in the following areas: veterans' benefits; bank accounts; membership in credit unions and building and loan associations; treatment for venereal disease (over 14); blood donation. A minor spouse may join an adult spouse in selling real property in their possession.

Age of consent: A male who has sexual relations with a female under 16 may be charged with statutory rape whether or not she consented.

Age of majority: All minors come of age at 18.

NEW JERSEY

Marriage: Without parents' consent—males and females, 18. With parents' consent—males, 18; females, 16; under this age court approval is required.

Contracts: Everyone over 18 may contract as an adult. Minors may make binding contracts in the following areas: necessities of life; veterans' benefits; insurance (over 15); loans for higher education; bank accounts; membership in credit unions and savings and loan associations; treatment for venereal disease and pregnancy. Married minors may consent to medical care. Any other contracts made by a minor are not binding unless they are reaffirmed when he or she reaches adulthood.

Age of consent: A male over 16 who has sexual relations with a female under 16 may be charged with statutory rape.

Age of majority: All minors come of age at 18.

NEW MEXICO

Marriage: Without parents' consent—males and females, 18. With parents' consent—males and females, 16; there are provisions for waiver in case of pregnancy.

Contracts: Everyone over 18 may contract as an adult. Minors may make binding contracts in the following areas: necessities of life; veterans' benefits; life, disability, and accident insurance and annuities (over 15); loans for higher education (over 16); bank accounts; membership in credit unions. Any other contracts made by a minor are not binding unless they are reaffirmed when he or she reaches adulthood.

Age of consent: A male who has sexual relations with a female under 16 may be charged with statutory rape whether or not she consented.

Age of majority: All minors come of age at 18 or upon marriage.

NEW YORK

Marriage: Without parents' consent—males, 21; females, 18. With parents' consent—males, 16;

females, 14 and court approval if under 16.

Contracts: Everyone over 21 may contract as an adult. Minors may make binding contracts in the following areas: necessities of life; accident and health insurance (over 18); life insurance (over 15); loans for higher education (over 16); bank accounts; membership in credit unions (over 15); blood donation. Married minors may make binding contracts with regard to land on which they are living or to which they are about to move. Minor veterans and their spouses may make binding contracts for loans for real property. Any other contracts made by a minor are not binding unless they are reaffirmed when he or she reaches adulthood. However, contracts made by a minor are binding if he or she is engaged in business.

Age of consent: A male over 21 who has sexual relations with a female under 17, or a male over 18 who has sexual relations with a female under 14, may be charged with statutory rape whether or not she consented.

Age of majority: All minors come of age at 21.

NORTH CAROLINA

Marriage: Without parents' consent—males and females, 18. With parents' consent—males and females, 16; there are provisions for waiver in case of pregnancy.

Contracts: Everyone over 18 may contract as an adult. Minors may make binding contracts in the following areas: veterans' benefits; life insurance and annuities (over 15); loans for higher education (over 17); bank accounts. A minor spouse may join an adult spouse in selling property they own jointly. Any other contracts made by a minor are not binding unless they are reaffirmed when he or she reaches adulthood or within three years thereafter. If a minor disaffirms a contract, all remaining money or property received because of it must be returned.

Age of consent: Either a male or female who has sexual relations with a previously chaste unmarried member of the opposite sex who is under 16 may be charged with statutory rape whether or not the younger person consented.

Age of majority: All minors come of age at 18.

NORTH DAKOTA

Marriage: Without parents' consent—males and females, 18. With parents' consent—males, 18; females, 15.

Contracts: Everyone over 18 may contract as an adult. Minors may make binding contracts in the following areas: necessities of life; veterans' benefits; loans for higher education (over 16); bank accounts; membership in credit unions and savings and loan associations; treatment for venereal disease (over 14); real or personal property in their possession. Any other contracts made by a minor are not binding unless they are reaffirmed when he or she reaches adulthood or within a reasonable time thereafter.

Age of consent: A male who has sexual relations with a female under 18 may be charged with statutory rape whether or not she consented.

Age of majority: All minors come of age at 18.

OHIO

Marriage: Without parents' consent—males and females, 21. With parents' consent—males, 18; females, 16.

Contracts: Everyone over 21 may contract as an adult. Minors may make binding contracts in the following areas: necessities of life; veterans' benefits; life insurance (over 15); loans for higher education; bank accounts; membership in credit unions; treatment for venereal disease and drug abuse; blood donation. A minor's agreement to pay an amount of money is not enforceable even it if is transferred to a third person who is unaware that the agreement was made by a minor.

Age of consent: A male over 18 who has sexual relations with a female under 16 may be charged with statutory rape whether or not she consented.

Age of majority: All minors come of age at 21.

OKLAHOMA

Marriage: Without parents' consent—males, 21; females, 18. With parents' consent—males, 18;

females, 15; there are provisions for waiver in case of pregnancy.

Contracts: Everyone over 18 may contract as an adult. Minors may make binding contracts in the following areas: necessities of life; veterans' benefits; life, accident, and health insurance (over 15); other kinds of insurance (over 16); loans for higher education (over 16); bank accounts; membership in credit unions and savings and loan associations; real or personal property in their possession. Married minors may make binding contracts for real estate acquired after marriage. Any other contracts made by a minor are not binding unless they are reaffirmed when he or she reaches adulthood or within a year thereafter.

Age of consent: A male over 18 who has sexual relations with any female under 16 or with a previously chaste female between 16 and 18, or a male under 18 who has sexual relations with a female under 14, may be charged with statutory rape.

Age of majority: All minors come of age at 18 or upon marriage.

OREGON

Marriage: Without parents' consent—males and females, 18. With parents' consent—males, 18; females, 15.

Contracts: Everyone over 18 may contract as an adult. Minors may make binding contracts in the following areas: necessities of life; insurance; loans for higher education; bank accounts; medical or dental treatment; hospital care; treatment for venereal disease (over 12); birth control information and services; blood donation. Any other contracts made by a minor are not binding unless they are reaffirmed when he or she reaches adulthood.

Age of consent: Either a male or a female who has sexual relations with an unmarried member of the opposite sex who is under 18 may be charged with statutory rape whether or not the younger person consented.

Age of majority: All minors come of age at 18 or upon marriage.

PENNSYLVANIA

Marriage: Without parents' consent—males and females, 18. With parents' consent—males and females, 16; under this age court approval is required.

Contracts: Everyone over 18 may contract as an adult. Minors may make binding contracts in the following areas: necessities of life; veterans' benefits; loans for higher education; bank accounts; medical and dental treatment; treatment for venereal disease, pregnancy, and drug or alcohol abuse. A minor spouse (over 17) may join an adult spouse in selling real property. Any other contracts made by a minor are not binding unless they are reaffirmed when he or she reaches adulthood or within a reasonable time thereafter.

Age of consent: Either a male or a female over 16 who has sexual relations with an unmarried member of the opposite sex who is under 16 may be charged with statutory rape whether or not the younger person consented.

Age of majority: All minors come of age at 21.

RHODE ISLAND

Marriage: Without parents' consent—males and females, 18. With parents' consent—males, 18; females, 16; under these ages court approval is required.

Contracts: Everyone over 18 may contract as an adult. Minors may make binding contracts in the following areas: necessities of life; veterans' benefits; bank accounts; membership in credit unions and savings and loan associations. A minor wife may join with her adult husband in selling property they own jointly.

Age of consent: A male who has sexual relations with a female under 16 who is not his wife may be charged with statutory rape whether or not she consented.

Age of majority: All minors come of age at 18.

SOUTH CAROLINA

Marriage: Without parents' consent—males and females, 18. With parents' consent—males, 16; females, 14; there are provisions for waiver in case of pregnancy.

Contracts: Everyone over 21 may contract as an adult. Minors may make binding contracts in the following areas: necessities of life; veterans' benefits; loans for higher education; bank deposits; membership in credit unions; medical treatment in certain situations; blood donation (over 18). Married minors can consent to medical or hospital care; a minor wife may join with her adult husband in selling property they own jointly. Any other contracts made by a minor are not binding unless they are reaffirmed when he or she reaches adulthood.

Age of consent: A male who has sexual relations with a female under 16 may be charged with statutory rape whether or not she consented.

Age of majority: All minors come of age at 21.

SOUTH DAKOTA

Marriage: Without parents' consent—males and females, 18. With parents' consent—males, 18; females, 16; there are provisions for waiver in case of pregnancy.

Contracts: Everyone over 18 may contract as an adult. Minors may make binding contracts in the following areas: necessities of life; veterans' benefits; loans for higher education; bank accounts; treatment for venereal disease. Any other contracts made by a minor are not binding unless they are reaffirmed when he or she reaches adulthood or within a year thereafter. If a minor over 16 disaffirms a contract, all money or property received because of it must be returned, with interest.

Age of consent: A male who has sexual relations with a female under 16 may be charged with statutory rape.

Age of majority: All minors come of age at 18 or upon marriage.

TENNESSEE

Marriage: Without parents' consent—males and females, 18. With parents' consent—males and females, 16.

Contracts: Everyone over 18 may contract as an adult. Minors may make binding contracts in the following areas: necessities of life; veterans' benefits; loans for higher education; bank accounts; membership in credit unions. Any other contracts made by a minor are not binding unless they are reaffirmed when he or she reaches adulthood or within a reasonable time thereafter. However, contracts made by a minor are binding if he or she misrepresented his or her age in making them.

Age of consent: A male who has sexual relations with a female under 18 may be charged with statutory rape whether or not she consented.

Age of majority: All minors come of age at 18.

TEXAS

Marriage: Without parents' consent—males and females, 18. With parents' consent—males and females, 16.

Contracts: Everyone over 18 may contract as an adult. Minors may make binding contracts in the following areas: necessities of life; life insurance and annuities (over 14 and with an adult's approval); savings accounts; membership in credit unions; treatment for venereal disease and drug abuse (over 13); blood donation. Married minors may contract as adults. Any other contracts made by a minor are not binding unless they are reaffirmed when he or she reaches adulthood or within a reasonable time thereafter. However, contracts made by a minor are binding if he or she misrepresented his or her age in making them.

Age of consent: A male who has sexual relations with a female under 17 may be charged with statutory rape whether or not she consented. However, if the female is over 14 and was pre-

viously unchaste, that is considered to be a mitigating circumstance.

Age of majority: All minors come of age at 18 or upon marriage.

UTAH

Marriage: Without parents' consent—males, 21; females, 18. With parents' consent—males, 16; females, 14.

Contracts: Males over 21 and females over 18 may contract as adults. Minors may make binding contracts in the following areas: necessities of life; veterans' benefits; insurance (over 15); bank accounts; membership in credit unions and savings and loan associations; treatment for venereal disease; blood donation (over 18). Married minors may contract as adults. Any other contracts made by a minor are not binding unless they are reaffirmed when he or she reaches adulthood or within a reasonable time thereafter. If a minor disaffirms a contract, all remaining money or property received because of it must be returned. Contracts made by a minor are binding if he or she is engaged in business or misrepresents his or her age in making them.

Age of consent: A male who has sexual relations with a female under 18 may be charged with statutory rape whether or not she consented.

Age of majority: Women come of age at 18, men at 21, or upon marriage for both.

VERMONT

Marriage: Without parents' consent—males and females, 18. With parents' consent—males, 18; females, 16; under these ages court approval is required.

Contracts: Everyone over 18 may contract as an adult. Minors may make binding contracts in the following areas: necessities of life; loans for higher education; bank accounts; membership in credit unions and savings and loan associations. Any other contracts made by a minor are not binding unless they are reaffirmed when he or she reaches adulthood or within a reasonable time thereafter. If a minor disaffirms a contract, all remaining money or property received because of it must be returned.

Age of consent: A male over 16 who has sexual relations with a female under 16 may be charged with statutory rape whether or not she consented. However, if both parties are under 16, they are both guilty of a misdemeanor.

Age of majority: All minors come of age at 18 or upon marriage.

VIRGINIA

Marriage: Without parents' consent—males and females, 18. With parents' consent—males, 18; females 16.

Contracts: Everyone over 18 may contract as an adult. Minors may make binding contracts in the following areas: veterans' benefits; life insurance (over 15 and with parental approval); loans for higher education (over 16); bank accounts; membership in credit unions; treatment for venereal disease and drug abuse; birth control (but not sterilization). Any other contracts made by a minor are not binding unless they are reaffirmed when he or she reaches adulthood. If a minor disaffirms a contract, all remaining money or property received because of it must be returned. Contracts made by a minor are binding if he or she is engaged in business.

Age of consent: A male who has sexual relations with a female under 16 may be charged with statutory rape.

Age of majority: All minors come of age at 18.

WASHINGTON

Marriage: Without parents' consent—males and females, 18. With parents' consent—males and females, 17; under this age court approval is required.

Contracts: Everyone over 18 may contract as an adult. Minors may make binding contracts in the following areas: necessities of life; life and disability insurance (over 15); bank accounts; membership in credit unions and savings and loan associations. Minor wives of adult husbands may contract as adults. A minor's contracts are considered binding if he or she does not disaffirm them upon reaching adulthood. If a minor disaffirms a contract, all remaining money or property received because of it must be returned. Contracts made by a minor are binding if he or she is engaged in business or misrepresents his or her age in making them.

Age of consent: Either a male or a female who has sexual relations with a previously chaste unmarried member of the opposite sex who is under 18 may be charged with statutory rape whether or not the younger person consented.

Age of majority: All minors come of age at 18, or upon marriage for women.

WEST VIRGINIA

Marriage: Without parents' consent—males and females, 18. With parents' consent—males, 18; females, 16; there are provisions for waiver in case of pregnancy.

Contracts: Everyone over 18 may contract as an adult. Minors may make binding contracts in the following areas: necessities of life; veterans' benefits; health, accident, and life insurance (over 15); bank accounts; membership in credit unions and savings and loan associations. Any other contracts made by a minor are not binding unless they are reaffirmed when he or she reaches adulthood.

Age of consent: Either a male or a female over 16 who has sexual relations with a previously chaste member of the opposite sex who is under 16, or a male who has sexual relations with any female under 10, may be charged with statutory rape whether or not the younger person consented. However, the penalties are much less severe for the older woman who seduces a boy than they are for an older man who seduces a girl.

Age of majority: All minors come of age at 18.

WISCONSIN

Marriage: Without parents' consent—males and females, 18. With parents' consent—males and females, 16.

Contracts: Everyone over 18 may contract as an adult. Minors may make binding contracts in the following areas: necessities of life; veterans' benefits; bank accounts. Any other contracts made by a minor are not binding unless they are reaffirmed when he or she reaches adulthood.

Age of consent: A male who has sexual relations with a female under 18 may be charged with statutory rape whether or not she consented.

Age of majority: All minors come of age at 18 or upon marriage.

WYOMING

Marriage: Without parents' consent—males and females, 19. With parents' consent—males, 18; females, 16.

Contracts: Everyone over 19 may contract as an adult. Minors may make binding contracts in the following areas: necessities of life; veterans' benefits (with an honorable discharge); insurance (over 15); bank accounts. Any other contracts made by a minor are not binding unless they are reaffirmed when he or she reaches adulthood.

Age of consent: A male who has sexual relations with a female under 18 may be charged with statutory rape whether or not she consented.

Age of majority: All minors come of age at 19.

11

Am I a Full Citizen?

No one in this country is truly a full citizen until he or she is accorded the same rights, duties, and privileges as every other citizen. Laws that treat men and women differently—whether the differences are discriminatory or "protective"—raise basic questions about the status of women as full citizens. They also raise questions in terms of the constitutional guarantee that all persons must receive the "equal protection of the laws."

This is a problem the Supreme Court has not really dealt with in its rulings relating to women. When decisions in the areas of discrimination against women and racial minorities are compared, the Court's attitudes and reservations about the role of women in our society become evident.

Beginning with the historic 1954 school-desegregation decisions in *Brown v. Board of Education* and *Bolling v. Sharpe,* the Court has consistently held that racial discrimination violates the equal protection clause of the Fourteenth Amendment or—when the discrimination is so outrageously unfair as to constitute a denial of liberty or property—the due process clause of the Fifth Amendment. The only exception allowed is in cases where it can be shown there is a "compelling" governmental interest in making distinctions on the basis of race. So far, the Court has acknowledged this compelling interest only twice. The first time was thirty years ago when the Court upheld the constitutionality of the Japanese internment programs during World War II. The second time was the 1972 decision permitting the racial discrimination necessarily inherent in re-drawing school-attendance zones to reflect the racial composition of a school district, as required by the *Brown* decision. This is not really an exception, however, as it is the *only* way desegregation decisions can be implemented.

Since racial discrimination can be constitutional only if it is necessary (not just one of several alternative methods) to accomplish something the government feels is essential, all racial classifications or criteria in a law are considered constitutionally "suspect." This means that any such law is subjected to the strictest possible judicial scrutiny when challenged as unconstitutional under the Fifth or Fourteenth Amendment.

The Supreme Court has never treated sex discrimination in this way. That is, the Court does not see women as a group deserving of the same constitutional protection it has taken great pains to extend to racial minorities. Perhaps the easiest way to understand this difference is to look at the sexual composition of the Court. But the second-easiest way is to look at two leading cases involving race and sex discrimination in juries.

In 1880, twelve years after the adoption of the Fourteenth Amendment with its guarantee of equal protection of the laws, the Supreme Court, in *Strauder v. West Virginia*, held that a black criminal defendant convicted by an all-white jury had been denied his constitutional right to equal protection of the laws because of a state law prohibiting nonwhites from serving on juries. Eighty-one years later, in 1961 in *Hoyt v. Florida*, the Supreme Court *upheld* a Florida jury-selection law challenged by a woman convicted by an all-male jury. The law excluded women from jury service unless they registered with the court clerk an affirmative desire to be placed on the list of prospective jurors. The Court in *Hoyt* justified this discriminatory treatment of women—both as criminal defendants facing male juries and as potential jurors—in this way: "Woman is still regarded as the center of home and family life. We cannot say that it is constitutionally impermissible for a State . . . to conclude that a woman should be relieved from the civic duty of jury service unless she herself determines that such service is consistent with her own special responsibilities."

The provision making it necessary for women to register with the court clerk before being eligible for jury duty has been removed from the laws of all states. Many states, however, still do not require a woman to serve on a jury, once she is called, if she does not wish to or if she is the mother of dependent children, choices that no state gives to men. The rationale for these laws is undoubtedly the same as the rationale behind the *Hoyt* ruling, which in turn harks back to *Muller v. Oregon* (1908) and *Goesaert v. Cleary* (1948) in the area of discriminatory practices against working women (see Chapter 8).

In 1971 the Supreme Court handed down a landmark decision which seemed to indicate that the Court was on the verge of treating sex discrimination as constitutionally suspect. In *Reed v. Reed* the Court ruled that an Idaho statute giving an automatic preference to men over women, all other things being equal, when there was a contest over who would be the administrator of a decedent's estate violated the equal protection clause of the Fourteenth Amendment. In

Reed, the contest was between Mr. and Mrs. Reed, the parents of the decedent. In agreeing with Mrs. Reed's constitutional argument, the Court noted: "To give a mandatory preference to members of either sex over members of the other, merely to [reduce the workload on probate courts], . . . is to make the very kind of arbitrary legislative choice forbidden by the Equal Protection Clause of the Fourteenth Amendment."

Then two years later, in *Frontiero v. Richardson,* the Supreme Court held unconstitutional a congressional statute that required a female member of the armed services seeking housing and medical benefits for her husband to prove his financial dependence on her but did not impose a proof-of-dependence burden on a man seeking identical benefits for his wife. *Frontiero* was an eight-to-one decision, with only Justice Rehnquist dissenting, but there was no majority opinion—that is, no opinion with which at least five members of the Court agreed. Justice Brennan, joined by Justices Douglas, Marshall, and White, argued that classifications in the law based on sex should be treated the same as those based on race. The opinion deserves quoting at length:

> There can be no doubt that our Nation has had a long and unfortunate history of sex discrimination. Traditionally, such discrimination was rationalized by an attitude of "romantic paternalism". . . .
> . . . . Our statute books gradually became laden with gross, stereotypical distinctions between the sexes and, indeed, throughout much of the 19th century the position of women in our society was, in many respects, comparable to that of blacks under the pre-Civil War slave codes. Neither slaves nor women could hold office, serve on juries, or bring suit in their own names, and married women traditionally were denied the legal capacity to hold or convey property or to serve as legal guardians of their own children. . . . And although blacks were guaranteed the right to vote in 1870, women were denied even that right . . . until adoption of the Nineteenth Amendment half a century later.
> It is true, of course, that the position of women in America has improved markedly in recent decades. Nevertheless, it can hardly be doubted that, in part because of the high visibility of the sex characteristic, women still face pervasive, although at times more subtle, discrimination in our educational institutions, on the job market and, perhaps most conspicuously, in the political arena.
> [A footnote at this point noted: "It is true, of course, that when viewed in the abstract, women do not constitute a small and powerless minority. Nevertheless, in part because of past discrimination, women are vastly underrepresented in this Nation's decision-making councils. There has never been a female President, nor a female member of this Court. Not a single woman presently sits in the United States Senate, and only 14 women hold seats in the House of Representatives. And . . . this underrepresentation is present throughout all levels of our State and Federal Government." Other footnotes have been omitted.]
> . . . Since sex, like race and national origin, is an immutable characteristic determined solely by the accident of birth, the imposition of special disabilities upon the members of a particular sex because of their sex would seem to violate "the basic concept of our system that legal burdens should bear some relationship to individual responsibility.". . . And what differentiates sex from such non-suspect standards as intelligence or physical disability, and aligns it with the recognized suspect criteria, is that the sex characteristic

frequently bears no relation to ability to perform or contribute to society. As a result, statutory distinctions between the sexes often have the effect of invidiously relegating the entire class of females to inferior legal status without regard to the actual capabilities of its individual members.

Justice Powell, joined by Chief Justice Burger and Justice Blackmun, agreed that there was unconstitutional sex discrimination in the *Frontiero* case. But he did not go along with Justice Brennan's conclusion that sex should be treated as a suspect classification like race, and in fact specifically refused to consider this issue. As Powell said in his opinion:

> The Equal Rights Amendment, which if adopted will resolve the substance of this precise question [of whether classifications based upon sex are suspect like those based upon race], has been approved by the Congress and submitted for ratification by the States. If this Amendment is duly adopted, it will represent the will of the people accomplished in the manner prescribed by the Constitution.

Thus it seems that Justices Powell, Burger, and Blackmun, at least, are content to avoid this question in the hope that the adoption of the Equal Rights Amendment will relieve them of having to make a judgment. If the amendment is never ratified, however, will these men reconsider their hands-off policy?

In 1974 the Court made two rulings that mark an unfortunate retreat from the unanimous 1971 *Reed* decision and Justice Brennan's opinion in the 1973 *Frontiero* case. The first of these sex-discrimination cases was

Geduldig v. Aiello. It was brought in behalf of women who were denied pregnancy benefits under California's temporary disability insurance program, even though the program covered other "voluntary" disabilities (such as orthodontic treatment and cosmetic surgery) and some disabilities suffered only or primarily by men (such as prostatectomies, circumcision, and gout). The majority opinion held that the pregnancy exclusion was not discriminatory on the basis of sex and did not deny equal protection of the laws to women because they would have been eligible for benefits if their inability to work had been due to something other than pregnancy.

The majority opinion in this case indicates the extent to which the Court still refuses to treat sex discrimination like racial discrimination. Consider whether the following kind of explanation would have been appropriate if the disability excluded had been sickle-cell anemia, a disease suffered only by blacks:

> California does not discriminate with respect to the persons or groups who are eligible for disability insurance protection under the program. The classification challenged in this case relates to the asserted under-inclusiveness of the set of risks that the State has selected to insure. . . . There is no evidence . . . that the selection of the risks insured . . . discriminate[s] against any definable group or class . . . . There is no risk from which men are protected and women are not. Likewise, there is no risk from which women are protected and men are not.

If this argument fails to convince the reader that California's exclusion of pregnancy does not discriminate against women, the majority opinion in *Geduldig* offers even more subtle reasoning (in a footnote) on why there is no discrimination in this case comparable to the discrimination found in *Reed* and *Frontiero*:

> This case is . . . a far cry from cases . . . involving discrimination based on gender as such. . . . While it is true that only women can become pregnant, it does not follow that every legislative classification concerning pregnancy is sex-based. . . . The lack of identity between the excluded disability and gender as such under this insurance program becomes clear upon the most cursory analysis. The program divides potential recipients into two groups—pregnant persons and nonpregnant persons. While the first group is exclusively female, the second includes members of both sexes. The fiscal and actuarial benefits of the program thus accrue to both sexes.

The difference, then, appears to be that it would be unconstitutional to exclude women by name from the disability insurance program but that it is all right to exclude a disability from which only women can suffer. Granted that there is a difference, the practical result is that such an exclusion *does* discriminate against women because of their sex.

Perhaps the underlying reason for the *Geduldig* decision, however, has less to do with sex discrimination than it does with economics. As the majority points out in the last footnote to the opinion, "Indeed, . . . data . . . indicate that both the annual claim rate and the annual claim cost are greater for women than for men. . . . 'Women contribute about 28 per cent of the total disability insurance fund and receive back about 38 per cent of the fund in benefits.'"

Justice Brennan, joined only by Justices Douglas and Marshall, argues in his dissenting opinion that there is sex discrimination in *Geduldig*: "By singling out for less favorable treatment a gender-linked disability peculiar to women, the State has created a double standard for disability compensation. . . . In effect, one set of rules is applied to females and another to males." Moreover, Justice Brennan notes, the majority's narrow approach to what constitutes sex discrimination signals a return to the philosophy expressed in the *Hoyt, Muller,* and *Goesaert* cases.

Kahn v. Shevin, the other 1974 sex-discrimination case, represents a return to paternalism. It upholds, by a six-to-three majority, the constitutionality of special treatment for women—in this case, giving a property-tax exemption to widows but not to widowers. The ideas expressed in the *Kahn* decision sound more modern and liberal than those in the 1908 *Muller* case, but the basic attitudes are the same.

Justice Douglas, author of the majority opinion, points out the continuing economic disparity between men and women and the special difficulty faced by an older woman trying to enter the job market. He then concludes that the widow's exemption does not deny widowers—even the poorest ones—equal protection of the laws because Florida's state tax law is "reasonably designed to further the state policy of cushioning the financial impact of spousal loss upon the sex for whom that loss imposes a dispro-portionately heavy burden."

The use of the word "reasonably" is sig-nificant. "Reasonableness" would not be the standard used in deciding whether a widower was denied equal protection of the laws if classifications based on sex—as the prop-erty-tax exemption only for widows clearly is—were considered suspect like those based on race. Justice Douglas, who agreed with Justice Brennan in *Frontiero* that sexual and racial discrimination are similar, apparently thinks the situation in *Kahn* is different. But what if, because of the continuing economic disparities between blacks and whites in this country, the property-tax exemption at issue was for widows *and* widowers who are black?

The *Kahn* case is interesting for several reasons. First, it raises a crucial question that all women concerned with sexual inequality must face: Should women accept favors be-stowed by male legislators and judges to "make up" for their traditional position of political and economic inferiority? Aren't those women who feel the *Kahn* decision is fair asking to be viewed—as the Court in *Hoyt* did—as "the center of home and family life" deserving of special protection from the burdens of the outside world?

A second point of interest concerns the reasons the justices give in support of their views, whether on the majority side or in dissent. Justice Douglas' position has already been noted. Justice Brennan, joined only by Justice Marshall, argues that the state's "cushioning" policy is the kind of interest that is sufficiently compelling to justify legis-lation extending a benefit to a group of per-sons classified according to their sex, in spite

of the fact that earlier he had considered sex a suspect classification. He notes, in his opinion:

> In providing special benefits for a needy seg-ment of society long the victim of purposeful discrimination and neglect, . . . the purpose and effect of the suspect classification is ame-liorative; the statute neither stigmatizes nor denigrates widowers not also benefited by the legislation. Moreover, inclusion of needy wid-owers within the class of beneficiaries would not further the State's overriding interest in remedying the economic effects of past sex discrimination for needy victims of that sex discrimination.

The only problem with the widow's tax ex-emption for Justice Brennan and Marshall, then, is that the tax statute should be even more narrowly written to benefit only wid-ows who are in fact the victims of sex dis-crimination—that is, "needy" widows.

The rationale of Justice Brennan's dissent raises in more concrete form the basic ques-tion posed earlier: Is this kind of judicial thinking one of the "gifts" women should accept in their efforts to overcome "the eco-nomic effects of past sex discrimination"? Perhaps it would be helpful to consider this question in light of the dissenting opinion of Justice White—the fourth vote in *Frontiero* for treating sex as a suspect classification:

> There is merit in giving poor widows a tax break, but gender-based classifications are suspect and require more justification than the State has offered. . . .
>
> It may be suggested that the State is entitled to prefer widows over widowers because their assumed need is rooted in past and present economic discrimination against women. But this is not a credible explanation of Florida's tax exemption: for if the State's purpose was

to compensate for past discrimination against females, surely it would not have limited the exemption to women who are widows. Moreover, even if past discrimination is considered to be the criterion for current tax exemption, the State nevertheless ignores all those widowers who have felt the effects of economic discrimination, whether as a member of a racial group or as one of the many who cannot escape the cycle of poverty.

As the *Kahn* and *Geduldig* majority decisions and Justice Powell's opinion in *Frontiero* all indicate, the Equal Rights Amendment is essential if women—and men—are going to receive equal protection of the laws regardless of their sex.

The Equal Rights Amendment has a long history. After a half century of struggle, the amendment finally received the necessary congressional approval when the House passed it in August 1970 and the Senate in March 1971. The first time congressional approval was sought was in 1923, and it had been sought repeatedly throughout the intervening years. Its adoption depends on ratification by at least thirty-eight states. As of early 1975, only thirty-four state legislatures had done so.

Proponents of the amendment were optimistic at first that the necessary ratification could be obtained in a reasonably short time. However, until the ascendancy of President Gerald Ford and his unexpectedly strong endorsement of the Equal Rights Amendment, there was good reason for the early optimism to fade. Twenty-two states ratified it in 1972. In 1973, however, only eight states came through with approval, and in 1974 there were only three. Who knows how long it will take for four more states to ratify?

The amendment provides that:

> Equality of rights under the law shall not be denied or abridged by the United States or by any State on account of sex.

> The Congress shall have the power to enforce, by appropriate legislation, the provisions of this article.

The Citizen's Advisory Council on the Status of Women, which was established by Executive Order 1126, has summarized the impact of the Equal Rights Amendment—should it ever receive the necessary ratification—on various state and federal laws as follows:

1. *Strike the Words of Sex Identification and Apply the Law to Both Sexes.* Where the law confers a benefit, privilege, or obligation of citizenship, such would be extended to the other sex. Thus, such laws would not be rendered unconstitutional but would be extended to apply to both sexes by operation of the amendment.

2. *Laws Rendered Unconstitutional by the Amendment.* Where a law restricts or denies opportunities of women or men, as the case may be, the effect of the Equal Rights Amendment would be to render such laws unconstitutional.

3. *Removal of Age Distinctions Based on Sex.* Some laws which apply to both sexes make an age distinction by sex and thereby discriminate as to persons between the ages specified for males and females. The ages specified in such laws would be equalized by the amendment. If the age limitation restricts individual liberty and freedom, the lower age applies; if the age limitation confers a right, benefit, or privilege to the

individuals concerned and does not limit individual freedom, the higher age applies.

4. *Laws Which Could Not Possibly Apply to Both Sexes Because of the Difference in Reproductive Capacity.* Laws which, as a practical matter, can apply to only one sex no matter how they are phrased, such as laws providing for maternity benefits and laws prohibiting rape, would not be affected by the amendment.

5. *Separation of the Sexes.* Separation of the sexes by law would be forbidden under the amendment except in situations where the separation is shown to be necessary because of an overriding and compelling public interest and does not deny individual rights and liberties.

This amendment would not only reinforce rights granted to all citizens by the due process and equal protection clauses of the Fifth and Fourteenth Amendments but also would place equal *responsibility* on them. No longer would women be favored or protected by legislation where men are not; all legislation would have to apply equally to both sexes.

It seems incredible that we are still deciding whether women should be equal under the law, which is what the debate on the Equal Rights Amendment is really about, whatever reasons are given for opposing the amendment. No group should be denied rights—or given special privileges—because of skin color or reproductive capacity. As long as women are not equal, they are not full citizens.

Glossary

abortion The induced termination of a pregnancy. Also, the spontaneous expulsion of a fetus before it is capable of sustaining independent life.

action A proceeding before a court in which (1) someone charged with having committed a misdemeanor or felony (subject to criminal law) or a tort (subject to civil law) is judged, or (2) a right is protected or enforced.

adoption The legally authorized taking of someone else's child into one's family and giving it all the rights, duties, and privileges of one's own child.

adoptive parent The adult who legally takes another person—usually a child, but sometimes another adult—into his or her family as a full-fledged member of the family. *See* adoption.

adult A person who has reached the age of majority, which is set by state law.

adultery Sexual intercourse between a married person and someone other than his or her spouse.

age of consent The age, set by state law, at which a young woman may agree to sexual relations without making her partner liable to a charge of statutory rape.

age of majority The age, set by state law, at which a person may fully and independently exercise his or her civil and personal rights.

alimony An allowance the court orders one spouse to pay to the other while they are legally separated or after they are divorced.

annulment A legal declaration that a marriage was never valid and never will be.

assault A physical or verbal attack on another person. Also, a threat of physical injury that is capable of being carried out.

bigamy The crime committed when someone willfully enters into a second marriage while still married to another person.

biological parent *See* natural parent.

chattel An article of personal goods; any property that can be moved.

civil Pertaining to the rights of private individuals and to legal proceedings concerning those rights. Used as a general category to distinguish a court, proceeding, or rule that is not criminal, military, or international.

civil action A lawsuit to recover money or property or to have someone discontinue wrongful acts; it is brought by one individual against another who is charged with having committed a violation of civil law.

claim A demand for compensation or for one's rightful due; an affirmation of a right.

class action A lawsuit instituted by one or more persons on behalf of themselves and all others who are in the same situation or who have suffered a similar wrong.

coercion The use of force or fear to compel someone to act against his or her will or better judgment.

cohabit To live together as husband and wife, whether legally married or not.

collusion A secret agreement between two or more persons to fraudulently deprive another of his or her rights.

common law The body of law originating in England that is based on custom, usage, and court decision rather than written codes, as distinguished from statutory law. In the United States, if there is no statutory law in a particular case, common law prevails.

common-law marriage An arrangement in which a man and woman agree to live together as husband and wife but do not go through a civil or religious ceremony or obtain a marriage license.

community property All possessions, holdings, and money each spouse acquires after marriage that are owned equally by both partners in those states with community-property systems.

complainant The person who applies to the court for legal redress against another; the plaintiff.

complaint In civil law, the formal charge brought by the plaintiff against the defendant setting forth all the facts on which his or her demand is based.

connivance Awareness of and active or passive consent to someone else's illegal act.

consortium The right of a husband and wife to the company, affection, and services of the other in their marital relationship.

contract A legally binding agreement between two or more parties by which one side does (or refrains from doing) or supplies something in return for money or a promise to do something by the other side.

corroboration Additional information offered to strengthen and support evidence or testimony given in a court trial.

crime An act or omission in violation of penal (criminal) law for which a punishment is prescribed by that law, and which is prosecuted in the name of the state. Crimes are divided into felonies and misdemeanors and are considered to be harmful to society as a whole rather than merely to another individual, as are torts (violations of civil law).

criminal Pertaining to the administration of the penal law as distinguished from civil, military, or international law. Also, one who commits a crime.

cross-action A suit brought by a defendant against a plaintiff based on a grievance growing out of the case the plaintiff originally brought to court.

custody The care, keeping, and possession of a thing or the guardianship of a person.

decision A judgment pronounced by a court on a controversy submitted to it.

default The failure to fulfill a legal obligation within a specified time or to appear in court in response to a summons.

defendant The person against whom relief is sought in an action or lawsuit.

delinquent Failure to do something required by law or obligation; also, the person who is at fault in this situation.

dependent Someone who relies on another person for support.

desertion The willful abandonment of a duty—or of a spouse and family without their consent—in spite of a legal obligation.

disinherit To deprive an heir of any part of an estate that would rightfully go to him or her.

dissolution The legal termination of a formal bond or contract. This term is used officially instead of "divorce" in a number of states.

domicile A person's legal residence; the place one makes his or her principal and permanent home for an indefinite period and to which he or she intends to return after an absence.

dower The portion of real property that legally goes to a man's wife upon his death for her use during her lifetime. *Also see* nonbarrable forced share.

due process of law The constitutional guarantee that limits the government's power to deprive a citizen of life, liberty, or property; specifically, legal proceedings conducted according to established rules and principles.

emancipate To release a minor from parental control and authority, thus giving the minor some rights and duties he or she would not ordinarily have until reaching the age of majority.

equal protection of the laws A constitutional requirement that the state extend to everyone within its jurisdiction the same duties and privileges granted by the laws of that state to all persons; specifically, a guarantee that the same rules of evidence and legal procedure will apply to all citizens.

equity Justice administered on terms of what is fair, ethical, and reasonable beyond any particular requirements of the law.

estate The entire amount of a person's assets and liabilities at the time of his or her death. Also, the nature and extent to which a person has interest in the ownership or use of real and personal property.

evidence Any proof legally presented in a court proceeding through witnesses, objects, or documents.

extreme cruelty Serious misconduct (physical violence or threats of it; treatment that endangers mental health) in a marriage. It is a ground for divorce in many states.

felony A crime that is prosecuted by the state, must be tried before a jury, and is punishable by a fine, imprisonment in a state prison or penitentiary, or death; some examples are rape, murder, burglary, arson, kidnaping. The difference between a felony and a misdemeanor is mainly one of the degree of seriousness of the offense and the severity of punishment.

grand jury A panel of from six to twenty-three persons convened in private session to investigate charges of criminal conduct, evaluate evidence, and determine whether an indictment should be filed.

guardian Someone who is legally charged with taking care of the person or property of another.

guardianship The obligation or authority of a guardian.

heir Someone who inherits real or personal property through a will or by the laws of intestate succession if there is no will.

homestead Real property that is protected from a forced sale to meet the claims of creditors as long as the property is occupied as a home.

illegitimate child A child born to a man and woman who are not married to each other.

immunity Exemption from performing duties the law requires, such as payment of taxes. Also, a guarantee against prosecution as a result of incriminating oneself if one agrees to supply information needed by the prosecution in a criminal action.

incompatibility Personality conflicts between a husband and wife that seriously disrupt a marriage. It is a ground for divorce in many states.

indictment In criminal law, a written statement charging someone with the commission of a crime, usually drawn up by the prosecuting attorney and presented by the grand jury.

inheritance All rights and property, both real and personal, that an heir receives either by will or intestate succession.

interest A share in the ownership of property or a business. Also, the compensation paid for the use of another's money.

intestate The condition of a person who dies without leaving a will, or who leaves a will that is not valid.

intestate succession The state laws governing the distribution of a deceased person's estate if he or she left no will.

issue All persons who descend directly from a common ancestor, such as children, grandchildren, great-grandchildren, etc.

joint tenancy Property owned by two or more persons in which each has an undivided share; the entire tenancy automatically passes to the surviving tenants on the death of one of them.

laws A body of rules and penalties governing the conduct of society that are enacted by legislatures and enforced by the courts.

lawful issue Under common law, children born to a man and woman who are legally married.

legacy Personal property—as distinguished from real property—left to someone in a will.

legitimate child A child born to a man and woman who are married to each other or which has been made legitimate by a legal method.

legitimation The act of legalizing the status of a child born to parents who are not married to each other.

liability An obligation that one is bound by law to perform.

life estate Real property that belongs to someone only as long as that person is alive; it does not become part of his or her estate at death.

life interest A share in property, short of ownership, held only for the duration of one's life.

majority *See* age of majority.

marital deduction A tax-free exemption of up to half the decedent's adjusted gross estate that one spouse may grant another in his or her will.

minor A person who has not reached the age of majority and is still subject to parental control and authority.

misdemeanor A crime that is less serious than a felony and is punishable by fine or imprisonment in a city or county jail rather than in a state or federal prison or penitentiary.

natural parent The woman (the mother) who gives birth to a child or the man (the father) whose impregnation of a woman results in the birth of a child. Such parents are also known as biological parents.

necessaries, necessities of life Those articles a person needs to sustain life; a precise definition depends on the manner of living to which the person is accustomed.

negligence The failure to do that which a reasonable and prudent person would do under the same or similar circumstances, or doing something a reasonable or prudent person would not do.

nonbarrable forced share That portion of a husband's estate, set by state law, that goes to a widow even if she is not included in his will or is left a very small amount; it has been substituted for the dower share in those states that have abolished dower.

opinion A statement by the court of the decision reached in a case, detailing the reasons and precedents upon which the judgment is based.

personal property All a person's possessions except for land, buildings, and business interests.

plaintiff The party which instituted a criminal or civil action. In a criminal prosecution, the state is the plaintiff.

precedent A court decision that becomes authority for a similar case that arises from the same or similar questions of law.

probate The process by which a will is validated and all disputes concerning it are settled.

probate homestead A parcel of land and/or a house set apart for the use of a surviving spouse and minor children out of the property of the deceased spouse.

proceeding The manner in which business is conducted before a court from its inception to the final judgment.

real property Land and whatever is built or growing upon it or is affixed to it.

rape Unlawful sexual intercourse with another person forcibly and against his or her will.

residence The place where one lives, either temporarily or permanently.

separate property Any possessions, holdings, or money acquired primarily by the effort of one spouse. In states that have community-property systems, any such property either spouse owned before the marriage is not included in the community property but is kept by the individual. In states that do *not* have community-property systems, property acquired both before and during the marriage belongs only to the spouse who received or acquired it.

separation A mutual agreement or court decree by which husband and wife decide to live apart for a period of time.

sodomy Anal copulation of one male with another. Also, anal or oral copulation with a member of the opposite sex or with an animal.

statute law That body of law that has been enacted by a legislature, as distinguished from common law.

statutory rape The charge a man is liable to if he has sexual relations with a young woman who has not reached the age of consent, whether she agrees or not.

stepchild The child of one of the spouses by a former marriage.

stepparent The spouse of the natural or adoptive parent of children by his or her former marriage.

suit A legal proceeding in a civil court to enforce a right or redress a wrong.

surname The family name, common to all members of a family.

tenancy in common The holding of real property by different titles, but each having an undivided interest in the whole.

title The right to ownership of property.

tort An act or omission caused by negligence or malice in violation of civil law, not including breach of contract.

trust Property held by one person for the benefit of another.

trustee The person appointed to administer a trust.

trustor The person who creates a trust.

unconstitutional Any practice that is held to be, by court decision, contrary to the provisions of the U.S. Constitution.

valid Anything that is legally binding, upheld by the courts, sound as to form and substance.

void Null; having no legal or binding force.

voidable Something that is not automatically void but which is capable of being declared void.

will A person's legal declaration as to the manner in which he or she intends to dispose of his or her estate after death.

witness One who personally sees, hears, or knows of a thing or occurrence; also, one who gives evidence under oath in a court proceeding.